WHY YOU SHOULD BE A SOCIALIST

WHY YOU SHOULD BE A SOCIALIST

NATHAN J. ROBINSON

ALL
POINTS
BOOKS

NEW YORK

First published in the United States by All Points Books, an imprint of St. Martin's Publishing Group.

Portions of this book have been adapted from articles first printed in *Current Affairs*.

Seahorse illustration by Nick Sirotich.

www.allpointsbooks.com

Library of Congress Cataloging-in-Publication Data is available upon request.

ISBN 978-1-250-20086-0 (hardcover)
ISBN 978-1-250-20087-7 (ebook)

Our books may be purchased in bulk for promotional, educational, or business use. Please contact your local bookseller or the Macmillan Corporate and Premium Sales Department at 1-800-221-7945, extension 5442, or by email at MacmillanSpecialMarkets@macmillan.com.

First Edition: December 2019

10 9 8 7 6 5 4 3 2 1

To the *Current Affairs* editorial team:
Aisling, Brianna, Brie, Cate, Eli, Lyta, Nick, Oren, Sparky, Vanessa, and Yasmin
and to all subscribers present and future

CONTENTS

WHY YOU SHOULD BE A SOCIALIST

Introduction

Millennial Discontent and the
Rise of a Democratic Socialist Alternative

IN THE LAST FEW YEARS, U.S. politics has been completely upended. The presidency of Donald Trump, which took politicians and commentators by total surprise, shattered a number of Washington orthodoxies. Very few experts thought that a vicious, loutish reality TV star was capable of rising to the nation's highest office. But they had misjudged political reality and forgotten the cardinal rule: *anything can happen*.

Trump's improbable rise to power was not the only political irregularity to occur over the last several years. While Trump was defeating the most powerful figures in the country's two major political parties, another unexpected phenomenon was occurring: the rise of a new radicalism on the left.

When Bernie Sanders began his campaign for the 2016 Democratic presidential nomination, nobody expected him to pose a serious challenge to Hillary Clinton. Clinton was the consensus choice of the party establishment, and influential Democrats openly said that it was "her turn."[1] Sanders was in the race as a protest candidate. Not only was he considered a marginal figure in Washington, lacking both connections and funding, but he did not have any of the characteristics that traditionally made one electable. He was old. He was from a tiny state known for hippies and cheese. He was not particularly photogenic, polished, or popular. And he was an avowed socialist in a country that had had a half-century Cold War between Good American Capitalism and Evil Soviet Socialism.

It was not, however, a year in which the traditional criteria of electability would matter especially much. Sanders, perhaps as much to his own surprise as anybody else's, quickly attracted a significant following. His radical message, stingingly critical of the existing Democratic Party, resonated strongly with progressives who felt let down by Obama and viewed Clinton as part of an uninspiring and possibly corrupt political dynasty. When the first primary contest came around, February 2016's Iowa caucuses, Sanders achieved a shockingly strong result, coming close to beating Clinton outright.[2] As Sanders began to fill stadiums with crowds, attracting a highly visible and well-organized following, it quickly became clear that the race would not be the "coronation" that Clinton had anticipated.

Clinton ultimately won the Democratic nomination, but it took a bruising fight. Sanders was no mere protest candidate; he was a serious competitor who won 23 contests to Clinton's 34. While Clinton received over 16 million votes across the various primaries, Sanders achieved a remarkable 13 million.[3] It was surprising enough that a socialist candidate could be anything more than a gadfly in a major party nominating contest. It was downright stunning that such a candidate could rack up nearly two dozen primary victories against one of the most experienced and well-connected members of the Democratic Party.

Sanders' unexpected rise to prominence represented an extraordinary shift in the political landscape. The nearest precedent was Eugene Debs' 1920 presidential run on the Socialist Party ticket. Debs achieved nearly 1 million votes despite being in prison for defying the World War I draft.[4] But even Debs didn't pose a serious electoral threat to the dominant parties, receiving only 3 percent of the general election vote. Sanders, who once recorded a spoken-word Eugene Debs tribute album and kept a portrait of Debs in his office while mayor of Burlington, Vermont,[5] achieved a far greater measure of success. He may not have started the political revolution that he often spoke of, but he came relatively close to poaching the presidential nomination from the party elite's preselected candidate.

The Sanders campaign was fueled by millennials, whose dissatisfaction with mainstream Democrats made them highly responsive to Sanders' progressive alternative. Clinton may have had more support than Sanders overall, but young people of all races and genders preferred Sanders over Clinton by large margins.[6] With the exception of Lena Dunham, it was hard to find many people under 30 who had much enthusiasm for Clinton, a candidate they associated with Wall Street, cronyism, and the Iraq disaster.

Sanders' success with millennials, while unanticipated by pollsters, did not occur purely because of Sanders' political skill. It happened because a revolt had been brewing among young progressives for years, as they had steadily grown more and more alienated from the Democratic Party mainstream. Ever since the Occupy Wall Street movement in 2011, young people in the United States had been becoming increasingly radicalized. Weighed down with debt, paying through the nose for health insurance, unable to afford to have kids, and frustrated by an undemocratic political system that implements the policy preferences of rich elites, millennials were both frustrated and tired. Sanders came along at just the right moment: they had been waiting for someone to say what was on their minds—that the economic and political systems were unfair at their core and needed a drastic overhaul.

But the Sanders campaign was just the start.

* * *

JOE CROWLEY HAD been in Congress for 20 years and was one of the highest-ranking members of the House Democrats. He was considered a serious contender for the party leadership and known in his New York City district as a well-connected part of the local Democratic machine. He was the sort of backroom deal–making congressman whose influence is disproportionate to his name recognition.

Alexandria Ocasio-Cortez was not an important figure in the Democratic Party. Far from it. She was a 28-year-old bartender and activist who had once interned for Ted Kennedy and had worked for Sanders' campaign.[7] A member of the Democratic Socialists of America (DSA), she was considered the longest of long shots in her primary contest against Crowley. Crowley had endorsements from powerful political organizations like the AFL-CIO, the Human Rights Campaign, and Planned Parenthood, along with dozens of prominent elected officials, including New York senator Kirsten Gillibrand.[8] The Crowley campaign spent $3.4 million to Ocasio-Cortez's $194,000.[9] Most major media outlets didn't even cover the race, since Crowley's victory seemed so certain. Crowley himself did not even bother to attend a debate against Ocasio-Cortez, sending a surrogate in his place.

Yet on June 26, 2018, Ocasio-Cortez received 57.1 percent of the vote to Crowley's 42.5. The year before, Ocasio-Cortez says, while she was scrubbing restaurant tables, she thought "the train of [her] fulfilled potential had left the station."[10] In January, Ocasio-Cortez would become the youngest woman ever to serve in the U.S. Congress and achieve instant, nationwide fame as a face of the millennial left.

Ocasio-Cortez's victory was impressive, even deeply inspiring, but not shocking. The Clinton-Sanders primary showed that the Democratic Party establishment was deeply unpopular and vulnerable, and that many primary voters were perfectly willing to get behind a socialist if they offered an alternative to the uninspiring, centrist politics that had destroyed the Democrats' popular appeal.

The national media has sometimes downplayed the extent of the Democrats' leftward drift. Just two days before Ocasio-Cortez won her primary, the *New York Times* published an article wondering why the candidates Sanders had endorsed had not been winning in larger numbers and suggesting that the socialist left was underperforming.[11] The same thing happened in August 2018: after a few left candidates in "purple states" lost primary elections, *Politico* published an article titled "Down Goes Socialism," arguing that left politics were only viable in deep-blue districts like Ocasio-Cortez's Bronx.[12] Yet, a few weeks after *Politico* declared the left moribund, Andrew Gillum won the Democratic gubernatorial primary in Florida, having pushed a "Medicare for All" policy of the kind favored by socialists as one of his key issues.[13]

In fact, the successes of the Sanders left have been striking. Before the Sanders campaign took off, the word *socialist* was still a political kiss of death, and advocating for Medicare for All or free college tuition was considered far too radical to be politically viable. In November 2017, however, *Washington Monthly* noted a startling transformation in what constituted the mainstream, writing that while, "not long ago, politicians advocating for single-payer health care were taken to be on the lefty fringe," it was now the case that "Democrats of every stripe, including some with plausible presidential aspirations, are using the term to describe what they think America needs now."[14] We even see headlines like "The Democrats Have Become Socialists,"[15] and not just from hyperbolic paranoid right-wingers. A few years ago, Bernie Sanders couldn't get any of his Senate colleagues to sign on to his single-payer plan, and now presidential candidates, from Cory Booker to Gillibrand, all insist they are Medicare for All supporters.[16] Single-payer healthcare has gotten so popular that it is now supported not only by a majority of Democrats, but, according to one poll, by a majority of *Republicans*. That shift can be attributed in large part to the effect of the Sanders campaign (as well as the Medicare for All activists who have been making the case to the public). Candidates who *don't* support signature pieces of Sanders' policy now find themselves on the defensive.

A number of progressive victories have been notched around the country. The Democratic Socialists of America (DSA) have launched numerous socialist candidates into national and local offices. In Virginia, Democratic Socialist Lee Carter was elected to the state House of Delegates. Dozens of members of the DSA have been elected to state and local offices, and the organization itself has grown to well over 50,000 members nationwide. There are even 300 DSA members in Houston. (Houston!) The *New York Times* reported in April 2018 that "many Democrats have begun to ask socialists for their support and adopt some of the D.S.A.'s platform on health care and pay."[17]

Around the country, socialists are starting reading groups, running publications, and knocking on doors for candidates. In Austin, they successfully "pushed to pass what has been called the first mandatory paid sick leave requirement in the South."[18] The Chicago City Council now has five socialists,[19] and Somerville, Massachusetts, is "dominated by a left-leaning wave."[20]

There are other signs of change beyond the election of socialists. Waves of teachers' strikes, even in red states like West Virginia, Oklahoma, and Arizona, have shown the rebirth of a kind of labor radicalism that has long been dormant. In Philadelphia, leftist public defender Larry Krasner won the race for district prosecutor by pledging to end mass incarceration and radically rethink the city's approach to criminal justice.[21]

The *New York Times* has tried to understand why socialism is taking off among young people, and the answers are about what you might expect. Young socialists are often struggling to make monthly thousand-dollar student loan payments (in addition to rent, health insurance, and every other damn thing). And they experienced "profound disillusionment with the Democratic Party" after 2016. As Houston union organizer Amy Zachmeyer told the reporter, "We want to see money stop controlling everything. That includes politics . . . That just resonates with millennials who are making less money than their parents did, are less able to buy a home and [are] drowning in student debt."[22] One defense attorney who is running for a judgeship in Texas said openly, "Yes, I'm running as a socialist . . . I'm a far-left candidate. What I'm trying to do is be a Democrat who actually stands for something, and tells people, 'Here's how we are going to materially improve conditions in your life.'"[23]

This is not the politics of several years ago. This bears little resemblance to Clinton-era "triangulation" or Tony Blair's "New Labour." There is, in the words of the song that plays over every documentary about the '60s, "*something happening here.*"[24]

*   *   *

MILLENNIAL DISCONTENT HAS its roots in the financial crisis of 2007–2008. It was hard for us to believe that capitalism was the magical, rational prosperity machine that free-market fundamentalists insisted it was when all around us we saw foreclosure and ruin. Even the libertarian magazine *Reason* admitted that the global economic collapse was a naturally radicalizing force, because many young people now "associate capitalism with crisis, not progress," and "some of capitalism's more dogmatic advocates have done it lasting harm."[25] *If this is capitalism,* many millennials thought to themselves, *I'll take something else, please.*

Occupy Wall Street was a natural expression of this rage and disaffection. Its slogan, "We are the 99 percent," accurately reflected the staggering disparities of wealth in the country, with a tiny fraction of people owning most of the actual wealth. To people saddled with tens of thousands of dollars in debt, the twenty-first-century economy seemed more feudalistic than meritocratic. Faced with a future that would consist of working endless hours to pay back impossibly large sums of money, many felt there was little to do except set up camp on Wall Street itself.

The "occupying" tactic was a reflection of just how alienated from the political system many members of the movement felt. In 2011, it didn't feel as if electoral politics held much hope for radical economic and social change. After all, Obama had been elected as a transformative candidate who supposedly came bearing hope and change. But the Obama administration swiftly appointed Wall Street–friendly cabinet officials, such as Larry Summers, and declined to criminally prosecute anyone in the finance industry responsible for the crisis.[26] Many prominent participants in Occupy Wall Street were anarchists, so thoroughly dispirited by the failures of the democratic process that they wanted to burn the whole system to the ground. It seemed like the only way to resist was to stand out in public and refuse to leave until they took you away. It wasn't exactly a political strategy, but it was *something*, at a time when it felt like something needed to be done. Soon, Occupy encampments had sprung up across the country.

It's important to understand just what Occupy Wall Street meant to those who participated in it. I was living in Massachusetts when Occupy began, and I spent some time at the Occupy Boston encampment. I still remember coming up from the Red Line subway station in the Financial District and setting eyes on the camp for the first time. It was breathtaking. The occupiers were not hippies or squatters; they were serious, intelligent people who felt it was necessary to make a powerful statement about the unity of the 99 percent and the level of popular dissatisfaction with the economy. They weren't just protesters, though. They had also created a community.

People who never visited the Occupy encampments missed the chance to see something extraordinary. The best way I can describe it is as an ecosystem. As I walked through the Boston camp for the first time, I realized they had everything: food tents, a medical tent, sleeping accommodations, a library, bathrooms, and meeting spaces. It felt like a genuine, self-sustaining community, built from scratch by people who had been alone and desperate until they had found one another. Occupiers were sometimes caricatured in the press as a bunch of lazy, rich hipsters. That was not what I saw there. Certainly, it was not an idle place. People had literally built a miniature city within the city, from which they planned actions, debated policies, resolved disputes, and organized all aspects of their daily survival.

Most impressively, all of this had occurred spontaneously, without any support from outside institutions. People had come together and built a community from the bottom up, improvising innovative solutions to the problems that face any group trying to take collective action. Occupiers experimented with new kinds of democratic procedures for their meetings, trying to balance their commitment to leaderlessness and equality with the need for results and efficiency. In *The Democracy Project*, anarchist anthropologist and prominent Occupy supporter David Graeber describes Occupy as offering a radical experiment in a new kind of participatory democracy.[27]

And yet, when I first stood in Boston's Dewey Square, looking over the remarkable, improvised tent city, it was also obvious that whatever it was the occupiers had built, it couldn't last. City authorities were never going to allow protesters to live in their parks indefinitely, and while the participants had built something powerfully symbolic, there was never a clear answer to the question, What happens next? There were contentious internal debates within the movement, but it was never able to achieve consensus on whether it wanted some new kind of economic system, an amendment to the U.S. Constitution, a package of legislation, or merely the right to remain in city parks indefinitely.

That lack of cohesion can only partly be blamed on Occupy itself. It was inevitable. One reason Occupy took the form it did was because the traditional organizations through which collective economic action could be taken, like unions and community groups, have steadily been disappearing.[28] It wasn't clear what you could do or what you could join if you wanted to change something. You couldn't change things through the electoral system; Obama's disappointing presidency had shown that.[29] So the occupiers were caught in a bind. The reason they couldn't come up with a good answer was that there *wasn't* one. As the months went by, and the activities of the camps turned more and more toward mundane matters of day-to-day survival (keeping the grounds clean, making sure there was food, maintaining the tents, resisting city attempts to clear the camps), the political energy of Occupy steadily dissipated. One by one, the camps were raided by police and their residents dispersed. When the final tents were taken down in the spring, it seemed as if Occupy hadn't produced much except a powerful statement and that important rallying cry: "We are the 99 percent."

Four years later, as Sanders ran for president, the same feelings that had caused people to gather at Zuccotti Park would come bubbling up once again. The movement had been dormant. But the anger hadn't gone away.

* * *

SOCIALISM HAS BEGUN to set the intellectual agenda, too. Ironically, even though Trump occupies the White House and Republicans dominate the federal and the state governments, ideological conservatism seems to be in retreat. One of the most peculiar features of contemporary politics is how unwilling conservatives are to actually defend many of their core ideas and policies. Take a look at headlines in the leading right-wing publications and you'll notice something: there's a lot of talk about Democratic hypocrisy and the crazy campus left, but there isn't much talk about *conservatism*. From *Breitbart* ("NBC Runs Heartwarming NFL Thanksgiving Commercial Featuring . . . Registered Sex Offender"), to the *National Review* ("Charles Manson's Radical Chic"), to the *Daily Wire* ("SJW Screams at Black Man Dressed as Peacock"), they publish little more than a litany of cultural grievances. Hardly anyone seems to want to be associated with the GOP's policy plans, and when conservative writers do try to stick up for them publicly, the result is underwhelming. Conservative Ramesh Ponnuru notes that some members of the right seem to be giving up on capitalism altogether.[30]

Bill Kristol, once one of the main "thinkers" in the conservative movement, doesn't even know what he believes anymore:

> The GOP tax bill's bringing out my inner socialist. The sex scandals are bringing out my inner feminist. Donald Trump and Roy Moore are bringing out my inner liberal. WHAT IS HAPPENING?[31]

(Dinesh D'Souza mocked Kristol for his betrayal of the cause. D'Souza's own recent intellectual output is a book literally arguing that the Democrats are Hitler.[32])

One of the problems conservatives are running into is that the policies associated with the American right, if presented honestly, are unpopular with the American public. Most people believe the federal government should guarantee healthcare coverage, with a plurality supporting a single-payer system.[33] I suspect the vast majority of people would be horrified by the consequences of pure free-market healthcare, in which people who couldn't afford to spend huge chunks of their income on insurance would either have to put their faith in GoFundMe or die. Yet, because the right is ideologically wedded to its belief in free markets, it has been incapable of actually proposing any feasible alternative to Obamacare. The party spent so long defining itself by its hatred of Obama, it fell on its face the moment it was given the opportunity to actually implement something. Likewise, twice as many people want to see corporate taxes *raised* as want to see them lowered,[34] but because the GOP has no ideas beyond cutting taxes and deregulation, the only thing it can do is scream about social justice warriors and liberal hypocrisy while trying to ram through an incredibly unpopular set of "reforms." Conservatives have no plan to deal with the catastrophic consequences of climate change, and no vision for the common good beyond "what the market decides." They are content to rationalize injustice rather than try to eliminate it.

By contrast, parts of today's left are vibrant and intellectually exciting. It's a great time to be a socialist, social democrat, or progressive, because these are the groups producing serious thoughts on how to solve social problems. This is not as obvious as it should be, partly because many prominent members of the Democratic Party have spent the past three years criticizing Trump rather than putting forward their alternative plans. But that's strange, because they *do* actually have positive ideas. Have a look at the 2016 Democratic Party Platform.[35] Hillary Clinton's campaign didn't talk about it very much, perhaps because it's a strongly Sanders-influenced document, but it's actually impressive. It goes through every area of policy and explains what the problems are, and what the Democrats intend to do about them. It includes plans like: strengthening overtime pay, stabilizing Social Security by taxing high-income earners, allowing the Postal Service to offer banking services, protecting net neutrality, toughening criminal enforcement against Wall Street executives, enforcing antitrust laws to stop corporate concentration, promoting the decriminalization of marijuana, guaranteeing lawyers for asylum-seeking immigrants, and offering debt-free college at public universities. It's not a list of complaints about Republicans; it's a set of clear, though simplified, policy priorities for how to fix the financial industry, campaign finance, education, healthcare, and civil rights. I don't agree with all of it (it contains a totally unnecessary disavowal of the Boycott, Divest, and Sanctions movement). But thanks to the left wing of the Democratic Party, and the success of the Sanders campaign in drawing attention to the actual issues that affect people's lives, it's the sort of serious statement of priorities that a party ought to have. (If we could only get all Democrats to talk about the platform as much as some of them talk about Russia . . .)

There's a very similar contrast in U.K. politics. The Labour Party under Jeremy Corbyn performed unexpectedly well in the 2017 British election in large part because it has adopted a clear set of values, visions, and strategies. The most important moment in the 2017 election was the release of Labour's policy manifesto, which was widely praised for its specificity: Labour said how many new affordable houses they planned to build, how they planned to allocate new funding for education, what new regulations on employment contracts they would introduce, and how they intended to pay for all of it.[36] By contrast, the Conservative manifesto immediately proved so unpopular that parts of it had to be dropped and the party had no real suggestions for how it intended to improve the lives of the young people who began flocking to Corbyn's Labour.[37]

It's an encouraging time to be a socialist in America. The majority of millennials are skeptical of capitalism and have warm feelings toward socialism and social democracy. A pollster from Harvard's Institute of Politics reported the surprising finding that "the only group that expressed net positive support for capitalism were people over 50 years old . . . The largest generation of Americans in history—millennials—have lost confidence. They are interested in finding a better way."[38]

The stigma of the word *socialism* is evaporating. The reasons for this are fairly obvious: it's hard not to laugh at paeans to the Free Market and Our Great American Democracy when the free market siphons every penny millennials earn and our "representative democracy" is neither representative nor democratic. If the right could explain to millennials how their beliefs would improve our lives, how they plan to generate economic growth without the benefits of that growth accruing to the already extremely rich, young people might not feel so sour toward capitalism. But since they *can't* offer such a plan, or at least one that isn't absurd on its face, the left looks more and more attractive.

On the ground, things are encouraging, too. Radical candidates are doing unexpectedly well in ways that would have been inconceivable a few years ago. It's no longer considered fantastical to think that Corbyn might one day be the U.K. prime minister, or that Sanders would have beaten Trump. Membership in the DSA has taken off, and independent left media outlets are growing their audiences. (Although, in order to remain viable, they depend on your subscription dollars.[39])

Of course, radical free-market conservatives still hold national political power, and for all Trump's bluster and ineptitude, he is doing an excellent job gutting the regulatory state and installing right-wing federal judges. But battles of ideas matter a lot: persuading people to believe in your politics is a prerequisite to getting them to actually support you, and far more left-wing beliefs are suddenly becoming mainstream. More and more doctors are supporting single-payer healthcare, and the "Green New Deal" has gone from a fringe concept to the preeminent proposal for how to take the next major step on climate change.[40]

I don't believe anyone who says that conservative power is in its death throes, or that Trump and the Republicans are floundering and 2020 will be an easy victory for Democrats. Overly optimistic predictions

had devastating consequences in 2016, and how the left does elector-
ally will depend on *what* the left does to convince people to vote for its
candidates. But one thing does seem clear: there is something strange
going on among conservatives. While they are more radical than ever
in certain ways, many conservative intellectuals appear half-hearted
about their own policies. Before the financial crisis, it would have seemed
inconceivable that libertarian-leaning federal judge Richard Posner
would write a book on the failures of capitalism.[41] Before Sanders, it was
inconceivable that an open socialist would come reasonably close to
winning a major-party primary, and that even some Republican voters
would find themselves rooting for him. When Kristol is talking about
his inner socialist and the *National Review* is conceding that hardly
any conservatives truly endorse free-market economics, the intellectual landscape is shifting. Conservative counterarguments to the left's
critiques seem increasingly flimsy and superficial, to the extent that they
bother to offer arguments at all anymore. Recently, the conservatives'
sole tactic consists of invoking the specter of the Soviet Union, which
persuades hardly anybody, since most people are capable of realizing the
difference between guaranteed healthcare and Stalinism.[42]

Socialists are having what Ross Douthat called in 2014 a "miniature intellectual renaissance."[43] Douthat thought intellectual popularity wouldn't translate into political popularity because ordinary people
weren't as upset and frustrated as socialism presumed them to be.
Events of 2016 blew a great big hole in that theory. The left is doing well
because millennials are tired of life in the gig economy. Young women
preferred Sanders to Clinton by a stunning 37 percentage points.[44] Our
ideas are doing well, and with the right incapable of offering alternatives, we'll only grow further.

If there is one certainty in politics, it is that nothing is certain and
nobody actually knows anything. Political reality changes quickly.
Pundits and experts can be absolutely certain that a particular event
won't happen, only to be dramatically proven wrong overnight. The
received wisdom of one moment can look like laughable delusion the
next. Nothing is harder to predict than the future, and that holds especially true in politics.

This uncertainty is both encouraging and terrifying. On the one hand, it means that seemingly impossible goals may be more reachable than we think. Hardly anybody thought there could be a black president. Hardly anybody thought there would be same-sex marriage in every state in the union. On the other hand, it means that the world is less stable than we may imagine it to be. People in the 1920s saw Adolf Hitler as a fringe figure, with little chance of ever attaining power. ("Hitler Virtually Eliminated" ran a *New York Times* headline from 1923.[45]) In just over ten years, he would amass almost total control over Western Europe. Likewise, in the 1980s, Ronald Reagan called the Soviet Union an "evil empire," but by 1992 it had disintegrated. The world changes very fast, and because human beings also get used to new situations very fast, it's sometimes hard to appreciate just how dramatic the shifts have been. Detroit was one of America's most populous and industrious cities in the 1950s, and today huge swaths of it are overgrown and abandoned.

All of this uncertainty should leave us both apprehensive and hopeful: hopeful because we never know what might be around the corner, and apprehensive because, well, we never know what might be around the corner, and the progress we take for granted is less stable than we might assume.

* * *

IN THIS BOOK, I want to convince you that everyone should join the political left and identify themselves as a democratic socialist. I want to show you, as thoroughly and persuasively as I can, that leftist politics are not just consistent and reasonable, but that elementary moral principles compel us all to be leftists and socialists. I intend to define, as clearly as possible, what I mean by words like *leftism*, *socialism*, and *principles*, and show you how left ideas work, why they're practical, and why the usual criticisms of them are false and/or frivolous. I also want to explain to you why democratic socialism has been gaining currency in recent years, and look at the changes in U.S. and global politics that are driving more and more people to embrace leftism.

I'm going to assume that you don't consider yourself a socialist. In fact, I'm going to assume that you're *extremely* dubious about socialism, and that when you hear the word you think something along the following lines:

Socialism is a discredited and naive ideology that was tried over and over again and failed. However pleasant it may sound in theory, in practice it is a nightmare. It means government control of resources, but sooner or later you run out of other people's money. It destroys innovation and produces dependency. People who self-identify as socialists do not understand economic reality, and their ignorance is dangerous. If socialists had their way, freedom would be destroyed and we would live in a dystopia.

Here, for example, are a few representative contributions from the comments section of a YouTube video explaining socialism:

Socialism works great . . . if your goal is genocide.

If you Marxist idiots love socialism so much move to Venezuela.

Socialism is economic snake oil and you are fools to believe that it has ever worked or ever will work.

Socialism is cancer!

Socialism, in all its forms and names, always leads to Authoritarianism. This happened in Cambodia, North Korea, the Soviet Union, Venezuela, Cuba, and China.

Socialism is really evil shrouded in the veil of something good.

Socialism is evil! End of story. Snowflakes.

Socialism always leads to mass starvation and genocide. Always.

It would seem I have quite a task ahead of me.

If you've opened this book, however, it means that you're at least willing to give me a chance to make the case. And I appreciate that, especially because political discussions are unimaginably tedious and we'd probably all rather be doing other things. I will do my best not to waste your time. I know that every moment you spend reading my words is a moment that you could be spending trying to pay off your debts, learning to be a pastry chef, or looking at pictures of baby sloths. (Wait! Please don't go!)

I'm going to try to answer a few simple questions here: What is the political left? What is socialism? How do they relate? Oh, and *why should anybody care*? What should compel us to adopt these ideas? What does it *mean* to adopt these ideas? Why do criticisms of the ideas fail? And how do we put the ideas into practice? (If we have time, we may get into the question, What is an idea? Let's hope we don't have time.)

Here's an important point I'm going to beg you to keep in mind as we proceed: don't get too hung up on the words themselves. Discussions about socialism usually quickly descend into debates over whether some particular thing is or is not socialism. (Is Norway socialist? Is Venezuela? Is the U.S. Postal Service?) We're going to have to go through that a *bit*, since it's part of figuring out what we're actually talking about. But ultimately, I'm more concerned with figuring out what to do, and I would much rather people say, "I think the ideas are right and we should adopt them, but they're not Socialism," than, "I agree that this is Socialism and I hate it."

In some ways, I've set myself up for a frustrating terminological debate by framing this book the way I have. I could have called it *Here Are Some Simple Things That I Think Are Very Obviously True and That We Should Believe Regardless of What We Call Them* and just tried to convince you that certain features of society are dysfunctional and can be fixed. Then, since you'd instantly see that none of the fixes I propose sound anything like the failed policies of the government of Venezuela, you could sign on to them without us ever having to relitigate an impossible, interminable, centuries-old debate about what socialism "is." (I put "is" in quotes because, if people disagree about a conceptual term, there's not actually a factual answer to the question of what it is, in the way that there may be an answer to what a book is or what a glass of water is.[46])

I've mulled it over extensively (if there is one thing I am good at, it is extensive mulling), and I've come to the conclusion that the words *socialism* and *leftism* are indispensable. Their meanings may be hotly debated, but so are the meanings of other words like *democracy, freedom, virtue,* and *organic.* And I think if we *lose* the *s* and *l* words, we lose convenient shorthands for the set of principles I'm defending and the common thread that binds ideas together as part of one tendency.

I've talked to many people who have said something along the lines of "Well, I agree with what you're saying, but do I have to call myself a *socialist* if I think that?" To which I answer: "No, you don't have to do anything. But I think you ought to call yourself a socialist, because if you agree with the ideas, then that's what you are." Likewise, if someone said, "I believe in the right of the people to govern themselves and participate in the important decisions that affect their lives," we would say, "Well, you believe in democracy, then." And if they replied, "No, my system is called 'potatoes'; I loathe democracy and this is totally different," we might humor them and indulge their terminology, but we'd know inside that they had endorsed democracy whether they chose to acknowledge it or not.

I'm going to proceed as follows: In Part I, we will discuss how examining the world honestly and humanely produces a "socialistic instinct," one that is frustrated by unnecessary injustices and unsatisfied with popular rationalizations of those injustices. We'll use that instinct to examine the world and try to understand precisely what features of contemporary political and economic systems are so revolting to the left sensibility. We'll also clear away some of the tempting myths advanced by defenders of free markets and social hierarchies.

Next, in Part II, I will talk about how that basic moral instinct can help us formulate a particular set of socialist principles—valuing solidarity, equality, and freedom. Then I will look at the long and honorable tradition of socialist thinking, paying particular attention to libertarian socialism and the great socialists of the United States. After that, I'll talk explicitly about the kind of vision and ambition that these principles produce, laying out some of the utopian ideals that are worth thinking about. Then, we'll get into some of the frustrating terminological discussions about *socialism, democratic socialism, libertarian socialism, social democracy, liberalism,* etcetera. (We will try to get this sorted out as quickly as possible, so that everyone can go home early.) Then, we'll see how conventional political ideas failed, and why the world needs a socialist political response. I'll explain what a strong left agenda would look like and give some suggestions for strategies to move it forward.

In Part III, I will deal with alternatives and criticisms. I'll explain why conservatism is cruel and liberalism is oblivious. I'll respond to common critiques of the left, examining why they all fail and everyone should reject them. I will conclude with a rousing call to arms for the new generation of democratic socialists who will make life better for billions of people around the world.

*   *   *

BEFORE I DO any of that, though, I'm going to tell you a bit about my own involvement with the democratic socialist tendency, and how I came to be running a modest, left-wing magazine called *Current Affairs*.

I'm one of many millions of people who have, over the course of the last decade, come to identify as an anti-capitalist. I had the same coming-of-age experience that many others did: watching my peers' parents lose their houses in the mortgage crisis, friends give up on any prospect of ever owning a house themselves, and people who wanted to be parents forgoing parenthood because raising a child seemed hopelessly unaffordable. I saw some disturbing things: people I had gone to school with, whose personalities had sparkled with creativity and curiosity, went into the workforce and became depressed, dulled, and directionless. They were so tired and jaded that all they felt capable of doing at the end of a workday was flopping onto the sofa and watching Netflix. Democracy itself had become something of a joke, as everyone knew that business and political elites, not the mass public, determined the contours of government policy. There was a widespread sense of fear, anxiety, and helplessness. People joked that they didn't know how long the human species had left, what with climate change and nuclear weapons and the steady piling up of mountains and mountains of garbage. The future seemed to hold, at best, something like the dystopia depicted in Pixar's *WALL-E*: a grim, desiccated planet strewn with flaming rubbish, nary a plant in sight, and the remaining human population reduced to passive, internet-addicted lumps.

But I didn't just see people who hated their jobs and dreaded the apocalypse. The financial crisis and its aftermath did not just lead to despair. They led to revolt, and many people began to question why their lives should be determined by vast, uncaring institutions over which they have no control. I saw the rebirth of a kind of humanistic, utopian worldview, one that bubbled up in Occupy and again in the Sanders campaign and is now a major force within the Democratic Party. I saw Ocasio-Cortez and Michigan gubernatorial candidate Abdul El-Sayed demonstrate resilience and a constructive alternative to the neoliberal consensus that had dominated for so long.[47] And I saw people who realized that they didn't *have* to live in a world where everything was privatized, everyone worked all the time, and if you couldn't pay your debts, you were shit out of luck. They envisaged a better world, in which people had more control over their lives; basic needs like healthcare, shelter, and food were guaranteed for all; and *retirement* and *pension* did not seem like forgotten, mysterious words from some long-dead civilization. All around the country, there were organizations, podcasts, blogs, and publications springing up to promote discussion of left politics.

I was particularly inspired by one project: *Jacobin*, a socialist magazine started in 2009 by 21-year-old George Washington University student Bhaskar Sunkara. Sunkara had watched the steady collapse and merger of local newspapers and the mass layoffs of journalists, and he had put together a glossy newsstand periodical that combined radical politics with quality design. In a few years, it had reached tens of thousands of print subscribers, and by 2013, the *New York Times* was writing about its influence. In "A Young Publisher Takes Marx into the Mainstream," the *Times* said that *Jacobin* "has certainly been an improbable hit, buoyed by the radical stirrings of the Occupy movement and a bitingly satirical but serious-minded style."[48] What *Jacobin* brought to left publishing was professionalism. The magazine looked and felt good, and it could sit alongside centrist periodicals like *The Atlantic* or the *New Republic*. Previously, the left had always lacked a certain slickness. Socialist publishing meant little zines on cheap paper and garish Geocities-like websites. Their aesthetics reinforced the perception that left ideas were fringe. *Jacobin* changed that. By hiring good designers and producing an object that would look stylish on people's coffee tables, Sunkara gave socialist politics an aura of legitimacy. I was stunned by what could be done just by putting in a little effort and copying the techniques of mainstream outlets.

If you wanted to start a nationwide print magazine in 1990, the first thing you needed was $500,000. Possibly more like $1 million. Before the internet, it was all but impossible to get the word out about your new venture without spending a large amount of money on advertising. And you certainly couldn't design the whole thing on a single PC. You would need a staff, advertisers, a distributor. If you were, say, a 26-year-old sociology PhD student with $150,000 in student debt, your prospects for getting a quality magazine off the ground without outside investment would be approximately nil.

In 2015, I was a 26-year-old sociology PhD student with $150,000 in student debt. I was not doing very well in my studies. I generally felt rather useless and spent a good deal of my time making self-published parodic children's books with socialist messages (e.g., *The Day the Crayons Organized an Autonomous Workers' Collective*).[49] Seeing what *Jacobin* had done caused me to think about the possibilities for independent left media. It hadn't had much funding or any real institutional support, and yet there it was, competing against national magazines and drawing the attention of the mainstream press. I wondered if I could do something similar.

One day in early September, I went down to the newsstand at a local Massachusetts bookshop. I picked up a stack of magazines, somewhat at random, and hauled them into the café. I started flicking through them, trying to figure out how magazines were made. I had written for a couple of magazines before, but I'd never actually tried to *make* one. Other than paper and printing quality, what was it that separated major periodicals from hand-stapled zines? What techniques did they use to make themselves look reputable?

I quickly realized that good magazine design actually boiled down to a few simple tricks: You needed to typeset and choose your typefaces well. You needed to have stylistic consistency. You needed to combine images and text in accordance with some basic design rules and use color elegantly. And you needed fancy drop caps, which are those giant letters that begin special paragraphs. Examining a copy of *TIME* magazine, I realized that none of this was hard to do. *TIME*'s visual and editorial content wasn't especially sophisticated, and yet it was one of the leading magazines in the country. *I could make* TIME *magazine in my living room,* I thought. (Arrogant, but correct.)

So I tried. I decided to take the next 30 days and see if I could rep-licate a newsstand-quality magazine on my home computer. I resolved to neglect my schoolwork, eat badly, sleep little, and see what I could churn out over a four-week frenzy. If I could make something that looked decent, I'd see where it led. If I couldn't, I'd forget the whole thing and get on with my schoolwork. I wasn't quite sure what I was trying to do, and had no particular ambition beyond trying this little experiment. But it somehow felt like what I ought to be doing.

I opened up Adobe InDesign and tried to replicate a few pages from *Wired* and the *New Yorker*. After half a day, I had some layouts that looked moderately similar to the originals. Then I tried a few more complicated designs. When those looked semirespectable, I began writ-ing some articles to fill the pages. Mostly opinion pieces, with a film or book review here and there. In my academic life, I was used to quickly churning out large volumes of needless words, so it was not difficult to fill seventy pages or so. I scanned some photos from old postcards to sprinkle in and liven up the visuals.

At the end of thirty days, I had something that looked remarkably like a magazine. Granted, many of its "articles" were long-winded, pompous, and boring ("The Philosophy of Buckminster Fuller as Ap-plied to the Present Day"). But when I had a copy of the thing printed, it looked a lot like something you might see for sale in a shop. I called it *The Navel Observatory*, an attempted pun about academic navel-gazing.

I still wasn't quite sure what to think about what I had done. Was I going to try to sell it? Was I going to make more of them? What was it, exactly? I showed it to friends and asked them what they thought. They liked it, they said, though they also seemed to wonder what I was doing with my life. I started to wonder how I could improve it, how it could attract subscribers, and how I could build a website. Soon, without re-alizing what I was doing, I was planning to publish an actual magazine.

It had been thrilling to put together a prototype. I realized that with printing costs lower than ever and social media allowing easy access to potential readers, it would be fairly inexpensive to put out a competitive publication. What's more, I thought I could put one together that was very different from anything else.

So, with the help of my longtime friend and flatmate Oren Nimni, I filmed an introductory video for a crowdfunding campaign. We promised a magazine that was fresh, fun, and thoughtful. We were both staunch leftists (Oren is something of an anarchist), but we thought we could write in ways that would appeal to people who were, well, extremely skeptical of leftism. Too many political publications seemed to be talking mostly to those who already agreed with their editorial positions. We wanted to appeal to those outside our little bubble, to help make the radical libertarian socialism we subscribed to seem friendly, feasible, and reasonable. As part of our plan to seem "respectable," I came up with a new name: *Current Affairs*. At first, I couldn't believe that no other magazine had ever been called *Current Affairs*. It seemed like it ought to have been taken. Evidently, though, it was so generic and boring that nobody had even thought to use it. For our purposes, that was fine. Generic and boring meant nonthreatening. We wanted a name that would imply we were a venerable, century-old media institution, one whose opinions could be trusted. (The name has had the desired effect. Because *Current Affairs* sounds like the sort of magazine that has been around forever, and that people ought to have heard of, many people actually pretend to be familiar with our work even if they aren't. "Oh, yes, *Current Affairs*. I've had a *Current Affairs* subscription for decades.")

Our Kickstarter campaign netted $16,000. This was enough to build a website and a subscription system and print the first issue. In the early days, I still wrote a number of the articles under implausible *noms de plume* (e.g., Tex Wonder, A. Q. Smith, Darcy McEwan), and we spent many hours on our living room floor bagging up magazines and shipping them out to subscribers. At first, these numbered only a few hundred. But with each additional issue, our numbers grew, until they were in the thousands and we were sending magazines to all 50 states and 20 different countries. Slowly but steadily, we are building a powerful independent competitor to other national political magazines. We have built a real editorial team, opened a physical office in New Orleans, and been quoted in bourgeois media like the *New York Times* and the *New Yorker*.

We did not rise out of nowhere, though, and it would be a mistake to think of our magazine as some kind of fluke. We exist in large part because there has been a ready audience for our kind of work. People have been losing trust in major media institutions and are desperately hungry for an alternative to the blaring mindlessness of cable news. This does not necessarily mean that they want nonpartisan media. They want something trustworthy, thoughtful, and enjoyable to consume.

The election of Trump was also, I have to admit, a turning point for the fortunes of left media. I feel somewhat like a disaster profiteer because Trump's election caused large numbers of progressively inclined people to wake up and realize just how important it is to have a vibrant, critical press. People horrified by day-to-day life in Trump's America sought outlets that could give them a bit of comfort, hope, and truth during difficult times. Here's how *The Ringer* explained some of the consequences for us and others:

> *Current Affairs* is part of a wave of print and digital independent leftist media organizations gaining steam after the November presidential election. Not only are heritage brands like *The New York Times* and *Vanity Fair* adding tens of thousands of subscribers; business is also booming for *Jacobin*, the colorful Marxist journal founded in 2010; *Chapo Trap House*, a darkly funny roundtable podcast made up of mostly Brooklynite, mostly male 20- and 30-somethings; and *The Baffler*, a magazine of cultural critique first established in 1988 . . . that's the closest predecessor to Robinson's project. All are helping fill a political vacuum that Hillary Clinton's loss created, or perhaps revealed to a wider public.[50]

Over the last three years, *Current Affairs* has published hundreds of articles by some of the left's most thoughtful and imaginative writers. We've written about elections, economics, architecture, *Star Trek*, nuclear weapons, Silicon Valley, the rise of Hitler, automation, financial scams, murder mysteries, Mardi Gras, loneliness, Palestine, and dozens of other topics that may not all seem political. To each subject, we bring a fair but opinionated perspective: we don't pretend to be neutral or objective, but we try to be scrupulous about not distorting the truth and always sourcing our factual claims. We also try to hear out the other side's argument, even as we mercilessly criticize it. We attracted a good deal of attention in February 2016 when I wrote an article warning that Trump would probably become president if the Democratic Party nominated Clinton instead of Sanders. (And, lo and behold . . .) We have also become known for our withering essays on popular conservative figures like Jordan Peterson, Ben Shapiro, Charles Murray, and Ann Coulter. The difference between *Current Affairs'* approach and that of other liberal or left publications is that we try to prove our case so thoroughly that even the strongest fans of these figures may come away a little unsure of themselves.

That approach is the one I intend to bring to this book. I have a strong viewpoint, but I understand that it is the writer's job to convince the reader—and to be interesting enough that the reader wants to stick around. I am not going to attempt to indoctrinate you, but to explain my own thinking and show you why so many millennials now call themselves democratic socialists. Perhaps you are already one of those millennials, and this book will mostly help to clarify what you already instinctively believe to be true. Perhaps you are among those skeptics who think we who embrace the term *socialism* are naive at best and outright dangerous at worst. I will endeavor to keep both types of readers in mind.

Alright, enough harrumphing and dithering! Let's get ready to become socialists together!

PART I

WHAT IS THE LEFT SO MAD ABOUT?

Revulsion, Curiosity, Moral Instinct

Orienting Ourselves in the World

> "My sense of the equality of men was based not so much on an aware-ness of the masses as on loneliness. I can remember lying awake at night thinking of this human condition in which everyone living, without the asking, is thrust upon the earth, where he is enclosed within himself, a stranger to the rest of humanity, needing love and facing his own death . . . [H]ow unjust it seems . . . that there should be men and women who are not permitted to explore the world into which they are born, but who are throughout their lives sealed into leaden slums as into living tombs. It seemed to me—as it still seems—that the unique condition of each person within life outweighs the considerations which justify class and privilege."
>
> —Stephen Spender,
> "Worshippers from Afar," *The God That Failed*

HERE IS HOW I CAME to identify myself as a member of the political left: I began to look at the world around me. Human beings are natu-rally oblivious, and we tend to outsource much of our thinking to other people. Famous studies have shown that most people can't even explain how simple everyday devices like toilets, zippers, and bicycles work. (We all say we can, and then when the examiner asks, "Alright, please explain how a toilet works," a lot of people go silent.) Many of us use computer technology every day without understanding the first thing about how it works or how it's made. Fortunately, this is not because we're stupid, but because the world is extremely complex and we tend to retain only the knowledge we actually need in order to navigate our

own lives. We forget everything we learned in school that proved useless, and we are too busy trying to survive to bother examining questions like, How do you build a submarine? Or, Who makes bricks? Or,
What is GDP, anyway?

Generally, I'm just as clueless as everyone else about the functioning
of the world. If you ask me how an iPad or a digestive system works, my
answer will be mumbled sheepishly and worthy of a D minus. But I am
also a person who tends to be unsatisfied when the questions I *do* have
don't seem to have satisfactory answers. And as I germinated into the
literate and curious adult I am today (by "literate and curious," I mean
"now I sometimes read the first paragraph of a newspaper article instead of just the headline"), I realized that certain aspects of the world
around me made very little sense. The simple, childlike questions that
entered my head didn't have satisfactory answers. Something seemed
deeply, troublingly *wrong*.

I did not understand wealth and poverty. I saw luxury retailers
offering the most ridiculous, unnecessary nonsense (Tiffany & Co.
sells a $490 sterling silver protractor[1]). I saw colossal amounts of
waste, from the 150,000 tons of uneaten food Americans discard per
day to the tens of millions of dollars' worth of fancy handbags that
Burberry was incinerating every year to keep their products scarce
and expensive. I saw people in my Florida hometown living in garish,
seven-bedroom McMansions while there weren't enough beds at the
local homeless shelter. I saw people buying new phones every year
and keeping the old ones in a drawer, while a few miles away, day laborers picked tomatoes, earning 45 cents for every 30-pound bucket.
I saw reports of Americans being charged $5,000 by hospitals for an
icepack and a bandage, or paying $1,200 a month in rent for a bunk
bed. And I couldn't understand why everyone wasn't constantly *enraged* by all this.[2]

The more you learn about what life is actually like for people at the
top and bottom, the more grotesque everything seems. If you want to
see what being super-wealthy really means, but you don't have the door
codes to get inside their lairs—sorry, homes—you can simply pick up a
copy of the *Wall Street Journal* and turn to its Friday real estate section,
which is literally called "Mansion." In Mansion, one can find illuminat-

ing descriptions of the kinds of houses currently for sale at the upper end of the market:

> To aid in entertaining, the house has four kitchens, one of which has a loading dock for catering trucks . . . There are two garages: the owner's garage, which connects directly to the house, and a guest garage that fits about 30 cars. A wine room, which doubles as a humidor, contains a wet bar and a champagne refrigerator, and there is an adjacent walk-in wine refrigerator. Off the master suite, there is a gym, a massage room and an indoor hot tub with a view of the river.[3]

Or, how about this comfortable estate:

> On over 13 acres, the property includes a roughly 28,000-square-foot, four-level main house. The home, which is partially built underground, contains a 4,700-square-foot gym with a climbing wall and locker room; a home theater; poker and billiards rooms; "pizza room" with a pizza oven and a disco with a dance floor and disco ball. There is also a safe room with panic buttons and a sliding Kevlar door.[4]

To be fair, a sliding Kevlar door does sound like the sort of thing you might need once the marauding proletarian hordes discover how you live.

Now, before you jump on me for criticizing people for spending *their* money however *they* like ("Who are you to tell me what to do with my hard-earned property? Didn't I earn it?"), I'd like us to look at a couple of other snapshots of contemporary economic life, of the kind that regularly pop up in the newspaper:

> A quick trot through current appeals on GoFundMe reveals campaigns for a network sports cameraman experiencing an unspecified "very serious health issue," a California toddler with "a fatal, progressive, neurodegenerative storage disorder," a 33-year-old rugby player with chronic heart problems and a young man, "one of the most caring and loving individuals that you will ever meet," who suffered brain and physical complications from a cardiac arrest.[5]

Another:

> During one heartbreaking moment of the life-or-death drama, the victim implored her rescuers not to call 911 because she said she couldn't afford the cost of the ambulance, the *Boston Globe* reported. "Awful scene on the orange line," [*Globe* reporter Maria] Cramer wrote. "A woman's leg got stuck in the gap between the train and the platform. It was twisted and bloody. Skin came off. She's in agony and weeping. Just as upsetting she begged no one call an ambulance. 'It's $3000,' she wailed. 'I can't afford that.'"[6]

Actually, these people have it comparatively well, since, globally, the American poor are actually among the world's wealthy. While the most extreme poverty has been decreasing around the world over the last several decades (good news!), there are still nearly 750 million people on Earth who can't afford the *very* basics and live on under two dollars a day.[7] Let's talk about the amount of preventable disease that goes unprevented because people can't afford or don't have access to necessary healthcare. Globally, there are still 1.5 million unnecessary deaths annually from vaccinable diseases, and the CDC has said that up to 40 percent of deaths from the five leading causes of death in the United States could be prevented.[8]

We all *know* that a lot of people die because they can't afford medical care, and we all *know* that these people are other people's mothers, fathers, coworkers, children, and friends. And we all *know* that instead of installing a fourth kitchen, the *Wall Street Journal* Mansion–dweller could have saved poor children from dying of malaria. And we all know that, therefore, the person's decision *not* to do this meant a child died who otherwise would not have. And yet despite knowing all these things, most people don't see this as a crime against humanity.

I've always found this puzzling. The distinction between murdering someone (taking an action that produces their death) and letting someone die (failing to take an action that would have prevented their death) has always seemed fuzzy to me. In both situations, your decisions are the reason that someone's death happens. And yet those who murder people get sent to prison, while those who merely let people die get put on the *Forbes* rich list.

Importantly, my own sense of disquiet did not begin as a political ideology. I didn't read Karl Marx and suddenly reinterpret old facts in a new light. It was a visceral, emotional reaction that came from encountering the facts. I couldn't reconcile certain features of society with my deepest moral intuitions, and none of the available rationalizations did anything to change that. The arguments that were put forth to justify the existing state of things seemed unpersuasive. In fact, they seemed like nothing more than excuses.

SOME EXCUSES AND THE REASONS THEY SEEMED FISHY TO ME

- **People are financially rewarded according to their economic productivity:** Billionaire hedge fund manager and bestselling author Ray Dalio has said that "people get what they deserve in life," and "how much money people have earned is a rough measure of how much they gave society what it wanted."[9] Whether this is true or false as an empirical matter (and it's false), it doesn't make me any less disturbed to see someone lose their teeth because they don't have enough money to pay for a dentist, or lose their job because they couldn't afford to fix their car, or have to return to work immediately after having a child because they can't afford to take time off. I cannot accept this notion of just deserts.

- **The rich deserve their riches because they were given to them through voluntary transactions:** This is the theory advanced by libertarian philosopher Robert Nozick in his famous Wilt Chamberlain example: if a million people pay a quarter each to watch Wilt Chamberlain play basketball, and he ends up far richer than anyone else, isn't this the fair result of voluntary exchange?[10] But getting your wealth legitimately doesn't justify hoarding it. Whatever entitlement we may assume people have to their earnings, theoretically, alleviating the deprivation of others seems far more important than preserving the right to wealth. Accepting that people voluntarily trade their money for basketball tickets does not mean accepting that it's just to have one person sit on a mountain of wealth while other people cannot afford insulin or an asthma inhaler.

- **If you don't succeed, it's because you didn't try hard enough:** This one is laughable. I saw people around me putting all of their energy into trying to keep afloat and still finding themselves deep in debt, exhausted from overwork, and lacking any semblance of a social life. Yet conservative commentator Ben Shapiro said, "If you fail [in America], it's probably your fault."[11] That sort of comment viscerally disgusts me, because anyone who has spent any time examining the country they live in knows that plenty of people fail for reasons completely beyond their control.

- **I worked hard, and I succeeded, so anyone can:** This is just a logical fallacy. "I won the contest so everyone could win it" is a bizarre thing to say. If sixty people compete for thirty positions, thirty people are going to lose no matter how hard they work or how good they are. The economist Henry George pointed this out in 1879: "The fallacy is similar to that which would be involved in the assertion that every one of a number of competitors might win a race."[12] Yet somehow, this argument persists. Ken Langone, the CEO of Home Depot, recently wrote a book called *I Love Capitalism!*, arguing that he's "living proof" that capitalism "works for everybody," since he's a billionaire who started off poor. "If I can make it, everyone can!" Langone said.[13]

People often seemed to simply be coming up with whatever flimsy rationalizations would allow them to avoid confronting the ugly truth: every day, we let others suffer, and we don't care. Nobody wants to admit that because it suggests that we, and many of the people we love and think of as good people, are actually bad people. After all, indifference and inaction in the face of suffering is monstrous. It's understandable why everyone would be desperate to avoid thinking of themselves that way. The sociologist Max Weber put it like this:

> The fortunate is seldom satisfied with the fact of being fortunate. Beyond this he needs to know that he has a right to his good fortune.

He wants to be convinced that he "deserves" it, and above all, that he deserves it in comparison with others. He wishes to be allowed the belief that the less fortunate also merely experience their due. Good fortune thus wants to be "legitimate fortune."[14]

Jack London—whose socialist politics are often forgotten—offered in *The Iron Heel* a more dramatic description of the kinds of stories that the oligarchy tells itself:

> They, as a class, believed that they alone maintained civilization. It was their belief that if ever they weakened, the great beast would engulf them and everything of beauty and wonder and joy and good in its cavernous and slime-dripping maw. Without them, anarchy would reign and humanity would drop backward into the primitive night out of which it had so painfully emerged . . . [T]hey alone, by their unremitting toil and sacrifice, stood between weak humanity and the all-devouring beast; and they believed it, firmly believed it.[15]

Justifications are one way of allowing ourselves not to be too disturbed. Sure, there are moms who have to choose between providing for their children and getting to see their children. "But if they didn't want that to happen, they shouldn't have had kids." There are countless ways to shift responsibility onto other people and avoid thinking that there's any duty on the part of bystanders to intervene. It's a free country. I sort out my life, you sort out yours. Why should I be responsible for what happens to you? I can come up with lots of reasons why it's not my fault, and therefore not my problem, if bad things happen to people who are not me.

Another way of avoiding a troubled conscience is to just be willfully blind to other people's hardships. Many decent progressives I know have trained themselves to walk past homeless people and barely notice them.[16] Nobody wants to hear how their food or phones are made.[17] Wealthy people do everything possible to never have to notice the humanity of those in other social classes. They put their children in private schools, live in gated communities, upgrade to first class, avoid public transit, and make sure the cleaning staff come in at night when nobody else is in the building. Ironically, they do these things because they *do* have consciences: if they had to confront the reality of inequality, they would be disturbed, because all the intellectual defenses seem pitiful when you're face to face with reality. If I was asked, point-blank, by a working mother, "How can you justify purchasing a new soft bathrobe when I can't pay for my son's asthma inhaler?," it would be hard for me to come up with an answer.

Sociology professor Rachel Sherman, in her book *Uneasy Street*, shows that upper-class families are actually embarrassed by their advantages.[18] Many she interviewed said things along the lines of "I know it's obscene" or "I can't justify it." Some had furniture delivered without the price tags because they didn't want the housekeeper to know what they had spent. They avoided explicitly discussing money, because it was uncomfortable, and would never describe themselves as rich, instead using euphemisms like "comfortable" or "fortunate." (Funnily enough, the *comfortable* euphemism has been in use since the last Gilded Age; Edith Wharton's 1905 novel *The House of Mirth* mocks the word and "the heiress's view of a colossal fortune as a mere shelter against want."[19]) Some, even those with millions in assets, referred to themselves as "middle class." One woman who lived in a $2.5 million home was offended when Sherman referred to her as "affluent." Another interviewee "was so uneasy with the fact that they lived in a penthouse that she had asked the post office to change their mailing address so that it would include the floor number instead of 'PH,' a term she found 'elite and snobby.'"

Of course, there is a very easy way for these families to instantly quell their anxiety. They could give their money to the less affluent! (Sorry, less "comfortable.") But at least they are aware, on some level, of the moral problem. They don't want to talk about money. They will react defensively to anyone who brings up the subject of their money. They'll keep it, but have to constantly stave off creeping feelings of guilt.

Not everyone is like this. There are some mega-rich people who love to conspicuously consume. Larry Ellison of Oracle bought the entire Hawaiian island of Lanai (it's not even a tiny island, it's one of the major ones!) and literally hired a "basketball retriever" to follow his yachts around, picking up errant balls from the water whenever Ellison shoots hoops on one of his custom, on-deck courts.[20] Still, even Ellison might squirm if you asked him to explain why he needs *two* yachts with basketball courts when 3,000 children still die of malaria every single day.

I am not yet making any argument about capitalism. I am not suggesting that these inequities have a solution, or making any proposals as to what causes them. I am just talking about a general moral queasiness that I felt when observing aspects of the world that seemed *wrong somehow*. I have been unable to keep myself from constantly putting different facts side by side and telling myself, "No, no, that can't be. That shouldn't be. If that were the case, people wouldn't be able to stomach it. They'd feel nauseated. They'd be ashamed of themselves."

EXAMPLES OF THE SORTS OF FACTS THAT I CAN'T HELP BUT THINK ABOUT CONSTANTLY

Children die of preventable diseases.
And yet there are Ferraris.

There are tens of thousands of homeless people in New York.
And yet there are tens of thousands of empty luxury condos bought as investment properties.

Amazon warehouse workers work long, exhausting shifts for little money and no benefits.
And yet Jeff Bezos, the richest man on Earth, has declared that he has no idea what he could possibly do with so much money other than build spaceships.

Hedge fund managers do not seem to actually produce anything.
And yet they make millions of dollars while teachers buy their own school supplies.

We are told we cannot afford generous public-sector pensions.
And yet we maintain 800 U.S. military bases in 70 countries around the world.[21]

Many people make money simply because they were born with money, or they make money from renting out property rather than working.
And yet wealth is supposedly linked to hard work and merit.

Some children are sent to private schools while other children go to public schools where the heat doesn't work and the desks are broken.

Yet, when the children who go to private schools grow up, they will feel as if they deserve their wealth.

The country you are born in seems to be a very strong determinant of how prosperous you'll be.

And yet people's birthplaces have nothing to do with their choices.

I fully realize that these thoughts are naive and childlike. I know there are plenty of people who will instantly snap at my simplistic reasoning. But I can't stop myself. Across every area of social life, I have been unable to content myself with the available justifications for the status quo. I can't see how anyone could be untroubled, and I think nearly everyone who confronts the actual facts *is* troubled. If you don't spend much time thinking about the fact that 47,000 people every year in the United States are so despondent that they commit suicide, you probably won't consider the possibility that there is something deeply cruel, alienating, and dysfunctional about our country.[22] But if, like me, you just can't get those deaths out of your mind, if they follow you and haunt you every day, you will always look around and feel that terrible sense of *wrongness*.

Some people are untroubled by the existing state of things. But if they thought more, if they questioned their assumptions and got closer to the facts on the ground, they might be more disturbed. If you don't *think* about what it feels like to be a frightened Guatemalan child in an immigration jail, you can comfort yourself with phrases like "securing our borders" and "enforcing our laws." If you know that child and see the reality underneath the words, it's much harder to be sanguine. One reason I am dubious about those who justify, say, solitary confinement is that they don't seem to do much thinking about what it feels like to be trapped in a box. It's easy to justify something if you haven't empathized with the person who experiences it.

When I was younger, I felt like I must be crazy for being unable to get past my horror. There are all sorts of clichés about how young people are natural bleeding hearts, until they actually *understand* the world. "If you're not a liberal when you're under 30, you have no heart, and if you're not a conservative when you're over 30, you have no brain." But I actually found the opposite to be the case. The more I learned, the more I investigated, the more skeptical I was of justifications of the status quo.

Take, for example, crime. As I've met and gotten to know more criminal defendants, I've realized that tough-on-crime grandstanding is much more difficult when you more fully understand the lives of prisoners. It's easy to talk about personal responsibility and say, "If you can't do the time, don't do the crime," if you only see the victims as humans and the perpetrators as monsters. Those who commit crimes, however, often turn out to be fairly similar to everyone else. I once sat in on meetings in a maximum-security prison in upstate New York, where a group of inmates had casual conversations with students from Yale Law School. From a transcript of the back-and-forth, it would have been difficult to tell which speakers were the prisoners and which were the law students.

I also used to correspond with a man named Robert Pruett, an inmate on Texas' death row who had been incarcerated continuously since the age of 15. Pruett was bright, funny, and loved to read works on psychology and philosophy. He had grown up in trailer parks, the son of a violent felon. In elementary school, he began using drugs, and by his teenage years, he was using cocaine and committing regular burglaries. In junior high school, Pruett was arrested as an accomplice after his father killed a man in their trailer park. Pruett was accused of involvement in his father's crime and sentenced to 99 years in prison.

An adult prison was a brutal place for a scrawny 15-year-old, and Pruett's life was characterized by extreme violence and trauma. When he was in his 20s, already without any hope of seeing daylight again, Pruett was accused of killing a prison guard and put on death row.

I read Pruett's autobiography when I was in law school, and was struck by just how intelligent and sensitive he was. He had taken a psychology course in prison and spent a lot of time ruminating on the question of how he had gotten to where he was: his father had committed the crime that first landed him in prison, and we don't choose our parents, but were there choices he could have made differently before age 15? Which ones?

As I read Pruett's writings, which were poignant and full of insight into the human condition, I couldn't help but think that if Pruett and I had been switched at birth, I'd be where he was and he'd be where I am. He was just as capable a writer, just as curious a reader. Yet here I am, with an expensive education and a happy career.

Pruett, meanwhile, was put to death in October of 2017.[23]

*   *   *

A FAILURE TO empathize is a failure to think.[24] Every other person is, of course, a conscious being just like ourselves, who goes through many of the same experiences we do. They eat, shit, worry, and fumble. (Yes, those are the four main activities of life.) The fact that all other humans are *human* is so obvious that it seems stupid to even mention it. But it seems to be the most easily forgotten fact in the world. Soldiers are trained not to see their victims as people with aspirations and families like themselves, but as the Enemy. (If they weren't, it would be difficult for them to do their job. Some people think this justifies the training, whereas I think it should make us question the job.)

During the Vietnam War, for example, U.S. troops were told not to call Vietnamese people "Vietnamese people." Instead, they were "gooks."[25] When Lieutenant William Calley was originally charged with mass murder after the My Lai massacre, he was accused of taking "Oriental lives," rather than just lives, and the top U.S. general in Vietnam said that the Vietnamese don't mourn their dead like we do. In fact, the entire U.S. portrayal of the Vietnam War offers an instructive lesson on how easy it is to avoid thinking about other people's lives. In television and movie accounts, press stories, and books, the war is almost always seen through American eyes, and the "tragedy" of the war is the nearly 60,000 Americans who lost their lives. But the number of Vietnamese people who lost their lives is in the *millions*. Because Americans have a pro-American bias and are simply more interested in our "own" people than "their" people, the effect of the war on the lives of the Vietnamese themselves is given far less attention than the effect of the war on American soldiers, politics, and culture.

Sometimes, dehumanization occurs because people talk about others as lesser creatures, as when the president talks about criminal immigrants as "animals," or when young black men are stereotyped as "thugs." But often, it occurs because we simply don't notice other people at all. The United States is thought of as a free country by its admirers, but it has millions of people in a vast correctional archipelago dotted across the map.

In the media, there is a very obvious hierarchy of coverage, in which some people's lives are considered worthier of attention than others. This is colloquially known as "missing white woman syndrome," but we actually have data showing just how great the variations are in the "news value" of a life. A 2007 study looked at over 5,000 natural disasters and 700,000 news stories that ran on the major news networks such as ABC, NBC, and CNN. It found that the loss of one European life was equivalent to the loss of 45 African lives, in terms of the amount of coverage generated. Deaths in Europe and the Americas were given tens of times more weight than Asian, African, and Pacific lives.[26]

Now, you might think this is natural or justified. Plenty of people can look at the prison statistics and think, *That shows the laws are being*

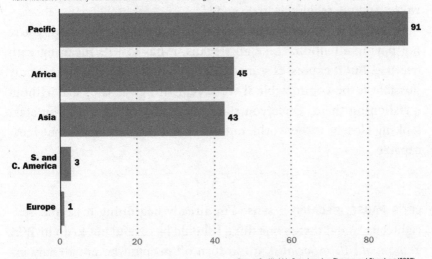

How many deaths does it take for a disaster in different continents to receive news coverage?

Ratio indicates how many casualties would make media coverage in major U.S. networks equally likely, all else equal

- Pacific — 91
- Africa — 45
- Asia — 43
- S. and C. America — 3
- Europe — 1

Source: Our World In Data, based on Eisensee and Stromberg (2007)
ourworldindata.org/how-many-deaths-make-a-natural-disaster-newsworthy/

enforced; or at differences in coverage and think, *Well, of course we care about our people more than others*; or at the expulsion of unauthorized migrants and think, *Well, a nation needs to protect its borders, you can't just open the borders, there have to be rules.* What I'm suggesting is that these responses are too easy; that they're reflexive and sound good but that if we try to get serious about applying our moral values consistently, they begin to seem much less persuasive.

Once you start asking simple questions, interrogating the seemingly obvious, phrases that seem like arguments begin to look like evasions. The flip side of "ignorance is bliss" is that knowledge is painful. Why should we care about people in our country more than we care about people in other countries? In what sense are nations real, and in what sense are they artificial? Why should we defer to the authority of laws we find unjust? Why should there be countries at all? Why should groups of people build walls to keep each other out? Why does everyone care so much about whether someone broke the law, regardless of whether breaking the law actually caused any harm? Shouldn't everyone be free to live in whatever country they like? And shouldn't everyone's life matter the same amount? Pretty soon you end up sounding like Thomas Paine, the most eloquent and humanistic of the Founding Fathers, who said that his values applied to everyone alike: "I view things as they are, without regard to place or person; my country is the world, and my religion is to do good."[27]

There's a left-wing slogan that says, "If you're not outraged, you're not paying attention." Like all slogans, it has lost its meaning with overuse. But it expresses something profoundly important: It is only possible to be comfortable if we accept things as they are without questioning them. Once you start paying attention, once you start looking closely at the world, outrage is not just reasonable but inescapable.

* * *

LET'S PAUSE, BECAUSE I sense I'm already beginning to sound self-righteous, and if there's one thing I should be careful not to do in *Why You Should Be a Socialist*, it's to turn off people who are already extremely skeptical of socialism by becoming too much of a scold. Before we say anything more about prison and death, I'd like to mention the upsides of puzzlement and the majesty of the universe.

It is sad to think about other people's pain, about the abuse and suicidal hopelessness that can exist behind any door we pass as we walk through our towns and cities. I think this turns a lot of people away from a left worldview. If you look at life around you, and all you see is global warming, nuclear weapons, suicide, deportation, wage slavery, factory farming, racism, and prisons, not only are you going to be unhappy yourself, but the people around you are unlikely to find you to be uplifting and engaging company. When leftists suggest that everyone should start paying more attention to other people's problems and miseries, we often seem like real downers. Indeed, I know many people who are simply consumed by feelings of hopelessness, especially every time they realize that Donald Trump is the president of the United States.

Becoming a humane, conscientious person does mean dwelling on global warming, nuclear weapons, suicide, deportation, wage slavery, factory farming, racism, and prisons. Waving these things away is not defensible. But cultivating one's intelligence and judgment also means recognizing the truly wonderful as well as the truly terrible. Not only is a bleak, brutal picture of the world unbearable to live with, it's also inaccurate. For there are many things here that are so wondrous and beautiful that contemplating them should make you want to cry. There are things that are thrilling, sublime, and very, very strange.

In fact, next time you are feeling down, I strongly recommend taking a trip to the nearest aquarium. While you are there, watching anemones undulate and jellies drift, think about just how curious the natural world is. We share the Earth with so many other animals, and they are *remarkably* weird.

Take the seahorse. Seahorses are astonishing creatures indeed. This is not just because the males give birth, or they don't have stomachs, or they're the slowest swimmers in the sea, or they can consume 3,000 shrimp a day, fascinating as those factoids may be. It's because . . . well, look at them. They look like *horses.* But they have nothing to do with horses! Where did they *come* from? What are they *doing* here? The ocean is full of creatures so curious that if we didn't know better, we would think they were from faraway galaxies.

All of which makes it that much more tragic that humankind threatens to destroy itself and the rest of life on Earth. It's because there are so many wonderful things that the terrible things are so devastating. I know the kind of bliss that can be enjoyed when one is free from worries about rent, medical bills, and the threat of violence, and it makes me viscerally angry that such joy isn't available to all equally. The more you appreciate coral reefs, the more scandalized you'll be when you read that they've declined in area by one-third since the 1980s and, "plagued by overfishing, pollution, and invaders," these "gardens of colorful sea life" have been "reduced to furrowed, lifeless plains."[28]

Leftists don't just see the problems in the world. We see the things that make it wonderful, which is one reason why we sound so paranoid about threats. In *Vanishing New York*, Jeremiah Moss harshly condemns the gentrification of New York City.[29] Moss can sound strident sometimes: under the plutocrat mayor Michael Bloomberg, developers built "glittering pleasure domes for the uber-wealthy," with chains displacing mom-and-pop stores, luxury condo towers replacing old brownstones, and a "corporate monoculture" taking the place of the quirky, funky city of old. Bloomberg himself was explicit about his goal to turn New York City into a place for the rich, saying, "We want the rich from around this country to move here. We love the rich people." And, "If we could get every billionaire around the world to move here it would be a godsend that would create a much bigger income gap." But while Moss' book is a complaint about what has gone wrong, it's also a love letter to the city of bohemian weirdness and rich ethnic culture that he sees slipping away. He dislikes gentrification because he adores the old delis, diners, and dives of his romantic New York City youth, and he's agonized to watch them close down one by one. Leftists can look like we're being negative and driven by hatred, resentment, and bitterness, when what we feel most deeply is warmth and tenderness.[30]

It's true, though, that this part of leftism often doesn't come across. We can get wrapped up in sanctimony and forget to explain why we're so worked up in the first place. If I grumble when I see what New York City developers have done, it's because I miss the accordion shop on Forty-Eighth Street, and if I criticize what Amazon has done to small book publishers, it's because I see how empty the bookstores in the French Quarter have become. If I seem enraged when I talk about the prison system, it's because the Texas Department of Corrections killed my friend, and I know what a brilliant person he was and how much he added to the world. If I talk about why it's a scandal that the United States doesn't have guaranteed parental leave, it's because I realize how much my own mother treasured the time she got to spend with me as a baby, and I feel rage when I think of parents deprived of that joy. Call it sentimentalism or moralizing or nostalgia or irrationality if you like, but it comes from a love for the world and those in it.

The leftist orientation I begin with, then, is one of deep appreciation of spectacular things and deep loathing for unjust and cruel things. It's easily dismissed as "bleeding heart"-ism, and, well, that's exactly what it is. People's hearts *should* bleed more! If your heart doesn't bleed, what the hell kind of person are you? On both left and right, those who tend toward weepy laments are trivialized as sentimentalists. Charles Dickens' supposed weakness as a novelist is that he gets carried away with being sad about orphans. But while sentiment needs to be tempered with cool reason, an emotional reaction to the things we see around us is a good place to begin.

Where do our feelings get us? For me, they lead to a disgust with the way atrocities are papered over with pleasant-sounding euphemisms. In "Politics and the English Language," George Orwell noted that nobody ever says, "I believe in killing off your opponents when you can get good results by doing so," but plenty of political actors *do* engage in and defend exactly that. When they're asked about it, though, they use evasive language to describe the acts. Orwell gave a made-up example of how an apologist for Stalin's purges would talk:

> While freely conceding that the Soviet regime exhibits certain features which the humanitarian may be inclined to deplore, we must, I think, agree that a certain curtailment of the right to political opposition is an unavoidable concomitant of transitional periods, and that the rigors which the Russian people have been called upon to undergo have been amply justified in the sphere of concrete achievement.[31]

This tendency is not a Soviet invention, though, and it persists in our own time. Our discourse is saturated with euphemisms, which are like a thick forest between us and the underlying facts of a situation. The Bush administration, of course, used the phrase "enhanced interrogation techniques" to refer to what any honest person would call torture. The Obama administration used the term "disposition matrix" to describe its kill list.[32] Intelligence agencies "neutralize" or "depopulate" rather than kill. People imprisoned forever are "indefinitely detained," solitary confinement is the "special housing unit," and killings by police officers are "officer-involved shootings." Comedian George Carlin said that euphemism was the language invented by "smug, greedy, well-fed white people" to "conceal their sins."

> Poor people used to live in slums. Now the economically disadvantaged occupy substandard housing in the inner cities. And they're broke! They're broke! They don't have a negative cash-flow position. They're fucking broke! 'Cause a lot of them were fired. You know, fired. Management wanted to curtail redundancies in the human resources area, so many people are no longer viable members of the workforce.[33]

If there is one place we should begin, it is with a resolve to not conceal sins, to not seal ourselves off from people's suffering by burying it under a mountain of vacuous bullshit. Euphemisms are an attempt to find pleasant words for an ugly reality, and in doing so, they allow their users to avoid feeling guilty or uncomfortable. This is why they are particularly common in the business world, where executives do not want to admit that they are ruining a lot of people's lives through mass firings and so discuss *restructuring, outsourcing, redundancy*, and *streamlining*. An *independent contractor* is a worker who has no benefits or guaranteed hours, and *increasing efficiency* often means making people do more work in less time.

When it comes to U.S. foreign policy, where the stakes are far higher, euphemisms can conceal deadly realities. Often, U.S. politicians talk of "promoting democracy" abroad, with *democracy* simply meaning "the governments that favor U.S. interests," regardless of whether those governments are actually democratic in any meaningful sense. Both Barack Obama and Donald Trump arranged billions of dollars in arms sales to Saudi Arabia, a country that imprisons—and even kills—political dissidents, and U.S. leaders are unwavering in their support for the government of Israel, even as it commits serious human rights abuses in Gaza.[34] Pleasant and noble phrases are used to justify U.S. actions abroad—we are the world's policeman, a city on a hill, a beacon of freedom—but when the facts are examined honestly, it turns out that we are, for the most part, simply a very powerful country pursuing its national self-interest.

Being an honest leftist requires one to have a nose for jargon and a determination to figure out what is actually going on. It means examining phrases like *national security* and *globalization* and ascertaining what they mean for real human beings. When we do so, we often find that the reality beneath the words is disturbing. The "freest" country in the world is also the one that imprisons the most people; the most "democratic" country in the world is one in which ordinary people's policy preferences matter little; and "security" can be invoked to justify almost any kind of brutality. You can rationalize nearly anything if you speak at the right level of abstraction. But my kind of humanistic socialism, unlike the authoritarian Soviet variety, begins with a resolute determination to find the truth, to care about human beings, and to not turn away from unpleasant facts or find ways to make them less discomforting.

Neoliberal Nightmares

Our Depressing and Unacceptable Present

"Is $30,000 a Month Too Much to Spend on Wine?"
—*Wall Street Journal*, March 14, 2017

"Husband of Teacher Killed in Texas Shooting Is Crowdfunding Medical Bills."

—*Vice*, May 21, 2018

NOW THAT I HAVE REPUDIATED "depressing leftism," let's return to some matters that are, in fact, extremely depressing. We cannot spend all day looking at seahorses and forget our responsibilities. I will try to avoid being maudlin. I am a hopeful person, and I promise I ultimately won't leave you feeling doomed. Part II of this book is very upbeat. Unfortunately, here in Part I, we have no choice but to confront a few dispiriting facts. That's because, in the words of an infamous picket sign from Occupy Wall Street, "Shit Is Fucked Up and Bullshit."

What is everybody on the left complaining about? Why are they so grouchy? Why can't they just shut up and enjoy the miraculous consumer products that surround them, from Amazon Echo to the personal surveillance drone? What is their *problem*? Even Barack Obama has said that, for all its problems, the twenty-first century is the greatest time to be alive in all of human history.[1] (Although, since Jim Crow only ended in the 1960s, that's a fairly low bar.) Manhattan Institute fellow Scott Winship said that he finds the complaints of the political left "bewildering" because "we have under 4% unemployment, middle-class incomes are at an all-time high, and poverty is at an all-time low."[2] Harvard's Steven Pinker has concluded that left-wing intellectuals must "hate progress," because they don't seem to appreciate that across the globe, life expectancy has grown, extreme deprivation has declined, and on average, people are more prosperous than ever before.[3] People who wish to dismiss leftist complaints often point out that today's poor people, at least in the United States, often have refrigerators and cell phones, something their ancestors never had.

But we shouldn't measure contemporary well-being against Great Depression–era poverty, just as we shouldn't measure it against life in the Ice Age or during the time of the Black Death. Instead, we should measure our achievements against our potential. It doesn't matter if far more people were homeless fifty years ago than are homeless today. It might be worth a brief self-congratulatory pat on the back. More important, though, is the question of why we still have homelessness if we have bountiful resources that are being squandered on luxury rubbish. By showing that things used to be worse, we still haven't explained why it's reasonable for Burberry to incinerate thousands of handbags, or why healthcare is so costly.

The idea of the twenty-first century as a paradise of progress is also naive. Certainly, there's much to admire about our time, and innovations like Twitter and the Roomba are the products of remarkable ingenuity. But statistics on human progress often miss crucial facts about the reality of people's lives. We may live in a more comfortable time than many others, but it is also a deeply precarious and frightening time.

It should be remembered, after all, that for all the amusing and informative tweets we send (500 million per day), we are also ransacking and destroying the natural world at an equally impressive pace. People do not enjoy hearing about environmental destruction, because over the years it has successfully been painted as some kind of hippy-ish concern. Climate change and the environment were barely brought up during the 2016 presidential debates. And yet, the issues could not be more serious, nor the stakes higher.

The Union of Concerned Scientists has warned that the coming consequences of climate change will include rising sea levels, increases in both flooding and droughts, longer and more destructive wildfire seasons, more devastating hurricanes, more intense heat waves, mass forest deaths, the increased spread of insect-borne diseases, the death of coral reefs, and mass die-offs of insects that could have severe, disruptive consequences for major ecosystems. Some experts have warned that humanity may be approaching a "tipping point" from which there is no return, where feedback mechanisms will cause perpetual, unstoppable rising temperatures that will pose an existential threat to all life on Earth. Over 15,000 scientists from 184 countries have issued a statement warning that because of our excessive resource consumption, we face "widespread misery and catastrophic biodiversity loss," and "soon it will be too late to shift course away from our failing trajectory."[4]

Though we've become very good at not noticing it, human beings have caused colossal amounts of destruction and death all around us. Wild animal populations have been decimated, and over the last 50 years, there has been a 58 percent decline in the population of vertebrates, including an 81 percent decline in freshwater animals. That means that "for every five birds or fish that inhabited a river or lake in 1970, there is now just one."[5] Some have argued that we are in the middle of a new mass extinction, one of the rare periods in Earth's history when species disappear at unusually high rates.[6]

The oceans are full of plastic, the rainforest is still diminishing, and we eat so many cows that over a quarter of Earth's entire land surface is now used for livestock. One small bit of good news is that we're succeeding in closing the "ozone hole," thanks to the decades of effort by environmentalists and scientists to ban chlorofluorocarbons.[7] But we are still overfishing, overgrazing, and overpolluting. And right when we desperately need to reverse course, the United States has elected a president who not only actively denies the existence of the problem, but is intent on rolling back the modest regulations that have kept environmental destruction from becoming much worse. The Republican Party, through its fanatical devotion to "cutting red tape" and "creating a favorable climate for business," is threatening the future of life on Earth. The Democratic Party, seeing no political gain from giving environmental issues their due weight, has long been complicit in allowing environmental concerns to be pushed to the side. Now everything's fucked. Good job, everybody!

Then there are nuclear weapons. In 1945, shortly after the United States obliterated two civilian populations with nuclear bombs, Albert Einstein warned that there was a very simple chain of logic that could spell humanity's doom: First, that another war between the great powers would be "likely to bring destruction on a scale never before held possible and even now hardly conceived." Second, "so long as there are sovereign nations possessing great power, war is inevitable."[8] In other words, the very existence of rival great powers means war will come sooner or later, and the destructive capacity of modern weaponry means such a war would have unthinkable consequences for humanity. This is also expressed in another, possibly apocryphal, quote from Einstein: "I do not know with what weapons World War III will be fought, but World War IV will be fought with sticks and stones."

It's actually very difficult to appreciate just what the nuclear threat means, especially as we are now so many decades removed from the last world war. In the 1940s and '50s, the threat of atomic annihilation was a prominent part of public discourse. It even seeped into popular culture—the six-disc CD box set *Atomic Platters: Cold War Music from the Golden Age of Homeland Security* collects nuclear-themed songs, including Muddy Waters' "Atomic Bomb Blues" and a gospel number called "Jesus Hits Like an Atom Bomb." All of this seems peculiar now, and the duck-and-cover exercises of the 1950s are a comical relic. But the weapons themselves are still there, armed and ready to be deployed the moment a world leader gives the say-so. Despite the Non-Proliferation Treaty, the United States and Russia each possess well over 6,000 nuclear warheads.[9] With some commentators agitating for a "new cold war," arms control should top the list of "Things Something Ought to Be Done About Rather Quickly."

I hope I don't need to remind you what this threat truly means. The bombing of Hiroshima killed 125,000 people in a flash. Since then, countries have developed and tested bombs a thousand times larger, bombs that could kill every living soul for fifty miles. It's so unbelievable that it

TOTAL NUCLEAR WEAPONS: 13,850

RUSSIA 6,490

UNITED STATES 6,185

FRANCE 300

CHINA 280

UK 215

PAKISTAN 150

INDIA 130

ISRAEL 80

NORTH KOREA 20

= 100 bombs

Source: World Nuclear Weapons Stockpile Report,
Ploughshares Fund (April 2019) https://www.plough-
shares.org/world-nuclear-stockpile-report

feels like science fiction. I can *tell* you that "all of Manhattan could be destroyed in less than the time it takes to blink," but it's hard to fully accept that that's true or conceive of it happening.

In part, this is because the threat is kept unseen. Former secretary of defense William Perry, who thinks people should be far, far more concerned than they actually are, has said that the issue is neglected in part because "the poised nuclear doom, much of it hidden beneath the seas and in remote badlands, is too far out of the global public consciousness."[10] Nuclear weapons are hidden away in remote areas or lurking beneath the sea on submarines. We may know they are real on an intellectual level, but they do not *feel* real because their impact is beyond the scope of what our imaginations can conceive, and they are totally invisible to us in our daily lives. We are walking around with a loaded gun to our head (and to the heads of everyone we love), but we don't react as we would if the gun were right in front of us. We can go about our ordinary lives pretending it isn't there, until the bomb goes off. But by then, of course, it's too late.

The United States recently received a haunting preview of how the first moments of a nuclear war might look. On January 13, 2018, just after 8 a.m., the people of Hawaii received an emergency alert via text, radio, and television. It read: "BALLISTIC MISSILE THREAT INBOUND TO HAWAII. SEEK IMMEDIATE SHELTER. THIS IS NOT A DRILL." Terrified residents ran about frantically, unsure of what to do. They sent goodbyes to their loved ones, huddled in bathtubs, and climbed into holes. In the 38 minutes before officials managed to alert the public that it was a false alarm, Hawaiians had an agonizing insight into what the last moments of their lives may feel like.[11]

Some people think that nuclear arms control is not an especially pressing issue. With U.S.–North Korea tensions somewhat lower for the moment, and globalization tying the great powers' economies closer together, some have suggested we are now in a global "Long Peace," in which large-scale conflict has disappeared.[12] This is a shortsighted view. For us to be safe, the peace cannot just be *long*, it has to be *eternal*. It's not enough that the world's powerful countries are getting along at the moment. They literally have to never go to war again for the rest of history. And if there is one thing we should have learned from the twentieth century, it is that conditions that seem permanent can often turn out to be fragile and temporary. One day, Berlin is a city of bohemian cabaret artists. The next, it is the center of the Third Reich. One day, the Soviet Union is a global superpower. The next, it has disintegrated. For us to feel safe, we must be assured that no nuclear-armed power will ever again be controlled by a fanatical and irrational government. Given the existence of Trump and Vladimir Putin, it's difficult to feel confident.

*   *   *

CIVILIZATIONAL SUICIDE, WHETHER through killing the planet or setting off nuclear weapons, is so serious that it makes everything else look trivial. Alone, these two issues should be enough to cause everyone to immediately join the socialists. After all, we're the only ones who treat these matters with the seriousness they deserve. Republicans deny that there's even a problem, and Democrats mutter something every now and then but still don't seem to feel much urgency. (You tell me how much time our "liberal" news networks like CNN and MSNBC spend talking about arms control policy and climate science.)

But there are plenty of other features of contemporary life that any sane and sensitive person should be troubled by. In the United States, with a higher gross domestic product (GDP) than any other country in the world, we have still somehow managed to inflict an impressive amount of unnecessary hardship on people. While less wealthy countries with strong social welfare states take good care of their residents, the United States' commitment to further enriching the already extremely rich has made parts of this wealthy country look almost postapocalyptic. Drive through Detroit or Newburgh, New York, and observe the senseless decay of once-great cities. In these cities, you can see the consequences of a system in which people with money lack any commitment to the welfare of their fellow human beings.

The defining feature of our age is inequality. Even economist Larry Summers, certainly no socialist, has noted that "the world's wealthy elite are more wealthy, more knit together, more separate from their fellow citizens, and probably more powerful than ever before."[13] Shortly before the financial crisis, Citigroup released a report concluding that these days, "the world is dividing into two blocs—the Plutonomy and the rest," with a small number of wealthy plutocrats "absorb[ing] a disproportionate chunk of the economy."[14]

People do not realize just how extreme the situation is. Empirical research from Harvard Business School has confirmed that Americans seriously underestimate just how much the wealthy have and how little the non-wealthy have.[15] The study found that people's ideal distribution of wealth was fairly egalitarian:

Top 20%	2nd highest 20%	Middle 20%	2nd Lowest 20%	Bottom 20%

0%   10%   20%   30%   40%   50%   60%   70%   80%   90%   100%

Then, it asked people what they thought the situation looked like in reality. This is where their guesses were, on average:

Top 20%	2nd highest 20%	Middle 20%	2nd lowest 20%	Bottom 20%

0%   10%   20%   30%   40%   50%   60%   70%   80%   90%   100%

In reality, the situation is far more extreme than that:

Top 20%	2nd highest 20%

0%   10%   20%   30%   40%   50%   60%   70%   80%   90%   100%

The bottom 20 percent own almost nothing. In fact, many of them have *less* than nothing, because they're also in debt.

The Institute for Policy Studies has found that the wealth of just the top three richest Americans—Jeff Bezos, Warren Buffett, and Bill Gates—is now greater than that of the entire bottom 50 percent of the population put together (160 million or so people).[16] In the United States, billionaires have been adding about 13 percent per year to their wealth, while rank-and-file workers have gotten about 2 percent. Oxfam has concluded that "82 percent of all the world's wealth created in 2017 went to the global top 1 percent," while "the poorer half of humanity—3.7 billion people—got nothing."[17] In the United States, the top 1 percent holds more wealth than the bottom 95 percent of families, and the bottom one-third of families own about 0 percent of the country's wealth.[18]

It's hard to actually conceive of what concentrated wealth to this extent actually means. In an essay called "Who Cares About Inequality?," my friend David Adler suggested that a good way to begin is just by appreciating how much $10 million is, in multiples of $10,000.[19] While large sums of money can be quite abstract, we all kind of know what $10,000 is and can think of things you could buy with it, like a used car. First, he says, look at $100,000:

$10,000 $10,000 $10,000 $10,000 $10,000 $10,000 $10,000 $10,000 $10,000 $10,000

Then, look at $1 million:

$10,000 $10,000 $10,000 $10,000 $10,000 $10,000 $10,000 $10,000
$10,000 $10,000 $10,000 $10,000 $10,000 $10,000 $10,000 $10,000
$10,000 $10,000 $10,000 $10,000 $10,000 $10,000 $10,000 $10,000
$10,000 $10,000 $10,000 $10,000 $10,000 $10,000 $10,000 $10,000
$10,000 $10,000 $10,000 $10,000 $10,000 $10,000 $10,000 $10,000
$10,000 $10,000 $10,000 $10,000 $10,000 $10,000 $10,000 $10,000
$10,000 $10,000 $10,000 $10,000 $10,000 $10,000 $10,000 $10,000
$10,000 $10,000 $10,000 $10,000 $10,000 $10,000 $10,000 $10,000
$10,000 $10,000 $10,000 $10,000 $10,000 $10,000 $10,000 $10,000
$10,000 $10,000 $10,000 $10,000 $10,000 $10,000 $10,000 $10,000
$10,000 $10,000 $10,000 $10,000 $10,000 $10,000 $10,000 $10,000
$10,000 $10,000 $10,000 $10,000 $10,000 $10,000 $10,000 $10,000
$10,000 $10,000 $10,000 $10,000

David also shows us what $10M looks like, and I'd like to show you myself, but it *goes on for four pages* and my publisher steadfastly refused to let me waste that much paper. That's just 10 million! Now multiply it by 10 again to get 100 million, which still only gets you one-tenth of the way to what a billionaire has. And for a few, the first billion is just the start! As David comments, this is "a powerful exercise, [because] we can see, from the piles of $10,000 that compose these larger figures, just how many 'good' and 'decent' lives can fit into the fortunes of the extremely wealthy." Photocopy this page, spread the piles of $10,000s out on your floor until you have Jeff Bezos' net worth, and then stand on it as you explain why the United States can't afford a renewable energy program. And yet *Financial Times* writer Chrystia Freeland found when she interviewed

wealthy people that "people making $5 million to $10 million defi-
nitely don't think they are making enough money."[20] The 1 percent
feel "deprived" when they look at the .01 percent. One telecom billionaire said $1 billion was the "minimum" he needed "to cover the fringe
benefits, the plane, the boat."[21]

However much you have, you can always desire more. Nobel Prize–
winning economist Angus Deaton showed that "the richer you are, the
more covetous you become."[22] There is some experimental evidence
that just having money actually makes you a greedier person. University of California psychologist Paul Piff has produced research showing that "the more money you have, the more focused on yourself you
become, and less-sensitive to the welfare of people around you."[23] Piff's
team has even concluded that people who drive luxury cars are less
likely to yield to pedestrians, since being on top gives people a sense of
entitlement and indifference.[24]

AMAZON: A VISION OF OUR FEUDALISTIC FUTURE

Bezos, the founder of Amazon, has a net worth of $150 billion, which is
about seven times larger than the GDP of Afghanistan and about half
the size of the GDPs of Israel and Hong Kong. Bezos is not known as
an especially charitable billionaire, though he did open a small fruit
stand on the streets of Seattle that gave out free bananas.[25] He has refused to sign Buffett's Giving Pledge and instead is using his money to
create the largest luxury home in Washington, D.C., by converting the
27,000-square-foot Textile Museum into a single-family residence.[26]
Bezos has said that "the only way that I can see to deploy this much
financial resource is by converting my Amazon winnings into space
travel."[27] (Really, Jeff? The *only* way?)

The company's treatment of its low-level warehouse employees has
long been notorious. Stockers and packers often work 11-hour shifts
and walk up to 20 miles a day.[28] They are forced to work overtime and
often go unpaid for required tasks. There is intensive surveillance, even
of bathroom breaks, and weaker workers whose productivity lags are
summarily fired.[29]

The company is constantly advising people "that you're being watched" and giving ominous warnings about the swift termination that will follow any attempt to steal from the warehouse. The company "installed big-screen monitors to broadcast streams of images of workers fired after they were caught stealing on the job," in which "employees are seen in silhouettes, stamped with the words 'Terminated' or 'Arrested.'"[30] And after losing a case that went to the U.S. Supreme Court, workers remain unpaid for the portion of their days spent standing in line for mandatory security screenings. For several years, *Gawker* compiled testimonies from people who had spent time in Amazon warehouses. The quotes were depressing: "I have never felt more disposable or meaningless than I do at Amazon," said one worker. "They do not care if you keel over on the line," reported another, who claimed to have observed multiple people pass out during their shifts.[31] (Indeed, at an Amazon warehouse back in 2011, so many people were collapsing in the summer heat that the company hired ambulances to sit outside and wait for workers to drop.[32])

Investigative journalist James Bloodworth has worked in an Amazon warehouse and wrote about what the job is really like.[33] Turns out, the answer is: it's awful. Bloodworth says it felt like a "prison" and confirms the stories about grueling shifts and security checks during bathroom breaks. The handheld devices they carried frequently transmitted "admonishments to speed up" and ranked workers from "highest to lowest in terms of the speed at which we collected the items." Break time was minimal, and at lunch, "you had about fifteen minutes to bolt down the food." Bloodworth would arrive back after lunch to find two or three managers "pointing at imaginary watches and bellowing peremptorily at anyone who returned even thirty seconds late [saying,] 'Extended lunch break today, is it?' [or] 'We don't pay you to sit around jabbering.'"

The atmosphere was suffused with jargonistic bullshit. You weren't supposed to call it a warehouse, but a "fulfillment center." Workers weren't fired, they were "released." (Given the prison-like conditions, that one might be accurate.) In fact, they weren't even workers, they were "associates." Bloodworth says that on day one management told them that Amazon was an egalitarian workplace because "Jeff Bezos is an associate and so are all of you." (Some associates are more equal than others, by about $150 billion.) Posters of happy employees had captions like "We love coming to work and miss it when we're not here!," though Bloodworth cites a survey of Amazon staff showing 91 percent wouldn't recommend working there, 89 percent felt exploited, 71 percent reported walking more than 10 miles per day, and 78 percent felt their breaks were too short. Workers were disciplined with points, and anyone who received six points would be fired—sorry, "released"—with points given out for being sick or late because the Amazon bus didn't show up.

Conditions are little better for Amazon's white-collar workers. A 2015 *New York Times* investigation found that Amazon's corporate headquarters was a brutal place to work.[34] Employees were intentionally pressed to their physical limits in a culture of ruthless competition and unreasonable demands for self-sacrifice. There was little sense of work-life balance, and workers were subject to intensive psychological pressure, "toiling long and late" and being "castigated for their shortcomings." "Nearly every person I worked with, I saw cry at their desk," one employee said. (Amazon pushed back hard on the *New York Times* investigation, arguing it was full of mistakes.) In the wake of the *Times* report, a group called Former and Current Employees of Amazon (FACE) formed in order to push the company for reform and attempt to form a union. A FACE representative told me that while there have been a few changes in HR practices since the *Times* exposé, "Amazon is still Amazon," and "people are still pushed to their limits."

Amazon warehouses have become symbols of twenty-first-century capitalism for good reason. They represent an extreme version of some very common tendencies, namely the ceaseless pressure on workers to be more productive, the stripping of benefits and dignity, and the increasing imbalance of power between workers and owners. In Amazon, we can see a bleak vision of a possible future, one that resembles a more technologically advanced version of medieval feudalism. Since wealth is power, the few extremely rich people at the top will have immense control over the lives of the majority.

It may sound outlandish, but it's already the reality at Amazon, where one man reaps billions of dollars in rewards from the constant labor of hundreds of thousands of exploited, low-level laborers. And across the economy, the imbalance of power between top and bottom is increasingly evident. In the United States last year, 41 percent of workers didn't have even *one day* of paid vacation,[35] and 36 percent didn't have a single day of paid sick leave.[36] The word *pension* has become a joke, as 50 percent of private-sector pensions have disappeared.[37] The absence of paid parental leave in the United States means that mothers and fathers often have to return to work immediately after the birth of a child, right at the point when they most need and deserve to spend time with their newborn. This lack of security has serious psychological effects on people. When you can't afford to take vacations, when you can't spend time with your child, and when you can't afford to get sick, your day-to-day existence feels more precarious and stressful.

WHY MILLENNIALS ARE MAD

People in my generation feel powerless and frustrated. We see things like Apple achieving a $1 trillion market valuation and then look at our own lives and wonder why so little seems to be "trickling down," even though we are working hard. Millennials are having far fewer children than previous generations, and American fertility rates have reached a record low.[38] When the *New York Times* surveyed young people to find out the reasons they weren't having as many children as they had wanted, the top ten answers were:

- Childcare is too expensive
- They want more time for the children they have
- Worried about the economy
- Can't afford more children
- Waited because of financial instability
- Want more leisure time
- Not enough paid family leave
- No paid family leave
- Worried about global instability
- Struggle with work-life balance

Notice a common thread? Almost all are related to economic factors. People have to work too much, and they don't have the time or money to have children. The reasons are informative because it's *not* that millennials don't want to have children. They're *interested* in having children, but there are material obstacles standing between them and parenting. This is tragic. Here we have tons of young people who would like to bring new life into the world and spend their time caring for and educating the next generation, but they can't. People are missing out on one of the most incredible human experiences, that of being a mom or dad, simply because they aren't allowed to share in the country's tremendous wealth.

Millennials' financial situation, generally, is dire. A study based on the Survey of Consumer Finances concluded, "Millennials earned lower incomes, were less likely to own a home, . . . had lower net wealth than their parents at the same stage in life," and "had amassed just half the net wealth baby boomers had at the same age."[39] The portion of government spending going to young people (such as Temporary Assistance for Needy Families) has decreased relative to the portion going to older people (e.g., Social Security), even as baby boomers have seen their wealth explode compared to millennials.

With these prospects, it's no wonder there have been major increases in depression among teenagers, and studies have shown that young people are more anxious and mistrustful than older generations. According to Malcolm Harris in *Kids These Days*, the young have "greater levels of restlessness, dissatisfaction, and instability."[40] Harris' picture of millennial life is bleak. While we have become more productive, we haven't actually seen the benefits of that productivity, and young people are increasingly put into a dog-eat-dog economic competition that leaves them stressed, exhausted, and broke. According to Harris, "increase[s] in average worker output, rationalization, downward pressure on the cost of labor, mass incarceration, and elevated competition have shaped a generation of jittery kids teetering on the edge between outstanding achievement and spectacular collapse."

As the economy becomes more competitive, it affects how children are being raised. From a very young age, many are being prepped to compete in the job market. Harris quotes a letter from a school explaining why the annual kindergarten play was being canceled: the children simply couldn't afford to waste two days practicing a play, since the school is "responsible for preparing children for college and [a] career with valuable lifelong skills," and "what and how we teach is changing to meet the demands of a changing world." This is especially true for the upper middle class. Decisions over how children should spend their time are now made with an eye to cultivating their "human capital," the knowledge, skills, and personality traits that will make them attractive to potential employers. One school Harris cites brags of its "kindergarten-to-career" pipeline, and since all leisure time has an "opportunity cost," children are given enormous piles of homework and deprived of recess. Some have called for an end to summer vacation because students "lose ground" during the break from school in the never-ending struggle to be college-ready. Everyone is involved in the "arms race that pits kids and their families against each other in an ever-escalating battle for a competitive edge." And the more schoolwork is designed to give students the skills that employers want, rather than those that cultivate a human to reach their full potential, the more education becomes a form of unpaid job training, that is, child labor.

Universities are the gatekeepers of social success and determine whether young people will end up in comfortable professions. "College admissions are the 'boss' of aspirational achievement," Harris says. The already well-off are favored in this competition: they know which little dances to perform in order to impress administrators. Working-class students will probably have to hold jobs during college, and their grades will suffer. They may have to work late into the night: a quarter of students at Wisconsin public colleges worked jobs between 10 p.m. and 8 a.m. More and more effort is required to get to the top of the pile—we've all heard how jobs that used to require a BA now require an MA, the MA jobs need PhDs, etcetera.

No wonder people my age feel a bit piqued when we see headlines like "Millennials Are Ruining America's Sex Life," pondering why young people seem to be having less sex and delaying the decision to have children.[41] One reason is that we're all worried and stressed, and have neither the time nor money to live the kind of fulfilled and functional lives that our parents' generation did. This is why we all collectively grumble when we hear Joe Biden saying he has "no empathy" for the complaints of young people. "Give me a break," Biden said of millennials who "think they have it tough."[42] One might well ask Biden how much student debt he was left with when he graduated from the University of Delaware in 1965, and how long it took him to pay it off.

Out-of-touch perspectives like Biden's are lampooned in the online meme "Old Economy Steven," which depicts a blue-collar worker in 1970s garb making cracks about millennials set against the reality of the changing economy. Some of the captions include:

- "'When I was in college my summer job paid the tuition'" / "Tuition was $400"
- "Loses job" / "Finds another one on the way home"
- "Bought a house in his 20s with a 9–5 job that didn't require a bachelor's degree" / "'Kids these days have it easy'"

It is remarkable that a meme has a better grasp of young people's economic lives than a Democratic vice president. Right there, you have an important clue as to why so many people under 30 are put off by mainstream Democratic Party politics and are turning leftward. I have seen the best minds of my generation depressed and saddled with debt.

THE INDENTURED LIFE

Debt is one of the defining features of contemporary American life. In 2019, household debt hit $13.67 trillion.[43] $1.49 trillion of that is student loan debt, which is held by 44 million people, who now graduate with an average of nearly $30,000 each.[44]

Many economists think debt is a good or neutral thing. Debt allows us to get things done: borrowing money helps us pay for things that we couldn't otherwise afford, and it's win-win for the lender and the debtor. In *Game of Loans*, economists Matthew Chingos and Beth Akers argue that the problem of student loans has been overstated because most students manage to pay off their debt and taking on the debt enables them to go to college.[45]

But debt on paper is different from debt in practice. In reality, debt has serious psychological consequences for debtors. In a poll by LendingTree, most debtors said that worries about their student loans affect their lives and even give them headaches.[46] Having $100,000 of debt hanging over you, gathering interest all the time, makes you feel exhausted and hopeless. At one point, I was paying $800 a month on my student loans *just to cover the accruing interest*. I'm not alone in that. In fact, $100,000 is no longer the high end of student loans. In May of 2018, the *Wall Street Journal* reported that there are 100 people in America who now have over *$1 million* in unpaid student loans. The *Journal* profiled a 37-year-old orthodontist who owes $1,060,945.42, and whose payments don't cover the interest.[47] Eventually, he can expect to see the amount double.

Mother Jones, in writing about the failures of federal loan forgiveness programs, gave some examples of the educational backgrounds and financial profiles of student borrowers, which show just how extreme the situation has become for many.

- University of New Mexico (bachelor's, 2006); University of Minnesota (master's, 2008); $70,000 owed at graduation; $50,000 paid back so far; $410 paid per month, on average; . . . $70,000 still owed today.
- Gettysburg College (bachelor's, 2005); University of Detroit Mercy (JD, 2009); $139,000 owed at graduation; $58,000 paid back so far; $640 paid per month, on average; . . . $161,000 still owed today.
- University of Utah (bachelor's, 2004); University of Denver (JD, 2012); $341,000 owed at graduation; $35,000 paid back so far; $530 paid per month, on average; . . . $410,000 still owed today.[48]

But the largest amounts of debt are not even necessarily the most unfair. Most people in default on their loans actually owe less than $10,000. In many cases, they were working-class students who went to for-profit colleges that gave them almost valueless degrees. For-profit colleges are an unacknowledged scandal: many bait prospective students into enrolling through flashy advertising campaigns, and then load them up with debt while giving them a product that does virtually nothing for their career prospects. (Unsurprisingly, Betsy DeVos' Department of Education is making it easier than ever for these institutions to bilk vulnerable students with false promises.[49])

There's a racial and gender component to this, too. Two-thirds of student debt is held by women, and black women have greater amounts of student debt than any other group.[50] This isn't because they get more valuable degrees, but because they're less able to afford college in the first place. Student debt is an extraordinarily unjust system: it punishes people who don't have wealthy parents. It's perverse, when you think about it: you can't just go and educate yourself. Instead, you have to sign up for decades of indenture just to secure a qualification necessary for slight advancement in the workforce.

The United States is a nation of debtors. Eighty percent of Americans currently have debt, in one form or another, and average household debt is continuing to rise all the time.[51] We can't actually quantify the harm this does to people. How many couples have arguments over their financial predicaments? How many sleepless nights do people spend, worrying that they won't be able to afford to keep their car running because their student loan payments are coming due? How does it feel to know that everything you receive is owed to someone else, and that you won't be able to get out of this situation for a dozen years or more? What does it mean to have a country in which *millions upon millions* of people feel like that? So many people are living in this state of permanent indenture, and we have somehow come to accept it as natural and inevitable.

JUST A WHOLE MESS OF OTHER PROBLEMS

This is, I know, the part of the book where a critic will say, "Robinson rehearses a litany of familiar problems, making the usual complaints." I can't help it. The situation demands it! And who am I to deny what the situation demands? The fact is, while we on the left have a justified reputation as grumblers, for too long serious things haven't been taken very seriously. As humanity careens toward environmental catastrophe and feudalistic inequality, someone had better make a fuss.

Race

Nobody likes to be called a racist, but anyone who looks at the facts honestly has to admit that the United States is still a very racist country. Why? Because the mere fact of being born a certain race makes a highly significant difference to your chances in life. If black America were its own separate country, and we examined its statistics, it would have a higher infant mortality rate than many developing countries, like Mexico and Libya.[52] I am sure you know the horrifying statistics about race and incarceration. There are twice as many black men in the criminal justice system today as were enslaved in 1850.[53] Just a few years ago, one in three black men could expect to end up in jail over the course of their lives.[54] Predominantly African American cities like Detroit, New Orleans, St. Louis, and Baltimore have poor health outcomes, anemic economies, and dilapidated infrastructure.

The statistics on wealth are downright shocking. Black Americans have, on average, $5 in wealth for every $100 that white families have, and the average black family would need 228 years to amass as much wealth as the average white family holds today.[55] In Boston, the average black family has about $8 in wealth (yes, that's *eight* dollars), while the average white family has about $200,000.[56] Generally, while white people own homes, black people do not. (In fact, just looking at averages can be misleading. Matt Bruenig has argued that when you dive deeper into the numbers, you find that the racial wealth gap is much larger than even the most widely publicized statistics suggest, since most black wealth is concentrated at the top.[57])

This wealth gap is the direct consequence of slavery; it has existed since the founding of the country. Many people dismiss the importance of "historical" racism in determining today's African Americans' lives. But it's impossible to deny. Around 60 percent of wealth in the United States is inherited,[58] and slavery was much more recent than people seem to think. (There are still people alive today who, in their childhood, knew people who were former slaves.) And that's just financial wealth: also passed down are social and cultural capital, that is, the connections and insider knowledge that help you get ahead in life.

As Bernie Sanders forcefully, and correctly, declared:

The racial wealth gap exists because slavery, segregation, Jim Crow and predatory lending stole wealth from African Americans. That racial wealth gap must be repaired, and institutional racism must be rooted out wherever it exists.[59]

There is some good news on race. In recent years, the life expectancy gap has finally diminished, with black and white people having similar life expectancies.[60] (The bad news is that this is, in part, because white people are living shorter lives thanks to opioid and alcohol abuse epidemics.) But until being born black or Hispanic gives you the same life chances as being born white, everyone should be committed to an explicitly anti-racist politics. People tend to think that racism is about "hate," and that if they don't "hate" people of color, they can't possibly be racist. "I don't have a racist bone in my body," you often hear them say. But racism is more about indifference and bias than hate: it's about subconsciously preferring people of your own race, advancing their interests, and not caring how your actions affect people of other races. This is the way in which white Americans are still deeply racist: they do not care that black children go to worse schools, that black mothers are more likely to die in childbirth, or that a giant historical injustice distributed wealth unequally across races.

Sex & Gender

I try to be sensitive to the complaints of men about the difficulty of their lives. I, too, am a man, and I, too, find life difficult. Mortality and the human condition can be a hell of a thing, and there are some problems men face that women do not (prostate trouble, the draft).

But in the #MeToo era, nobody should have any doubt that there are specific gender-based harms that affect women more than men. Not only is there still a substantial gender pay gap (yes, it's real), but the entire experience of being a woman involves significant burdens that men not only never have to endure, but *never even notice the existence of*.[61] Anybody who doubts this should pick up a book like *Everyday Sexism*, which chronicles the innumerable instances in which the fact of gender intrudes on people's lived experiences.[62] Women and gender nonconforming people are not just routinely harassed and threatened, they are ignored, belittled, and excluded. A century after women's suffrage was achieved, we are still far from achieving equal representation in government. While certain fields have more than rectified their gender disparities (in psychology departments, for instance, women often outnumber men three to one),[63] women still have higher rates of poverty and lower net worths. Everything from student debt to domestic violence disproportionately affects women, to say nothing of a sexist culture that demeans those who defy gender expectations or cannot meet impossible beauty standards.

I have only touched here on gender injustice, which is even worse for transgender individuals, who experience homelessness, bullying, and suicide at unconscionable rates. Nobody looking out over the social landscape can say that meaningful gender equality has been achieved, and anyone who isn't a feminist isn't a socialist.

Militarism

The United States likes to think of itself as a force for good in the world. Our record over the past half century, though, has been shameful. We are the largest global arms dealer and supply morally repugnant dictatorships like Saudi Arabia. We have repeatedly overthrown democratically elected leaders and supported unconscionable acts of violence, from Indonesia's mass murder of communists to Saudi Arabia's ongoing bombing campaign in Yemen. The Vietnam War killed several million Vietnamese people, and the Iraq War killed 500,000 Iraqis.[64] U.S. intervention in Central America over the course of decades led to permanent instability.[65] We like to forget our own role in shaping the geopolitics that come back to bite us in the ass: North Korean anti-Americanism results from, in part, the fact that we destroyed 90 percent of the country's capital with bombs in the 1950s,[66] and the U.S. overthrow of the democratically elected Iranian government in 1953,[67] and our support for a repressive dictator, partly explains why the phrase "Death to America" can still be heard in Tehran. The United States has built a sprawling military empire that pursues its own interest and does as it pleases, regardless of the consequences for other nations.

Immigration

Every day, there are nearly 40,000 people in immigration detention centers in the United States.[68] Few of these people have committed any crime, beyond illegally setting foot on the wrong patch of land. And while the Trump administration is rightly lambasted for having cruelly stolen children away from their parents, the deportation regime has been separating families for a very long time. Every time a parent is swept up by Immigration and Customs Enforcement (ICE) and sent back to their "home" country, a family is separated. Barack Obama's administration deported hundreds of thousands of people,[69] and each of those deportations represents a human life thrust into chaos by the state. When we talk about "illegal immigrants" being deported, we're talking about ordinary people trying to eke out a living, who are swept up by armed agents and sent away. This was, of course, not how it worked for most of the country's history: it used to be that you could simply get on a boat, get checked for diseases, and then join the American family. The strict legal/illegal distinction is a recent development (ICE itself has only existed since 2003), and we have created a regime in which ordinary people must constantly worry about being asked for their papers, without anybody seeming to notice just how authoritarian such a concept is.

Animals

Anyone who is honest with themself must realize that the mass killing and eating of animals raises deep and discomforting moral questions. Animals can suffer, they can feel emotions, they can have desires and joy. And yet, while we would be horrified to see someone torturing or killing a dog, we accept the mass killing of hundreds of billions of animals of equal intelligence and sophistication. The left often neglects animal rights issues, but based on the scale of death and suffering involved, the industrial farming of animals may well be one of the most important moral issues of our time.[70]

General Despair

There are over 47,000 suicides in the United States every year. This number has been steadily increasing. Economists Anne Case and Angus Deaton have directly linked the American suicide epidemic to the bleak, unequal social and economic landscape. It is, they say, a "failure of spiritual and social life that drives people to suicide," concluding that "if we can only generate good lives for an elite that's about a third of the population, then we have a real problem."[71]

The economic roots of the suicide epidemic are obvious. Consider how Gene Sprague felt in the last days of his life. Sprague, a gentle 34-year-old punk rocker, had suffered from severe depression since his mother died during his youth. He had long talked about killing himself, and when asked what he wanted to have for breakfast, would sometimes reply, "Death." His suicide, therefore, did not come as much of a surprise. But consider what Sprague wrote in the last entry on his blog before he jumped from the Golden Gate Bridge:

> I have not heard from the future employer, I have not received a plane ticket to fly to Texas to interview for that job (I was supposed to leave tomorrow), I have completely run out of money, I am out of cigarettes, I am completely out of food, my eBay auctions have not been bid on, and I think my ferret is dying.[72]

Sprague had been suicidal for many years. But he only went through with the act once his material circumstances became unbearable, once a perfect storm of minor miseries added up. Case and Deaton call this "cumulative distress." Poorer people's mental health has been on the decline, and their access to care is minimal. The worse off you are financially, the more distress you're going to build up.

Recently, increased attention has been given to so-called deaths of despair in the United States. After many years of continuous growth, life expectancy in the United States has actually been *dropping* overall.

Widening Inequality In Life Expectancy

Life expectancy for 50-year-olds within a given year, by quintile of income over the previous ten years.

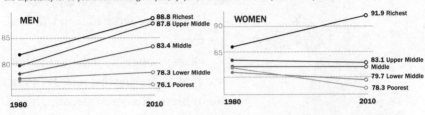

Source: World Economic Forum https://www.weforum.org/agenda/2015/09/how-income-affects-life-expectancy/

This is thanks, in part, to increases in suicide and alcoholism, as well as an explosion in drug overdose deaths, of which there are now 70,000 a year.[73] That's more than the entire number of Americans killed during the whole Vietnam War. And it's happening *every single year.*

One of the most disturbing features of the changes in life expectancy is that they vary considerably by income level. Poor people are living shorter and shorter lives, and rich people longer and longer ones. Between the very bottom and the very top, there is now almost a 15-year gap in average lifespan. To me, this feels like one of the most serious existing injustices. For your wealth to determine not only your level of comfort, but *literally how much time you will spend on Earth*, seems grotesque. Will we eventually see a far greater divergence, in which the bourgeoisie live two or three decades longer than proletarians? If present trends continue, we will.

On the whole, it's rough out there. Extreme poverty may have dropped, and the economy may be growing, but many millions of people are spending their whole lives trying to stay afloat, with little time to enjoy themselves. An Urban Institute survey found that "40 percent of American families struggled to meet a basic need last year—food, health care, housing or utilities."[74] Millions are faced with a choice between basic nutrition and paying rent.[75] The number of people who kill themselves annually is greater than the entire population of Burlington, Vermont— the equivalent of a 45,000-person town just popping out of existence every year.[76] Corporate profits are soaring, yet many people's wages are barely keeping up with inflation, and it costs more than ever to pay for basic housing, healthcare, and college. Every year, tens of thousands of people are forced into bankruptcy by their medical bills, and a trillion dollars

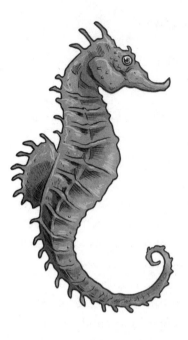

in student debt is forcing a generation of college graduates to put off parenting and sometimes move back in with their parents.

Okay, enough. I could go on, but I am already hearing that reviewer's voice in my head: "Robinson's seemingly endless list of greivances, which he thinks we shall find illuminating rather than exasperating, will be news to nobody."

Let us pause once again to appreciate the majestic seahorse. Hopefully, this picture of the wonderful creature will give us the spirit and fortitude we need to get through the next bit, in which I say the word *neoliberalism* repeatedly.

* * *

YES, NOW WE have to talk about neoliberalism. I'm sorry. I wish we didn't; but we do.

What the hell is neoliberalism?

I hate that word. I really do. First, it's misleading. As Noam Chomsky points out, the phenomenon called neoliberalism is neither new nor liberal. Second, it sounds academic and pretentious, and it can be lazily used to describe just about everything under the sun. If you're not careful with a word like that, it can become an all-purpose slur that you can deploy at will. Run out of tortillas? Curse you, neoliberalism. Subway running late? Fucking neoliberalism. (*Actually*, problems in public transit infrastructure are directly linked to . . . well, never mind for now.)

And yet, there is no other word that properly describes the tendency. The term refers to a set of ideas that have become conventional wisdom among political elites since the 1980s, in particular the belief that "free markets" are magnificent and capitalism should be set free to do pretty much whatever it pleases. This was once an extreme right-wing view (it makes Dwight Eisenhower look like Friedrich Engels). But in the

1980s and '90s, it became the "Washington consensus." Deregulate and privatize everything. Even the "liberal" parties, Bill Clinton's Democrats in the United States and Tony Blair's Labour Party in the United Kingdom, embraced the free-market agenda, calling themselves "New Democrats" and "New Labour," respectively. Larry Summers, who advised both Clinton and Obama, said, "Any honest Democrat will admit that we are now all Friedmanites."[77] Think about that: it means that both parties followed the ideas of Milton Friedman, a free-market economist so radical that he resented the existence of a government postal service.[78] Gone were the old Labour principles of collective ownership and the redistribution of power from capitalists to workers. To the extent government had any valuable role to play, it was simply in making markets work.[79] Stephen Metcalf of *The Guardian* called it the "idea that swallowed the world."[80]

Wendy Brown, in *Undoing the Demos*, says that there has been a "ubiquitous" embrace of "neoliberal rationality," and it has profoundly changed politics around the world.[81] This "rationality" is the idea that government should be run like a business, which means in part that everything has a price and should be judged accordingly. When you start to think this way as a policy-maker, trying to quantify everything and maximize return on investment, you end up governing very differently. If a public school is a "negative asset," shut it down. The democratic populace, Brown says,

> disintegrates into bits of human capital; concerns with justice bow to the mandates of growth rates, credit ratings, and investment climates; liberty submits to the imperative of human capital appreciation; equality dissolves into market competition; and popular sovereignty grows incoherent.

What does that mean in practice? Well, here's an example of this kind of "rationality." *Forbes* published an opinion piece called "Amazon Should Replace Local Libraries to Save Taxpayers Money."[82] The writer, Panos Mourdoukoutas, said that public libraries are not cost-effective. Taxpayers are subsidizing public spaces that are not used enough. Instead, we should turn libraries over to corporations, who can run them more efficiently. Librarians were appalled by the *Forbes* article, and rightly so. But this idea follows logically from neoliberal principles. You measure "value for money," and if a public asset isn't providing it, hand it over to the private sector. This is not the traditional leftist way of thinking about libraries. Leftists don't say, "Is this asset performing?" They say, "People need to be able to access knowledge, and a public library is an important component of a community, whether or not many people frequent it." We care about unquantifiable values as well as quantifiable ones, while neoliberal thinking tends to view anything you can't measure as insignificant.

What's striking about neoliberal rationality is that *both* liberals and conservatives embrace it. It has become the water in which we swim. For example, last year, a book by libertarian economist Bryan Caplan came out called *The Case Against Education*.[83] Caplan argues that public schools are not good investments because they do not actually produce a "return" for students in the form of useful job skills. Caplan believes that the school system should be privatized and, to a great extent, dismantled, because it is "inefficient" in producing good job market outcomes. It's not surprising that he thinks that; Caplan is a free-market libertarian, so we might expect him to see schools as little more than factories for efficiently manufacturing value for the job market.[84]

But here's the part that shows you the bipartisan nature of neoliberalism: Caplan's strongest *critics* accepted that premise. In response to Caplan's book, liberal writer Kevin Carey wrote an article in the *Washington Monthly* harshly dismissing Caplan's ideas.[85] Carey said that education *is* a good investment: there is a "strong relationship between average scores on international tests and the growth rates of national economies," and public schools improve students' long-term productivity. In this debate, we can see what the neoliberal consensus means in practice. Everyone agrees that we should measures schools by whether they produce a return on investment, but the left argues that they do and the right argues that they don't. Neoliberalism is that buried premise: that maximizing human capital output is the correct way to figure out whether a school is any good. It's not about whether students become humane and thoughtful citizens; it's about economic growth. The debate is not framed as a conflict of values but an empirical discussion about whether or not something contributes quantitatively to the economy. Unfortunately, because a lot of things the left advocates do *not* necessarily make people more productive, but simply make society more fair, neoliberal discussions nearly always favor free-market conclusions.

The term *neoliberalism* captures the tendency of people who are nominally on the left to make arguments based on conservative economic premises. For example, Republicans argue that their tax cut will increase GDP, reduce the deficit, and reduce taxes for the middle class. Democrats reply that the tax cut will not increase GDP, will not reduce the deficit, and will not reduce the middle-class tax burden. Both parties are arguing around a shared premise: the goal is to cut taxes for the middle class, reduce the deficit, and grow GDP. But traditional liberalism, before the "neo" variety emerged, would have made its case on the basis of different premises. Instead of arguing that Democrats are the party that will reduce the middle class's taxes, traditional liberalism would make the case that taxes are important because it's only through taxes that we can improve schools, infrastructure, healthcare, and poverty relief. Instead of participating in the race to make government smaller, old liberalism is based on a set of moral ideas about what we owe to one another.

Let me go through a few news stories that demonstrate the neoliberal character of our age. They don't necessarily *seem* related, but I think they *are* related.

- **The Return of Private Fire Services:** During the 2017 California wildfires, according to the *Wall Street Journal*, some people received more fire protection than others.[86] Insurers sent in private firefighting forces to protect valuable homes, and only those homes that had signed up for special policies were coated in fire retardant. The use of private firefighters for the wealthy has apparently grown over the past decade. A 2007 report documented insurer AIG's use of a Wildfire Protection Unit to serve its Private Client Group, a plan "offered only to homeowners in California's most affluent ZIP Codes—including Malibu, Beverly Hills, Newport Beach and Menlo Park."[87] Here, we have "efficient" firefighting: everyone gets just as much fire protection as they're willing to pay for, rather than fire protection being equally guaranteed to all.

- **Prisoners for Sale:** In rural Oklahoma, a program called Christian Alcoholics & Addicts in Recovery (CAAIR) supposedly operates as a diversionary treatment program for drug offenders that judges can sentence defendants to as an alternative to prison.[88] In reality, CAAIR operates a labor camp, in which residents work long hours in slaughterhouses for large food companies. There is no real treatment to speak of, and CAAIR pockets the workers' wages. Sometimes those sent there haven't even committed drug offenses. It appears to exist simply to provide convict labor for large corporations. This is an example of neoliberal criminal justice: maximize the return you get on your prisoners. The corporation gets profitable labor, and the state saves money that would have had to be spent on corrections. Everyone wins! (Except the prisoner, but if they didn't want to do the time, they shouldn't have done the crime.)

- **Goodbye History, Hello *League of Legends*:** The University of Akron recently announced that it would be cutting 80 different programs, both at the undergraduate and graduate level, including its history and sociology PhD programs.[89] This isn't because the university is out of money. In fact, at the same time they announced that they're spending $750,000 to build a new facility for "esports" (aka video games). In explaining its decision, Akron said that few students enrolled in the programs it was cutting, whereas the video game program would attract more participation. Students are therefore "customers," and the university exists not to offer knowledge, but to satisfy market demand. In fact, public universities increasingly operate like businesses and are bloated with administrators drawn from the private sector. Schools have hiked tuition through the roof and paid for huge legacy construction projects instead of improving instructor compensation. The "adjunct-ification" of academia has meant that instructors are poorly paid and have little job security. The share of budgets allocated to teaching has declined. Many universities seem to be portfolios of assets rather than educational institutions, with "ever-expanding real estate holdings, hospitals, corporate partnerships, and sports teams that are professional in every sense of the word—except that the players work for free."[90] None of this makes any sense if you think of a university as a place for learning and study. But if you run it like a business, the logic is obvious: cut labor costs (salaries) and dump negative assets (the history department). We are seeing deep cuts to research budgets at public universities, in part because it's difficult for a lot of researchers to justify themselves under "market logic."

• **Kids 4 Cash:** In 2008, there was a scandal in Wilkes-Barre, Pennsylvania: Two local judges were accused of taking kickbacks from a private juvenile detention center in exchange for sentencing children to that facility. The judges ruined thousands of young people's lives, imprisoning them for offenses as minor as cursing or creating a satirical MySpace page about their school's vice principal. The judges were indicted and convicted over the scheme, and there was understandable moral outrage about the case: kids were being sent to a cockroach-infested prison because judges had been bribed. And yet the case was only an extreme example of something that goes on every day, the major difference being that, in this case, the misconduct was actually illegal. One of the Wilkes-Barre judges defended himself, saying, "Look, this was a finder's fee. We needed this center built." And while it's uncommon for judges to be given "finder's fees," there is plenty of profit in criminal justice. The private prison industry in the United States is huge, and there is a tremendous amount of lobbying by prison companies against any measure that would reduce occupancy.[91] Legislators receive hundreds of thousands of dollars from corporations like CoreCivic (formerly the Corrections Corporation of America). Coincidentally, these same legislators never enact criminal justice reforms that would meaningfully reduce the profitability of the prison industry.

In each of these news stories, we see a similar tendency: maximize, maximize, maximize. Values like fairness, democracy, and wisdom all disappear. Instead, everything becomes quantified, and market values predominate. This is neoliberalism: what happens depends on the market and almost nothing else. The courses a university offers are based on what the market wants: if that's video games rather than history, so be it. Criminal laws are based on what best serves the profits of the prison industry, and who gets fire protection depends on who can *pay* for it. Community is not valued in a society like this. Money rules absolutely.[92]

The logical conclusion to this kind of society is terrifying. In Boots Riley's satirical dystopian film *Sorry to Bother You*, we see a vision of what such a place might look like. Riley depicts a world in which most people are in debt and struggling to make a living, while a few incredibly rich people at the top live lives of unbelievable luxury and decadence. (So far, so familiar.) Against this backdrop, a company called WorryFree offers people a tantalizing bargain: it will wipe out their debts and give them guaranteed housing, food, and healthcare. All they have to do is agree to come and work at the WorryFree campus, for life. They sign their lives over to the company, and in exchange the company takes care of their essential needs. It's the same bargain that once led many people to sign up for lives of indentured servitude and that still leads migrant laborers to accept exploitative work arrangements. But Riley shows us that if we keep going the way we're going, there's no reason such a thing couldn't happen in our own time and place. After all, wouldn't you want to be worry-free? It's tempting for desperate people to accept the deal. Yet this free-market solution ends up reproducing slavery: we all end up owned by a company, and the company's profits determine the course of our lives.

There is one more salient feature of neoliberalism that is essential in identifying it in the wild: fake social progressivism. This is one of its most sinister traits, because it helps unjust institutions appear benevolent and forward-thinking. To illustrate what I mean, consider the following real headline: "The U.S. and Israel Are Trying to Cure Breast Cancer with Tasteful Pink Fighter Jet."[93] That's it in a nutshell. Two repressive governments tried to illustrate their progressive bona fides by painting a *machine of death*. You'll notice that tendency over and over: an institution that is *inherently* hierarchical and unjust tries to defuse criticisms through superficial changes. A corporation, for instance, will not increase the rights of its ordinary workers or eliminate racial and gender pay gaps, but it might introduce racial and gender diversity on its board of directors.

One distinguishing difference between neoliberalism and plain old nineteenth-century free-market capitalism is this tendency to try to improve the "image" without changing the substance. Wall Street votes Democratic now, holds diversity trainings, and deplores outright bigotry. But they still won't hesitate to profit off the victims of a natural disaster or close a factory to make a buck.

Finally, a caution against "totalizing" words to describe everything under one umbrella. Some socialists attempt to link everything together under one System: racism, sexism, capitalism. I am not this kind of socialist. I certainly see common tendencies that cause a wide variety of ills: greed, prejudice, obliviousness, etcetera. But I'm reluctant to lump lots of small things together as part of one Gigantic, All-Explaining Phenomenon. I use the term *neoliberalism* only with the most extreme reluctance and in full awareness that it may cause you to close this book and write me off. (I promise, it won't recur after this chapter.)

* * *

ALRIGHT, THAT WAS all very grim. I am sorry. I am not a grim person by nature. But, well, if we're going to be serious, we have to face up to Unpleasant Facts. And many facts are deeply unpleasant. The whole "serious existential threats to the future of our species" thing needs to be discussed.

Let us not, however, throw our hands up in despair just yet. We will find our way out of this mess. Please bear with me. First, however, I want to make one or two observations about capitalism, to clear the way for convincing you to embrace socialism.

The Army of Psychopathic Androids

How Capitalism Works

"We must make our choice. We may have democracy, or we may have wealth concentrated in the hands of a few, but we can't have both."

—Louis Brandeis, quoted in
Mr. Justice Brandeis, Great American (1941)

"The few own the many because they possess the means of livelihood of all . . . The country is governed for the richest, for the corporations, the bankers, the land speculators, and for the exploiters of labor. The majority of mankind are working people. So long as their fair demands—the ownership and control of their livelihoods—are set at naught, we can have neither men's rights nor women's rights. The majority of mankind is ground down by industrial oppression in order that the small remnant may live in ease."

—Helen Keller, "To an English Woman Suffragist,"
Manchester Advertiser (1911)

"God gave me my money."

—John D. Rockefeller, *Woman's Home Companion* (1915)

IF A CORPORATION WAS A person, they might be the worst person you have ever met in your life. They might manipulate you into doing things you didn't want to do, take advantage of your weaknesses, lie to you if it benefited them, and show zero regard for basic standards of moral conduct. Then again, they might not, so long as it was to their advantage to treat you well. That's a crucial fact about those who serve only themselves: It's not that they'll never be nice to you or will never do anything to help you. It's that the moment you cease to be of use to them, they will abandon or betray you.

Economist Milton Friedman wrote a classic article called "The Social Responsibility of Business Is to Increase Its Profits."[1] Friedman made his own position very clear: a corporation exists to serve its shareholders, period. The shareholders own the business, and the managers' "responsibility is to conduct the business in accordance with [the shareholders'] desires," which are generally "to make as much money as possible" within the boundaries of the law. Friedman was criticizing businessmen who talked of their companies as having a "social responsibility," for example, to help the environment or improve their communities. Friedman said that even to use this phrase means "preaching pure and unadulterated socialism," and executives "who talk this way are unwitting puppets of the intellectual forces that have been undermining the basis of a free society." Friedman's position sounds extreme. But he argued that any businessman who considers responsibilities beyond profit is, in effect, taking money from the company's owners. Anything a company spends on, say, sponsoring a new ice rink for neighborhood children is frittering away that which rightfully belongs to the owners.

If corporate executives follow Friedman's recommendation, what happens? Well, Friedman is quite literally endorsing a pathological pursuit of profit. Profit is all that the executive should think about. It doesn't matter if people's lives are made miserable as a result, or if a few rare animal species are wiped out. As long as it's legal and makes money, do it.

To see what this kind of thinking leads to, we can look at Coca-Cola. President of Coca-Cola International Ahmet Bozer was once quoted as saying, "Half the world's population has not had a Coke in the last 30 days . . . There's 600 million teenagers who have not had a Coke in the last week. So the opportunity for that is huge."[2] According to the *New York Times*, a former Coke vice president said that the company's goal "became much larger than merely beating the rival brands; Coca-Cola strove to outsell every other thing people drank, including milk and water. The marketing division's efforts boiled down to one question . . . 'How can we drive more ounces into more bodies more often?'"[3] As a result of this policy, Coca-Cola has specifically targeted poor areas around the world. Coca-Cola's former North American president Jeffrey Dunn was horrified by what he saw when he toured one of the impoverished districts the company was trying to flood with Coke. "A voice in my head says, 'These people need a lot of things, but they don't need a Coke.' I almost threw up." When Dunn raised his concerns and tried to change the business, he encountered "very aggressive" resistance and was fired.[4]

Coca-Cola is just doing what Friedman said it should. As a chairman of GM is alleged to have once said, the job of GM is to make money, not cars, and beverage companies operate the same way. So do drug companies. Internal documents revealed Purdue Pharma, the makers of OxyContin, were constantly seeking new ways to get people addicted to their product. Former president Richard Sackler wrote that the company should "measure our performance by Rx's by strength, giving higher measures to higher strengths."[5] Lawsuits against Purdue have charged that the company "knew that putting patients on high dosages of OxyContin for long periods increased the risks of serious side effects, including addiction," yet "promoted higher dosages because stronger pain pills brought the company and the Sacklers the most profit."[6] Perhaps most despicably, as tens of thousands of casualties mounted, Sackler encouraged the company to blame addicts for their own problems, despite the company's deliberate efforts to get them hooked. "We have to hammer on abusers in every way possible. They are the culprits and the problem," he wrote in an internal email. He objected to "criminal addicts . . . being glorified as some sort of populist victim."[7]

There is a logic to this. You might think that it would be in a company's interests to ensure that people don't die. But it isn't always. Ecologist Paul Ehrlich quotes a Japanese journalist who tried to explain why Ehrlich was wrong to assume whalers would have an interest in keeping whale populations high:

You are thinking of the whaling industry as an organisation that is interested in maintaining whales; actually it is better viewed as a huge quantity of capital attempting to earn the highest possible re-turn. If it can exterminate whales in ten years to make a 15% profit, but it could only make a 10% profit with a sustainable harvest, then it will exterminate them in ten years. After that, the money will be moved to exterminating some other resource.[8]

The profit-seeking corporation isn't *always* an extermination ma-chine. Adam Smith famously argued that the pursuit of self-interest could be beneficial to all: the baker wants my money, and I want her bread; therefore, it's in her interest to sell me bread and my interest to pay for it. The pursuit of profit is a powerful force for satisfying people's wants, and it's one reason I can go out and choose from hundreds of brands of shoes and find the one that suits my feet just right.

But there are also some truly perverse consequences to the un-checked pursuit of self-interest. It leads, for one thing, to exploitation, that is, taking advantage of people's deprivation. If I see that you are desperate for work, I won't offer you any more than the bare minimum necessary to get you to work for me, even if that isn't nearly enough to live on. Smith admitted that companies were always careful to avoid paying their workers any more than they had to: "Masters are always and everywhere in a sort of tacit, but constant and uniform combina-tion, not to raise the wages of labour above their actual rate."[9] That's why, after Donald Trump's gigantic corporate tax giveaway of 2018, we didn't see companies sharing the proceeds with their workers. Instead, they were a windfall to corporate shareholders, who took home boat-loads of extra profits even as workers continued to be paid far less than they needed to live on.[10]

In the early twentieth century, Frederick Taylor published *The Principles of Scientific Management*, one of the most influential busi-ness books of the last hundred years. His system, which became known as Taylorism, applied the ruthless principle of efficiency to the process of running an organization. It advocated timing every part of the pro-duction process, trimming here and there to make sure that maximum productivity was being extracted from workers. The philosophy quite literally treated workers as indistinguishable from "cogs," in that as far as the organization was concerned, they were simply a statistical unit that created a certain daily output, an output that should be increased by whatever means necessary.[11] When people talk about capitalism's wondrous efficiency at improving productivity, they are often talking about disregarding the humanity of laborers and being willing to inflict any amount of fear and misery if it helps the collective.[12] Certainly, this process is effective. But threatening a person at gunpoint is also effective, and unless we have a theory of what is and is not acceptable, a quest to improve results at all costs will lead to gross violations of people's dignity.

Historically, some have assumed that this tendency would cause capitalism to self-destruct. Karl Marx believed that the pressure to exploit workers would make them more and more poor and miserable, at which point they would rise up and overthrow the capitalists. But the capitalists turned out to be wilier than Marx thought. They knew full well that there is a limit to what you can extract from people without them turning on you, and the lessons of the French Revolution were well learned. That's why, in response to sixty years of labor agitation for the eight-hour workday, Henry Ford finally introduced it in the 1920s. When people point to the "increase in living standards" that capitalism has brought to the average worker, they frequently neglect to note that these increases have come as concessions to worker demands for a greater share of the country's prosperity. If a company could get away with it, it wouldn't pay its workers at all, and it's only when it can't get away with it that it generously expands pay and benefits. We see this at Amazon, which frequently defends itself against charges of exploitation by citing the benefits it offers to its full-time workers, benefits that its temporary workers don't receive. If Amazon's public image continues to worsen, it will offer workers more *only* to the extent that doing so benefits the company.

* * *

INTERESTINGLY, THERE IS no reason why a corporation *has* to be a profit-maximizing machine. Corporations aren't found in nature. Governments "incorporate" them and set the rules by which they can operate. In many ways, corporations are an extremely generous gift from the state to investors. The law grants shareholders "limited liability," meaning that they're not fully legally responsible for the actions of the company they own. That is a highly unusual arrangement; in other spheres, you're fully liable for what's done with your property.

Corporations are downright bizarre entities: legally, they are artificial people that exist to maximize profits for other people, while shielding them from legal liability. Even if Friedman is right that, given the design of the institution, a corporation should maximize shareholder value, it's unclear why we would design such an institution in the first place. Why would you create legally artificial people with no moral responsibilities and a pathological devotion to their own self-interest and set them loose on the world? This is like building an army of psychopathic androids!

The answer is that *we* didn't actually design this institution. The American corporation evolved over time. Originally, it was an institution chartered by the government to carry out a specific set of functions for the public. You might charter a corporation to, say, build a bridge. But over time, the institution evolved as the legal doctrine of "corporate personhood" was developed. Yet, as late as the 1970s, few people thought corporations existed as pure profit-maximization machines. It was with the "shareholder revolution" of the 1980s that Friedman's conception of the corporation's function developed and a notion took hold that there was a legal duty to put shareholders above all other stakeholders.

Nobody went out and tried to raise an army of psychopathic androids. But that's what we've got. And now they're endangering us all.

There is a thought experiment called the "paperclip maximizer" that is often used by those who are concerned about the risks of artificial intelligence.[13] The paperclip maximizer is a machine programmed to do one thing: manufacture as many paperclips as possible. It is built to innovate new ways of making office supplies more efficiently. And yet, that's not what the machine does. Instead, it destroys the world. Why? Because it's only programmed to do *one thing*: build paperclips. And it doesn't care about anything else. At first, this might work quite well. It finds new materials and creates paperclips out of them, and everyone has more paperclips and is happy. Soon, though, things go quite wrong. The machine starts turning *everything* into paperclips. It has one mandate, and it follows it to the letter. It turns people into paperclips. It turns the whole *universe* into paperclips. That is, after all, its job.

The paperclip maximizer is science fiction. But it captures an important concept that should make us very dubious about profit-maximizing corporations. If you only give an organization one mandate and tell it to forget everything else, you might get the mandate fulfilled, but at a terrible price. If you build an artificial legal person and tell it to go and make as much money selling Coke as possible, it may hydrate many millions of people. But it may also market Coke to children, start offering 46-ounce bottles as single servings, and try to destroy every other beverage.

On a global scale, the consequences are existentially threatening. Look at climate change, for instance. The maximization of growth for fossil fuel companies will ultimately destroy large parts of the planet. These companies have distorted scientific fact, lobbied extensively, and done everything in their power to ensure that nothing is done about climate change, since it would threaten their organizational mandate. In the pursuit of growth, corporations routinely inflict serious environmental damage with a high human toll, but these "externalities" do not matter to them. In fact, if they're taking Friedman seriously, they *cannot* matter and it would actually be *irresponsible* to consider anything other than the corporation.

It's very obvious, given that we live on a planet with finite resources, that endless growth is impossible. And yet we have created artificial entities that exist to pursue endless growth, that cannot stop themselves from doing so. Like the paperclip maximizer, this is a recipe for civilizational suicide.

CAPITAL AND THE PHILOSOPHY OF PROPERTY

Nineteenth-century philosopher Pierre-Joseph Proudhon famously wrote, "Property is theft."[14] The phrase is a paradox because it seems strange to even speak of "theft" without having a concept of "property." But for Proudhon, property *was* a paradox.

Proudhon asked us to consider where property came from in the first place. We all know what it *is*, or think we do. I own my shirt and my books, which means that I have the right to dispose of them how I wish. I can destroy them. I can sell them. I can carry them from place to place, and nobody else has the legal right to control them. If someone else tries to exercise the same rights as I have, by destroying or selling them, they have stolen from me.

Where did I get my right from? Well, I got it because I bought my possessions from others. I exchanged one thing I owned (money) for another (stuff). Where did the people I bought from get *their* right? Well, they bought it from someone else, and so on and so forth. However, Proudhon asks us to consider how property came about in the beginning. Why are there even property rights at all? How did the world go from being "unowned" to "owned"? When our ancestors were single-celled creatures, or fish-beasts, or even *homo erectus*, the world wasn't owned, so why is it owned now?

The answer is that at various points, certain pieces of the world have been "claimed." For Proudhon, however, that claim has no natural legitimacy. It's unclear why, looking at an unowned world, I should be able to take part of it for myself *and demand that other people recognize my right*. By what right do I get to exclude people from certain parts of the world, and where does that right come from? Proudhon says that there *is* no such right, and that by claiming I can exclude others from using the world's resources (because they are "mine"), I am stealing from them. Hence, "property is theft," meaning that the very thing property rights supposedly do (protect people's right to use things), they actually abrogate completely by denying people's right to share in the world's resources.[15]

In fact, the origins of private property are often even more unjust than that. If we trace back existing property to its roots, we find much of it originates in conquest, and it's hard to say that we should respect property rights when the property itself is stolen. Texas was stolen from Mexico, and the United States was stolen from its Native population. In England, the commons were seized and privatized in the enclosure movement. There was no "right" to any of this, except to the extent that *might* makes right. That doesn't mean that nobody should be entitled to keep anything they currently own. But it does mean that we should raise a skeptical eyebrow at people who get furious at any perceived infringement on "their" property rights.

Nineteenth-century economist Henry George pointed out that property rights were especially questionable when it came to land. If I make a birdhouse with my bare hands, we might think it logical that I should be the one who gets to decide what to do with that birdhouse. (Though, if I stole the wood to build the birdhouse from a person who chopped down a tree on land they did not own, the answer becomes much murkier.) But nobody created the land. The only way land is originally turned into property is through seizure, and seizure does not establish a particularly compelling claim. For George, that meant that taxes on land were the most just form of taxation, because the land belonged to all. Landlords do not create wealth, they merely benefit from their ownership of something that they have no right to own in the first place.

The sanctity of property rights forms a major part of the intellectual defense of capitalism. But while there may be a pragmatic case for respecting parts of the existing property regime, there is very little "natural" right, and there is nothing sacred about property. Everything we control derives ultimately from a historically illegitimate seizure of either the commons or the possessions of people who were too weak to protect themselves.

* * *

Let's talk about capital itself. Under our capitalist system, many people make money not by working, but by having money. Thirty percent of income in the United States is capital income.[16] It accrues to people based on their investments. We may, of course, find this perfectly legitimate, and the argument made in its defense is that investors "risk" their money by investing and are therefore entitled to the rewards that accrue when those investments pay off. Nevertheless, the amount of passive income devastates two core dogmas that are used to justify inequality:

1. People work for their money.
2. If people do not work for their money and get "handouts," they become lazy and dependent.

A significant fraction of the wealthy's wealth is not the product of their labor. They earn it in their sleep because they have money to invest. Now, I don't think this in and of itself is a bad thing. I think it's *fine* for people to get money they haven't worked for, because I'm a socialist! But the idea that only hard work produces wealth is balderdash. Sean Hannity, for example, makes a large amount of money from rental properties he owns in poor neighborhoods.[17] Hannity himself does not do anything to earn this money. He probably could not even tell you where the buildings are. Whoever manages Hannity's money takes care of the entire process of collecting rent and maintaining the buildings, and Hannity doesn't even need to hear a word about it. Hannity is reaping a good chunk of poor people's salaries, without actually *doing* anything. He simply allows his money to be used in exchange for receiving even more money. The "risk" he takes is trivial.

If we believe all of the arguments that are made against welfare, this should make Hannity lazy. After all, when people don't work for their money, when it's just *given* to them, they have no incentive to work and they become freeloaders. This was the theory behind Bill Clinton's "Welfare-to-Work" initiative and the conservative pushes to attach work requirements to social benefits. But this theory only ever seems to apply to poor people. Nobody ever says it about, for example, Dan Bilzerian, a wealthy heir who spends his life posting Instagram pictures of himself driving sports cars, flying on private planes, and sharing hot tubs with porn stars.[18] Instead, the poor are lectured on the importance of "hard work," while the rich enjoy the unearned "universal basic income" that would supposedly have such catastrophic effects on the moral fiber of welfare recipients.

Capital income is a significant driver of inequality. Poor people simply do not own stocks and are unable to invest in assets that will allow them to make money in their sleep. And once your money makes money, that money makes even *more* money, further contributing to the cycle of inequality. By contrast, indebted people spend all their money paying off their debts. Most single-parent households, for instance, have no savings or other assets, and "after debt payments, poor families are constrained to spend the remaining income on items that will not produce wealth."[19]

We have the belief that people should earn their money through hard work. But that is not capitalism, which gives people their money according to how much capital they invest. Passively earning income can be a beautiful thing. But let's hear a little less about the importance of hard work from people whose money does the work for them.

MARKET INEFFICIENCY

There is a principle everyone is taught in Economics 101 and then is swiftly encouraged to forget. It is called the principle of marginal utility, and it means that beyond a certain point, every additional unit of a good provides less satisfaction. If you give me a piece of chocolate, I may enjoy it a lot. If you give me a second piece, I will enjoy it, but perhaps a little less than I enjoyed the first, since the difference between no chocolate and a piece of chocolate is greater than the difference between one piece of chocolate and two. Each additional piece of chocolate thereafter will be slightly less satisfying to the point where I will feel I've had *quite* enough chocolate and will decline even if you offer me more.

What the principle of marginal utility means is that something is often more useful to people who have less of it than to people who already have a lot of it. If I am a gardener and I do not have a wheelbarrow, I will find a wheelbarrow very valuable. If I already have five wheelbarrows, an additional wheelbarrow will be quite unnecessary and possibly an inconvenience.

This concept is simple, but its implications are actually extremely radical. A dollar is worth far more to someone who has no dollars than to someone who has a billion. To Jeff Bezos, a ten-dollar bill on the ground may be of so little additional value that it's not even worth the effort for him to stoop to pick it up. For a homeless woman, that ten-dollar bill may be the best thing that happens to her all day. What this means is that wealth creates much more utility if it goes to poor people than if it goes to rich people.

From a utilitarian perspective, the optimal maximization of total welfare would involve a significant redistribution of wealth from the top to the bottom. If you take $10,000 from Elon Musk's bank account and put it in the account of a farmer in Myanmar, Musk may not even notice the absence, but the farmer's life will be totally altered. The failure to redistribute wealth, then, creates significant economic inefficiencies. It destroys incalculable amounts of potential utility by not putting wealth to its optimal use. We may believe that this waste of utility is justified by our conception of property rights, or we may have other arguments against redistribution based on its consequences, but we must accept that all other things being equal, we are squandering our resources.[20]

MARKET IMMORALITY

Deferring to the judgment of the free market in allocating resources is morally odious as well as inefficient. Sentimental types like myself often react with horror when advocates of free markets say things like "morality has no application to market interactions under the conditions of perfect competition" or "the first principle of economics is that every agent is actuated only by self-interest."[21] The legitimizing of "self-interest"—aka, a callous indifference to the needs and desires of others except insofar as they serve you—creates a society that is intolerable to live in. Selfishness is unpleasant to be around, and people like Ayn Rand and Friedman make *bad friends*.

But there is also empirical evidence that markets undermine compassion. In *The Moral Economy*, Samuel Bowles reports on studies showing that when ordinary relationships become "transactional," people's morality erodes. He cites a famous study of a daycare that introduced a fine intended to reduce the number of parents who showed up late to pick up their child. Instead of reducing late pickups, the fine *increased* them, because people no longer felt a moral obligation to show up on time. They thought they could buy their way out of having to be a decent person. There's even evidence that just by studying economics, with its implicit sanctioning of greed, people become less generous to others. That's not surprising, since in economic textbooks, trying to secure an advantage over others is transformed, in Bowles' words, "from a moral failing to just another kind of motive, like a taste for ice cream."[22] Many economists even treat price gouging, such as trying to get as much money out of disaster victims as you can, as a perfectly legitimate form of "maximizing mutual self-interest."[23] (The disaster victim gets a bottle of water, and I get $1,000. Everyone wins!)

John Stuart Mill said that economics was concerned with the

human "solely [as a] being who desires to possess wealth."[24] But that's not what we are, and we should be very careful about embracing that ugly picture of human motivation, since we may end up tempted to believe it!

WHAT'S WRONG WITH INEQUALITY?

Many billionaires now realize that inequality is a crisis. In 2014, investor Nick Hanauer warned his "fellow plutocrats" that "the pitchforks are coming for us."[25] BlackRock executive Larry Fink, in his annual letter to corporate executives, warned, "Those with capital have reaped enormous benefits," while "many individuals across the world are facing a combination of low rates, low wage growth, and inadequate retirement systems."[26] At the annual Davos conference, where the world's super-elites gather to schmooze and plot, several talks have focused heavily on the inequality problem, though without much attention to the role the conference itself plays in reproducing the problem. (The Davos attendees did, however, learn how the other half lives by engaging in an elaborate role-play of the "refugee experience," in which they "pretended to flee advancing armies."[27] Interestingly, Marie Antoinette once did something similar, keeping a fake rustic village on her grounds where she occasionally dressed up as a peasant for fun.[28])

There are, however, some outright defenders of inequality. Steven Pinker, in *Enlightenment Now*, says that equality is "not a fundamental dimension of human well-being."[29] He cites the philosopher Harry Frankfurt, whose book *On Inequality* suggests that it's actually *irrational* to care about inequality.[30] Frankfurt's argument is that it doesn't matter whether some people have a lot more than others. It only matters whether some people do not have enough. We should care about *poverty*, not inequality. This may seem like a trivial distinction, but Frankfurt and Pinker insist it's important. After all, you could have a situation of perfect equality in which everyone is poor (there will be economic equality after the apocalypse, for instance). They argue that instead of focusing on making people equal, we should focus on making poor people less poor, even if we end up making rich people even richer in the process.

Frankfurt and Pinker are wrong to think that inequality doesn't matter in and of itself. To see why, think about voting. In a democracy, every person theoretically has an equal vote.[31] If some people were given two votes rather than one, however, those people would have twice as much power to affect political decisions. Wealth operates very similarly to votes, as a "bidding contest" to determine how different bits of property will be used. But in these "market elections," people have very different numbers of "votes," that is, wealth. Larry Ellison, for instance, owns the entire Hawaiian island of Lanai. He gets to determine what happens on it, and the residents don't, because they can't afford to buy the island. This is similar to a feudal system, in which the lord is in charge by virtue of his greater wealth. Democracy, on the other hand, is predicated on equality: everyone gets to participate equally because we all have a stake in the outcomes of political decisions. Objecting to inequality is just applying the same principle to the market that we would to the government.

Along similar lines, Warren Buffett has said, "The poor are not poor because the rich are rich."[32] This is false, and quite obviously so. The argument made here is that leftists are wrong to think of the economy as a pie in which one person will get a smaller slice if another person gets a larger slice. They even have a name for this type of thinking, the "fixed pie fallacy." It's a fallacy, they say, because *unlike* a pie, all of our portion sizes can grow simultaneously. The fact that the rich are getting richer does not mean that the poor are getting poorer, because if the economy grows, both the wealthy and the poor can get richer simultaneously.

It's true that the size of the overall economic pie isn't constant. It's fallacious, though, to think this means that the poor aren't poor because the rich are rich. If I'm getting slightly richer and you're getting *much* richer, your vast riches still constitute a mountain of wealth that could be used to, say, provide good public schools or give working mothers paid maternity leave. Every dollar that the rich choose to or are permitted to keep is a dollar that isn't going into the economies of Flint, Michigan, or Gary, Indiana.

Those, like Frankfurt and Pinker, who argue that economic inequality doesn't matter don't see the way money confers social power.

That power is "zero sum," in that when you have more of it, I necessarily have less of it. If you and I start with one vote each, and you are given three more votes, while I am given one more vote, my power has decreased relative to yours, *even though* my total number of votes has increased. Money operates similarly. The more say the rich have in society, the less the poor have, even if everyone's income is rising at the same time.

CORPORATE POWER

Corporate power has important implications for people's freedom. Friedman's book *Capitalism and Freedom* famously argued that "economic freedom," that is, free markets, and "political freedom," that is, civil liberties, went together. But if we look at people's actual lives, the promised freedom seems like a joke, because employers have so much power over their employees' lives. Employers can decide what their employees wear, who they can talk to, when they can pee, and what they can say on social media. In the United States, we have complete at-will employment in most states, meaning that if you do *anything* to tick off your boss, they can send you packing and rob you of your livelihood.

You have very few rights at work. In society at large, you have protected rights: the government cannot abridge the First Amendment's protections of your freedom of speech, and the Fourth Amendment means it cannot invade your privacy with unreasonable searches and seizures. None of that applies on the job: an employer can fire you not just for what you say *at* work, but what you say off the job. This creates an environment in which people are often as scared to voice their opinions as they would be in a police state; as a magazine editor, I've had plenty of prospective writers beg me to let them publish under pseudonyms because they were afraid that their employers would fire them if they were found to have publicly expressed their political opinions.

Chris Bertram, Corey Robin, and Alex Gourevitch explain the endless, nefarious ways in which employer power operates:

> Outside the prison or the military . . . it's difficult to conceive of a less
> free institution for adults than the average workplace . . . Employers

[demand that employees] hand over passwords to their Facebook accounts, and fire them for resisting such invasions. Employers secretly film their employees at home. Workers are fired for supporting the wrong political candidates ("work for John Kerry or work for me"), failing to donate to employer-approved candidates, challenging government officials, writing critiques of religion on their personal blogs (IBM instructs employees to "show proper consideration . . . for topics that may be considered objectionable or inflammatory—such as politics and religion"), carrying on extramarital affairs, participating in group sex at home, cross-dressing, and more. Workers are punished for smoking or drinking in the privacy of their own homes. (How many nanny states have tried that?) They can be fired for merely thinking about having an abortion . . . [or] for being raped by an estranged husband.[33]

Bertram et al. also point out that because the government is constrained by the Constitution, private action can be used to punish people in ways the government can't. For example, during the McCarthy era, very few Americans were actually sent to *jail* for having communist sympathies. But many were investigated by their employers. The Hollywood Blacklist was a private-sector form of repression: studios wouldn't give work to people suspected of holding certain political beliefs. These private punishments, which do not come with the due process rights that defendants get in public criminal cases, can be just as effective in silencing dissidents. Political philosopher Elizabeth Anderson has even gone so far as to compare corporations to "communist dictatorships," in part because they are surveillance states where the desires of the individual are subordinated to the mission of the collective.[34]

Corporations have nothing resembling the democratic decision-making that holds governments accountable. As an employee, your right to decide what the company does is usually nil. You don't get to vote for your boss, and if you disobey them, you can find yourself without a paycheck! It's worth considering what we'd call a country that was run along the same political lines as a company is.

All of these problems become much worse as corporations become more monopolistic. When a company is the only game in town, it has total power to dictate terms. The libertarian defense of corporate power is that we hand over our rights "freely"; nobody *makes* you sign up for Facebook or get a job in an Amazon warehouse. Friedman's famous documentary series lauding capitalism is called *Free to Choose*. When a few companies win the market competition and own all the brands in a particular industry, choice becomes meaningless, and consumers exercise no meaningful power to decide which company should rule over them.

Mainstream economists recognize the negative consequences of monopolies. Yale's Robert Shiller, a moderate who defends most features of capitalism, has said that we "will need to be vigilant to prevent the concentration of economic power, and we should work to disperse the ownership of capital even further."[35] When capital becomes concentrated in just a few companies, those companies develop formidable political power as well. Nobody can compete with them in terms of lobbying, and thanks to Supreme Court decisions like *Citizens United*, corporations are able to exercise their resources however they like to manipulate the political discourse.

The result is that government policy is set according to the wishes of the wealthiest residents rather than the will of the majority. Political scientists have confirmed that the desires of ordinary people in the United States have almost no effect on policy-making, a finding that should be somewhat shocking considering that we supposedly have "self-governance." Instead, corporations have been "particularly effective at using the tools of a political democracy—where, in theory, the majority should rule—to protect its minority privilege."[36] Even the taxes that we do have are routinely avoided, and an entire "income defense industry" exists to help the wealthy avoid paying the sums that they are required to pay. If "the people" pose too much of a threat to a corporation's finances, the corporation will just threaten to take its ball and go home. This is what happened in Seattle, where the city had to drop plans to impose a relatively minor tax on employers after Amazon threatened to leave the city.[37] Corporate power is so great that cities must beg companies not to leave, offering as many tax breaks and other incentives as the company demands.

The growth of monopolies and oligopolies in the United States has been downright extraordinary. All of the major eyeglass retailers (LensCrafters, Sears Optical, Sunglass Hut, Pearle Vision) are part of the same company,[38] and 90 percent of America's domestic beer production is controlled by two companies.[39] Google has a virtual monopoly on searches, and Facebook, YouTube, Apple, and Twitter each dominate their respective markets. This means they have total power to dictate terms. *Current Affairs* itself depends heavily on Facebook and Twitter to distribute its content. If either site were to ban our magazine, our business would almost certainly collapse overnight. These two companies hold our fate in their hands, and if they tell us we have to do something, we would have to seriously consider doing it. We remain in their favor, for now, but a benevolent dictator is still a dictator.

Friedrich Hayek, one of the foremost intellectual defenders of capitalism, wrote, "So long as property is divided among many owners, none of them acting independently has exclusive power to determine the income position of particular people."[40] But when property is *not* divided among many owners, they do have the power to determine people's income positions. In *Capital Moves*, Jefferson Cowie tracks the growth in the power of employers and the declining power of labor unions, and shows the consequences. RCA, for example, simply moved its capital elsewhere whenever workers threatened to gain the upper hand:

> Each of RCA's plant relocations represents the corporation's response to workers' increasing sense of entitlement and control over investment in their community. Capital flight was a means of countering that control as the company sought out new reservoirs of controllable labor.[41]

Ironically, the concentration of capital means that one of the great fears about socialism—that decisions about what to sell would be made by small, unelected groups of bureaucrats, rather than determined by competition—is increasingly coming true under capitalism. As economist Rob Larson writes, "Rather than the 'planned economy' of socialism that haunts Friedrich Hayek's dreams, it is corporate monopoly and oligopoly, and their industrial organizations, that are the main source of today's central planning."[42] Instead of the government determining which speech will be heard and which product features will be offered, the decisions are made by Mark Zuckerberg and Twitter's Jack Dorsey, whom nobody ever voted for.

* * *

MANY PEOPLE, ESPECIALLY those who are extremely wealthy, do not necessarily deny that we live in an economic system in which greed is rewarded and modesty punished. They just don't see a problem with it. Friedman, when asked if he ever had any doubts about capitalism, replied, "Do you know any economy that doesn't run on greed? You think Russia doesn't run on greed?" (So, no, no doubts at all.) Hayek called it a "misfortune" that many had "defended free enterprise on the ground that it regularly rewards the deserving," since it so frequently doesn't.[43]

Plenty of the super-wealthy, though, do think they deserve what they have. Even Buffett, one of the few billionaires alleged to have a conscience, has said that the rich should not be called "undeserving" because "most of them have contributed brilliant innovations or managerial expertise to America's well-being."[44] Chrystia Freeland, in her book *Plutocrats*, quotes several highly successful investors defending their right to riches.[45] Billionaire Leon Cooperman says the rich are not "a monolithic, selfish, and unfeeling lot who must be subjugated by the force of the state . . . we employ many millions of taxpaying people, pay their salaries." JPMorgan Chase CEO Jamie Dimon says, "Acting like . . . because you're rich, you're bad—I don't understand it." Bond trader Dennis Gartman went even further:

> We celebrate income disparity and we applaud the growing margins between the bottom 20 percent of American society and the upper 20 percent for it is evidence of what has made America a great country. It is the chance to have a huge income . . . Income disparity? Feh! What we despise is government that imposes rules that prohibit or make it difficult to make even more money.

At their core, these millionaires and billionaires believe that their money is theirs because they earned it, and the government has no "right" to take it away from them. They should get to spend it. Furthermore, they should not be criticized for their success. They should even be praised, because they are the "job creators" who get things done. Freeland quotes Wyoming businessman and conservative politician Foster Friess, who says, "I think we ought to have taxes as low as possible . . . [I]f you look at what Steve Jobs has done for us, what Bill Gates has done for society, the government ought to pay *them* . . . I've never seen poor people hire many people. So I think we ought to honor and uplift the 1 percent, the ones who have created value." Right-wing economist Ludwig von Mises put this somewhat more bluntly in a letter to Ayn Rand, in which he praised her for being willing to tell the "masses" that "you are inferior and all the improvements in your conditions which you simply take for granted you owe to the effort of men who are better than you."[46]

There are several important fallacies at the heart of this view. First is the conflation of market value and moral desert. Second is the idea that taxes are an illegitimate appropriation of "your" money. Third is the idea that capitalists build the fortunes of the workers, rather than workers building the fortunes of capitalists. Fourth, it is incontrovertibly true that being rich *does* make you a bad person. And fifth, the reason Friess hasn't seen many poor people hiring anyone is that . . . never mind, I won't insult your intelligence.[47]

It should be very clear why we can't mix up what you're "worth" in a market sense with what you're "worth" from the standpoint of your usefulness to your fellow creatures. It's an old observation that the people who do the least pleasant and most necessary work (such as cleaning up other people's shit) are the least compensated, while the useless children of the superrich are able to live off inheritances. And conflating the two types of worth often leads to policies that border on the eugenic: valuing "productive" immigrants over "nonproductive" ones, for instance, results in excluding the disabled, sick, and elderly.

We can also look at specific examples of vital contributions that go uncompensated. Very few of the programmers and tinkerers who pioneered the internet, for example, got rich from their endeavors. Tim

Berners-Lee, who created the World Wide Web, does not get paid each time we use it. Wikipedia has vastly expanded basic access to the repository of human knowledge, but has not yielded a fortune for its creator, Jimmy Wales. Even libertarian PayPal billionaire Peter Thiel has admitted that when it comes to scientific, technological, and medical innovation, the innovators themselves often receive about zero percent of the reward.[48] Why? Because innovators are not businessmen. They pursue their creations for the thrill of discovery. The people who get rich are the ones who learn to monetize that discovery, the ones who can talk the innovator into signing over their rights in exchange for a small lump sum. How many people at the top of the Forbes 400 actually invented something? What did Buffett invent? Ray Dalio? George Soros? The Koch brothers?

It's worth touching briefly on this idea that the government, by taxing people, is taking away something that belongs to them. Some people use the idea that they "own" their incomes to question the entire idea of "distributing." Don Watkins and Yaron Brook, for instance, suggest that there is no such thing as distribution, only *illegitimate seizure*: "Wealth is not distributed by society: it is produced and traded by the people who create it. To distribute it, society would first have to seize it from the people who created it."[49] But all of this ignores the role that government plays in setting up the market to begin with.[50] Money exists because of government; it is made *by* the government. And the government is responsible for creating the conditions under which all wealth creation is possible. Your pre-tax income cannot *entirely* be "yours," because in order for you to have an income at all, there must be a large, powerful government, and for there to be a government there must be taxation.[51] The government is involved in setting the rules of the economic game in a myriad of different ways, from defining how corporate charters work to defining liability rules to setting up ways of discharging debts in bankruptcy. The government is not a parasite, it is responsible for making sure that wealth can be created in the first place.

*   *   *

NOBODY COULD ACCUSE Frederick Douglass of minimizing the horrors of slavery. He wrote brilliantly and movingly about what it was like to be owned by another human being, and the physical and psychological degradation that was inflicted by slave masters. But Douglass knew that mere freedom from being owned wasn't enough. Real freedom meant freedom from being exploited, as well, because even if one was nominally "free," in an unequal society one could still be dominated by one's employer. Douglass spoke of "wage slavery" and was very clear that the power to compel people in a free market could be as coercive as slavery itself.

> Experience demonstrates that there may be a slavery of wages only a little less galling and crushing in its effects than chattel slavery, and that this slavery of wages must go down with the other . . . The man who has it in his power to say to a man you must work the land for me, for such wages as I choose to give, has a power of slavery over him as real, if not as complete, as he who compels toil under the lash.[52]

The twenty-first century is not, thankfully, as brutal to most working people as the late nineteenth century was. (Unless you are a Chinese iPhone assembler or a construction worker in Dubai.) But Douglass' principle should be taken very seriously: The free market is not necessarily free. Whether people are free depends not just on whether they own themselves, but whether others have power over them in practice.

*   *   *

NOTHING I HAVE said here is in any way new. In fact, it is depressingly ancient. The same defenses of capitalism have been put forward for centuries, with the same criticisms from leftists, followed by the same replies from capitalists, followed by the same rejoinders from the leftists. Everything you might say in response to my points here has already been said, with leftists having already replied to your response. In fact, if you want to know just how predictable the course of these back-and-forths is, pick up a copy of *At the Café*, a 1922 book by Italian anarchist Errico Malatesta. The book is a series of dialogues between a socialist, a capitalist, and several others. The capitalist makes all the objections Friedman would reiterate forty years later, though Friedman was only ten years old when Malatesta was writing.

AMBROGIO: Owners and workers contract freely for the price of work, and when the contract is respected no one can complain . . .

GIORGIO: But you are speaking of a free contract! The worker who does not work cannot eat, and his liberty resembles that of a traveller, assaulted by thieves, who gives up his purse for fear of losing his life.

AMBROGIO: All right; but you cannot use this to negate the right of each person to dispose of their property as they see fit . . . The law recognizes their right to it.

GIORGIO: Ah! If it is only the law, then even a street assassin could claim the right to assassinate and to rob: he would only have to formulate a few articles of law that recognized these rights. On the other hand, this is precisely what the dominant class has accomplished: it has created laws to legitimize the usurpations that it has already perpetrated, and has made them a means of new appropriations.[53]

And so on. I would invite those readers who have prepared elaborate, multipoint rebuttals to my observations to consult Malatesta's book. There, they will likely find that Ambrogio has already made their arguments for them and been exhaustively dealt with.

PART II

WHAT IS SOCIALISM AND WHY IS IT GOOD?

Solidarity Forever

A Set of Principles

"A socialist is just someone who is unable to get over his or her astonishment that most people who have lived and died have spent lives of wretched, fruitless, unremitting toil."

—Terry Eagleton, *Ideology: An Introduction*

"On a basic level, I am a socialist because I simply cannot fathom reconciling myself to a society where so many needlessly suffer because of circumstances beyond their control; where human dignity is distributed on the basis of luck and a social caste system is allowed to permeate every aspect of daily life; and where all of this is considered perfectly normal and acceptable in a civilization that has split the atom and sent people to the Moon."

—Luke Savage, "Liberalism in Theory and Practice," *Jacobin*[1]

"We are here to help each other get through this thing, whatever it is."

—Kurt Vonnegut, *A Man Without a Country*

SO FAR, ALL I HAVE really argued is that outrage is necessary. I have rejected the idea that we should reconcile ourselves to human misery and accept *excuses* for the status quo. I have suggested that having a functioning conscience means being troubled by the pain of others and resolving to do something about it.

This may not sound like much. Everyone, no matter what their politics, will insist that they share this orientation. They will be angry that

I'm presenting it as somehow radically left wing. "Concern for the un-fortunate is not socialism," as U.S. vice president Hubert Humphrey once said. But while Humphrey might technically be correct, I think genuine concern does at least *entail* socialism. (Moreover, I think a lot of people are lying when they say they are concerned for the unfor-tunate, and are actually concerned with the *appearance* of being con-cerned for the unfortunate.)

Let's start here with a few questions. More than half of millennials describe themselves as more sympathetic to socialism than capitalism.[2] What do they mean by these terms? What are they actually endorsing? Do they want to live in the Soviet Union? Do they want a centrally planned economy in which there is a government bureau for every product and the type of cheese you are able to buy depends on what the Bureau of Cheese has decided to make available that week?

I haven't asked them all, but I suspect this is *not* what they want. Instead, I think they are socialists of Terry Eagleton's description: people who are simply unable to get over the unfairness and brutality of the world, and who refuse to accept intellectual rationalizations for greed, bigotry, and hierarchy. They don't like how undemocratic and unequal the world is, and they refuse to accept that this is the best we can do.

That, in and of itself, is not an endorsement of a specific "alternate" economic system. Instead, it's a kind of instinct: an instinct of solidar-ity and a disagreement with a number of consensus beliefs about how wondrous and fair certain features of capitalism are. You will find that if you speak to these young people, many of them will have a dif-ficult time articulating what *exactly* they mean by socialism. That's not because they're stupid. It's because they are looking for a term that em-braces a wide number of different feelings they have and allows them to show how disgusted they are with economic and political life in the twenty-first century.

Twenty-first-century socialism expresses a commitment to a cer-tain set of values, values that are diametrically opposed to the dog-eat-dog, laissez-faire capitalism that both the Democratic and Republican parties seem to have fully embraced. It's an expression of horror at "avoidable misery"—at long hours with low pay, at dying because you can't afford medical treatment, at police shootings, at families being separated at the border. Not all of this is strictly economic. Instead, it springs from the solidarity ethic that sees all human fates as tied together, that says, in the words of Eugene Debs, "while there is a lower class, I am in it; and while there is a criminal element, I am of it; and while there is a soul in prison, I am not free."[3] The socialist does not accept that we are simply *individuals* who can freely pursue our self-interest, unencumbered by any duties toward our fellow creatures. For the socialist, in the words of an old labor slogan, "an injury to one is an injury to all."

Before today's socialists develop their theories, they start with facts and observations. For example, I have a friend who teaches second grade in Detroit. She buys her own school supplies—in fact, 94 percent of teachers end up spending their own money on school supplies.[4] She told me that her kids are lovely and they are smart, but they just do not have what they need in order to learn. Many of them come to school hungry, some are often homeless and don't know where they'll be spending the night. Separate from the issues that come from poverty at home, the school just isn't able to provide them what they need. My friend has about 30 students in her class, and because some of them are severely autistic, she spends all her time trying to keep order. At the end of the week she despairs because she wishes she could have taught them something but doesn't feel like she's been able to do her job. All this is made worse by the fact that the city's schools are dilapidated and there isn't enough money to pay for the basics. Forget having a good music program or decent sports equipment. Detroit recently estimated that its schools need $500 million worth of repairs, and the city admitted that it's not going to happen.[5] Here's a description of conditions in one of the elementary schools in 2016:

> The gym is closed because half of the floor is buckled and the other half suffered so much rainwater damage from the dripping ceiling that it became covered with toxic black mold. Instead of professionally addressing the problem, a black tarp simply was placed over the entire area like a Band-Aid. That area of the school has been condemned. The once beautiful pool sits empty because no one has come

to fix it. The playground is off-limits because a geyser of searing hot steam explodes out of the ground. What do our kids do for exercise with no gym, playground or pool? They walk or run in the halls.[6]

I was thinking about my friend's school when I went to give a talk at Phillips Academy in Andover, Massachusetts. Phillips Andover is the richest private school in the country, with a $1 billion endowment. Both George W. Bush and his father attended. It has 30 different sports programs, a world-class library, a dining hall like a cathedral, idyllic grounds. It's an amazing place: it's everything you'd ever want a school to be, and the students will all go on to be extremely successful. The school brings in experts from all over the world to give talks—they paid for my travel and offered me a substantial speaking fee.

How can one see such a place and then see a school in which the gym has been condemned and there is lead in the water and not become enraged? Whatever we might think about how people earn success, when you're young, you don't really *earn* much of anything. The kids in the Detroit school system are there because of an accident of their birth, and the Andover kids largely because of an accident of their birth. We all know that there is no element of justice in whether a 10-year-old is hungry and homeless, because children have very little control over their lives. The statistics on youth homelessness are staggering—in the United States, 4.2 million young people are going to spend at least some part of each year not knowing where they're going to sleep that night.[7] (And while we often discuss the United States alone, when we start looking at the rest of the world, where the nation of your birth is such a strong determinant of your future income, things become just unfathomably unfair.)

This is where the socialistic instinct starts. Jack London explains in his essay "How I Became a Socialist" that it was not because he had read Karl Marx and accepted the dialectical materialist conception of history.[8] It was because he went out into the world and realized that not everyone was like himself, and that the things he told himself about why some people deserved more than others simply broke down once he actually got to know people. He says that when he was young, at first,

I looked on the world and called it good, every bit of it . . . This op-
timism was because I was healthy and strong, bothered with neither
aches nor weaknesses, never turned down by the boss because I did
not look fit, able always to get a job . . . And I looked ahead into long
vistas of a hazy and interminable future, into which, playing what I
conceived to be MAN'S game, I should continue to travel with un-
failing health, without accidents, and with muscles ever vigorous . . .
I could see myself only raging through life without end like one of
Nietzsche's blond beasts, lustfully roving and conquering by sheer
superiority and strength. As for the unfortunates, the sick, and ail-
ing, and old, and maimed, I must confess I hardly thought of them
at all, save that I vaguely felt that they, barring accidents, could be
as good as I if they wanted to real hard, and could work just as well.

What changed his mind? London went out tramping. He went from
the west, where jobs were plentiful, to the east, where they weren't, and
he says, he "found [him]self looking upon life from a new and totally
different angle."

I found there all sorts of men, many of whom had once been as good
as myself and just as blond-beastly; sailor-men, soldier-men, labor-
men, all wrenched and distorted and twisted out of shape by toil and
hardship and accident, and cast adrift by their masters like so many
old horses. [I] shivered with them in box cars and city parks, listening the while to life-histories which began under auspices as fair as
mine, with digestions and bodies equal to and better than mine, and
which ended there before my eyes in the shambles at the bottom of
the Social Pit.

London's socialism was formed by getting out of his bubble and
actually trying to understand lives that were different from his own.
And that's where millennials begin, too: not with economic theory, but
with a sense of solidarity, a deep understanding of, love of, and sym-
pathy with your fellow human beings in very different circumstances,
and wanting nothing for yourself that you do not also want for them.
A socialist is, first and foremost, not just perturbed by injustice, but

horrified by it, really truly sickened by it in a way that means they can't stop thinking about it. For them, platitudes like "we can't do anything about that" or "that's just the way of the world" are just not acceptable.

* * *

IT IS PERHAPS worth distinguishing between a *socialist ethic*—anger at capitalism over its systematic destructiveness and injustice—and a *socialist economy* that rearranges the way goods are produced and distributed. A socialist ethic is both more and less than a socialist economy: it is less than because it does not necessarily have a specific blueprint for exactly how society should operate. But it is more than because it is not just an economic system; it is also a way of looking at the world, one that does not allow you to pass by a jail or a homeless encampment or an Amazon fulfillment center without being stirred to political action.

The Polish scholar of Marxism Leszek Kolakowski, who was bitterly disillusioned by communism, once helpfully distinguished between socialism as an ideal and socialism as a system:

> [It would be] a pity if the collapse of communist socialism resulted in the demise of the socialist tradition as a whole and the triumph of Social Darwinism as the dominant ideology . . . Fraternity under compulsion is the most malignant idea devised in modern times . . . This is no reason, however, to scrap the idea of human fraternity. If it is not something that can be effectively achieved by means of social engineering, it is useful as a statement of goals. The socialist idea is dead as a project for an "alternative society." But as a statement of solidarity with the underdog and the oppressed, as a motivation to oppose Social Darwinism, as a light that keeps before our eyes something higher than competition and greed—for all these reasons, socialism—the ideal, not the system—still has its uses.

In fact, just as Kolakowski feared, the collapse of communism has indeed meant the triumph of a kind of Social Darwinist ideology and the disappearance of the socialist ideal. Not only has the Soviet Union disappeared, but so have labor unions and social welfare programs.

It may seem as if, by using words like *fraternity* to describe the socialistic ethic, I'm draining socialism of its substantive meaning. If
it's just a "statement of solidarity with the underdog," then is it really
anything it all? Is the only difference between a socialist and a non-
socialist the fact that a socialist is, in Eagleton's term, "horrified"? Is
anyone who is "concerned for the unfortunate" a socialist?

I do think Kolakowski's use of *fraternity* is too vague. Socialism does
start with a feeling of connectedness and compassion, but this solidarity
and concern are just the first principles. One's socialism is meaningful,
and *not* just a rhetorical affirmation of where one's sympathies lie, only
to the extent that it involves a determination to actually alter the conditions that one deplores. It's not just about acknowledging the problems,
but about committing oneself to finding the solutions. Socialism is also
utopian, in that it believes transformative changes are possible.

Socialism leads not just to substantive convictions, but to radical
ideas about how the world ought to and can be. From its humanitarian sympathies, it derives a vision: it seeks a world in which people do
not go to war; there are no class, racial, and gender hierarchies; there
are no significant imbalances of power; there is no poverty coexisting
alongside wealth; and everyone leads a pleasant and fulfilled life. That's
not the world we currently live in, which is unequal, violent, and full of
poor people. Socialists will not rest until we have averted environmental catastrophe and eliminated suicide, malnourishment, and tyranny,
whether that of the autocrat or of the boss. That's *ambitious,* but it's
hardly some vague statement about loving the underdog.

It might seem like a cop-out to define socialism more by what it is
against than what it is for, and more by abstract values than concrete
prescriptions. I don't think it actually is, though, because concrete prescriptions vary from situation to situation, while the underlying values
remain the same. So, for example, in the long term, believing in equality may mean that everyone should have an equal stake in the country's
wealth. But in the short term, it may mean using the regulatory powers
of the state to ensure that lenders do not discriminate against black
borrowers, or restricting corporations' ability to contribute money to
election campaigns, so that they don't have an unfair advantage over
less well-off people. It might involve taxing wealth and redistributing

it, but it might also involve actions that have nothing to do with the government at all, such as forming a union in your workplace in order to give employees a greater say over what happens in the company. We could create a long list of different ideas that flow from socialism's abstract values, the values being what seemingly disparate policy goals all share in common.

*   *   *

A COMMITMENT TO expanding democracy is at the core of all good socialist thinking. Democracy is the principle that people ought to have a say over decisions that affect them, and that they should be in control of their own lives rather than being subjected to the wishes of powerful economic and political elites. Not everyone believes in democracy; one prominent libertarian philosopher, Jason Brennan, has even written a book called *Against Democracy*, which argues that the masses are too stupid and ignorant to make decisions for themselves and should be ruled over by the wise and learned.[9] (I swear I am not exaggerating, go read the book.)

Socialists not only believe in democracy, we believe it ought to be expanded. In the contemporary United States, democracy is very limited. Assuming you're a citizen over the age of 18 without a criminal record and with the proper documentation and not living in D.C. or Puerto Rico, you get to vote for a congressperson. But money is extremely important in elections, meaning that rich people are far more able to sway the outcomes than poor people are. This reduces democracy because it limits the degree to which people have control over their government. That's why you find democratic socialists like Bernie Sanders talking incessantly about campaign finance reform and trying to come up with ways to constrain the influence of money in politics. It's very difficult to do this, however, because money is very powerful and the only *real* way to equalize people's power is to equalize people's wealth. A highly economically unequal society can never be a politically equal society.

But socialists are also interested in expanding democracy to cover the economic sphere itself. Workplaces are highly undemocratic. If, for example, a manufacturer decides to close a factory and move it overseas, the workers in that factory don't get to "vote" on that decision. They are simply subjected to it against their will, no matter how much labor they put into building the factory or how devastating the factory's closure will be for their community. Full ownership includes the right to make decisions about what happens to some piece of property and to decide what happens to anything it produces. Workers do not own their factories, so they don't have any decision-making rights. The idea of "economic democracy" means they *should* get these kinds of decision-making rights.

Socialists have advocated numerous ways of democratizing the economy, from setting up worker cooperatives to nationalizing major industries. There are whole books on what aspects of this could look like, for example, Gar Alperovitz's *America Beyond Capitalism* or Richard Wolff's *Democracy at Work*. At the core of economic democracy is the notion that control should not be vested in a small group of people, but in the people who do the labor. Managers and owners shouldn't decide what the workers have to do, the workers should decide what managers have to do (or if they need managers at all). And they should own the workplaces themselves.

Here, we can see why the authoritarian "socialist" regimes of the twentieth century did not deserve to be called socialist at all. In the Soviet Union, workers had very limited control over their workplaces. They were told what to do by party functionaries. Socialism does not mean control by the government, it means control by the people, and if the government is not responsive to the will of the people, it's "socialistic" in the same way that Kim Jong-Un's Democratic People's Republic of Korea is "democratic." This is also why, while I and many others use the term *democratic socialism* to draw a distinction between our ideas and the hideous so-called socialism implemented under Joseph Stalin, ultimately the term should be redundant. Socialism is a term for economic democracy, so an undemocratic system doesn't deserve to claim the name.

You will notice that I am not providing a blueprint for what socialism will look like. This is because my kind of socialism does not have blueprints. It is not a fixed picture of how every single thing ought to look. Rather, it's a set of principles that we use to measure whether society is operating fairly and guide us as we move toward a better world.

* * *

AT THIS POINT, I think I know what you are probably screaming. If you are, as I have assumed, extremely skeptical of the socialist position, you may well be worked up into a borderline sputtering rage. Your thoughts will probably be somewhat similar to those expressed by the Canadian philosopher Joseph Heath, who explained why the simplistic, moralistic view of the world held by young leftists is wrong in approximately a bajillion ways.

> When I was younger, I thought that questions of social justice were easy. It seemed to me that there were two sorts of people in the world—those who were basically selfish, and those who were more generous and caring. Insofar as there was injustice or suffering in the world, it was because those who were selfish had managed to see their interests prevail . . . Anticapitalism therefore struck me as being a straightforward moral imperative . . . Now that I'm older, I think there are so many things wrong with this view that I wouldn't even know where to begin enumerating them.

Heath says that "many different factors" changed his mind. The first factor was his time spent in Asia, "seeing what an incredible force for development even a poorly structured market economy can be." Next was "meeting people outside my immediate circle of left-wing acquaintances" and finding "the system" was comprised of "people pretty much like everyone else," with "the usual mix" of selfishness and selflessness. The last factor was "reading economics" and trying to find "alternatives to the existing order of things." Heath concluded, "For any ridiculous, destructive, or unjust state of affairs," typically one will find an "understandable reason" why it continues. The problem is generally not, he says, that we "lack the will to fix our problems," but that we "don't know how."[10]

Heath's position is a rearticulation of the old cliché "if you're still a socialist after 30, you have no brain." It is a direct challenge to the view I subscribe to, which is that anti-capitalism is *absolutely* a moral imperative. I take it very seriously. But Heath's top reasons for abandoning the "easy" view are entirely unpersuasive to me. Let's remember what he says changed his mind:

1. Spending time in Asia and realizing that market economics could be helpful and governments were often incompetent.
2. Meeting people and realizing that they had a mixture of selfish and altruistic motivations.
3. Reading economics and realizing that there are reasons why injustices persist and we don't know how to fix them.

Numbers one and two strike me as almost wholly irrelevant. A pragmatic anti-capitalist realizes, like Karl Marx did, that the further development of capitalism is sometimes a necessary precondition for a more egalitarian society, and libertarian socialists are highly concerned with government corruption and abuse. Second, it's absolutely true that seeing the world as divided into purely good and purely evil people is a mistake, but it can still be true that there are "much better" and "much worse" people, and that the much worse people have disproportionate amounts of power. I, too, think most people are a mixture of selfish and altruistic, but I also think that the proportions of each vary considerably. There are people I know who spend their lives in the service of others, and there are others who spend their lives attempting to exploit others. Those in the former group sometimes do selfish things, and those in the latter group sometimes do kind things, but this does not mean that everyone is the same. Having Donald Trump in charge of a government is different than having Nelson Mandela in charge of one. There is good in this world, and there is evil, and almost nobody is purely one or purely the other, but some people feel solidarity and compassion and attempt to make others' lives better, and other people are Ayn Rand.[11]

Heath's third point articulates a kind of pessimism. Once you understand economics, he suggests, you realize that many human problems are insoluble. He says that those who issue the usual banalities about poverty in a world of riches fail to appreciate the world's complexity. They latch on to simplistic solutions: "Industry is polluting? Make them stop. Employers not paying enough? Get them to pay more. People are poor? Give them more money . . . Most of the mistakes that people on the left make," Heath says, "involve failures of self-restraint—an unwillingness to tolerate moral flaws in society, even when we have no idea how to fix them and no reason to think that the cure will not be worse than the disease."[12]

To me, this usefully articulates one of the main factors distinguishing a socialist from a liberal like Heath. The socialist is indeed, as Heath says, unable to accept injustices. We can't let the issue go. To the socialist, the fact that "we have no idea" how to solve a problem does not countenance resignation, but resolve. It's not good enough to say that there is a "reason why unjust states of affairs persist." A socialist is a person, as Eagleton notes, who refuses to get over their horror.

For some socialists, this may indeed mean an unjustified faith in simplistic solutions. Impose a tax on corporations that immediately gets passed on to consumers and ends up hurting the very people we want to help. Or we set price controls and then a market goes haywire. Heath spends much time lamenting the "economic illiteracy" of the left, who, he says, see law as a kind of magic wand that can get rid of social ills by banning them.

But we don't actually face a choice between doing stupid things and giving up. In fact, saying "I once thought capitalism was bad, but then I realized I couldn't think of an alternative" is shoddy thinking. If you can't think of an alternative, that doesn't mean capitalism isn't bad, it means you need to *think harder*. The fact that we don't know how to cure a disease doesn't mean it isn't a disease or that it's not worth searching for a cure. Socialists do not have to be able to present an alternative; what we have to present is a recognition of the problem and a commitment to finding that alternative. This is how innovation works: you start with the question, not the answer. If we are on a riverbank and someone proposes building a bridge to the other side, we do not give up on the idea of building a bridge merely because we haven't figured out how to do it yet.

Instead, this is where imagination comes in.

A Better World

Envisioning Utopias

"When one came straight from England the aspect of Barcelona was something startling and overwhelming. It was the first time that I had ever been in a town where the working class was in the saddle . . . Waiters and shop-walkers looked you in the face and treated you as an equal. Servile and even ceremonial forms of speech had temporarily disappeared. Nobody said 'Señor' or 'Don' or even 'Usted'; everyone called everyone else 'Comrade' and 'Thou', and said 'Salud!' instead of 'Buenos dias' . . . The revolutionary posters were everywhere, flaming from the walls in clean reds and blues that made the few remaining advertisements look like daubs of mud . . . [I]t was the aspect of the crowds that was the queerest thing of all. In outward appearance it was a town in which the wealthy classes had practically ceased to exist . . . All this was queer and moving. There was much in it that I did not understand, in some ways I did not even like it, but I recognized it immediately as a state of affairs worth fighting for."

—George Orwell, *Homage to Catalonia*

"If others can see it as I have seen it, then it may be called a vision rather than a dream."

—William Morris, *News from Nowhere*

LATELY, EVEN *STAR TREK* HAS given up. When series creator Gene Roddenberry originally spoke of his ambition for the show, he said openly that he had a political purpose: he wanted to show people a future very different from the present, a place where "this world's petty nationalism and all its old ways and old hatreds" had disappeared.[1] Roddenberry said that the "common man and common woman has an enormous hunger for brotherhood," and that they "are ready for the 23rd century now." *Star Trek* presented a society that had become, essentially, communistic. All human wants were satisfied, without competition, markets, or consumerism. As *Trekonomics* author Manu Saadia says, it is a world where "achievements are more important than the accumulation of wealth," and Patrick Stewart's Captain Jean-Luc Picard says of humanity, "We have grown out of our infancy. The accumulation of things is no longer thought to be the point of life."

But as the United States has become more unequal, and socialistic political philosophy has faded, the *Star Trek* franchise itself has seemingly become disillusioned. As my colleague Lyta Gold has written, the latest series, *Discovery*, seems downright pessimistic about humanity's future. The "post-scarcity utopia . . . is nowhere to be seen."[2] Life is once again violent, brutal, and competitive. As one character says, "The future came, and hunger and need and want disappeared. 'Course, they're making a comeback now." *Star Trek*'s abandonment of its utopian vision is part of a trend toward dystopian film, television, and literature. As people have felt more bleak and hopeless, and socialism has disappeared as a major political force, culture has come to reflect this kind of pessimism. The future is no longer "diplomacy in space"; it's *The Hunger Games* or *The Purge*. In 2018's *Ready Player One*, Earth of 2045 has been so devastated by pollution, overpopulation, and climate change that people escape into virtual reality.

* * *

ONCE UPON A time, people did dream of alternate tomorrows.

The history of utopian literature is both rich and neglected. Since the time of Plato, writers have thought deeply about what "ideal" societies might look like and sketched them out in words. Plato himself, in *The Republic*, depicted a perfectly governed city ruled by wise and educated philosopher-kings, in which justice is universal and poetry is banned.[3] Thomas More's *Utopia* showed a kind of communistic society where resources were shared freely.

In the nineteenth century, this kind of writing was not fringe. It was popular with readers. Edward Bellamy's *Looking Backward* was a bestseller, spawning multiple sequels and responses. It so captivated his contemporaries that hundreds of "Bellamy clubs" sprung up around the country, dedicating themselves to actualizing his vision. Unlike Karl Marx, who refrained from actually offering clear ideas of what a future society would look like and how it would work, Bellamy dared to make the fantastical seem feasible.

As a novel, there's not much to *Looking Backward*: a Bostonian falls asleep and awakens in the year 2000, where he is shown around a future socialist society. But Bellamy goes into detail about the operations of the new Boston, presenting a world in which labor is minimal, goods are distributed equally among all, crime is treated as a medical issue, and everyone retires at age 45.

> "Do you mean that all share equally in the national wealth?" Julian asked incredulously.
>
> "Certainly," replied the doctor. "And in return, we require precisely the same measure of service from all: namely, the best service it is in his power to give."
>
> "And supposing all do the best they can," said Julian, "[and] the amount of the product resulting is twice as much from one man as from another?"
>
> "That has nothing to do with the question of desert," the doctor answered. "All who do their best, do the same. A man's endowments, however godlike, merely fix the measure of his duty. [And although we reward excellence and diligence with public praise and increased responsibility,] you must not imagine that we consider such things a motive likely to appeal to noble natures. Such persons find their motives within, not without, and measure their duty by their own endowments, not by those of others."[4]

William Morris' *News from Nowhere* is similar in its structure: a visitor finds himself in the England of the future, where there is no government, no church, and no wage labor. People simply give each other whatever they need. Morris' community is a place where art is valued far more highly than commerce, and people mostly seem to spend their lives trying to create beautiful objects to treasure. Morris' visitor is astonished to see an artisan carving a beautiful wooden smoking-pipe, and even more astonished when the artisan offers to give it to the visitor *for free*. Morris depicts a world where everyone's needs are met, and people can simply dedicate themselves to the higher pleasures of life.

Some utopias were more fantastical than others. Charles Fourier, whose views were so popular that they spawned an entire Fourierist movement, believed everyone would live in specially designed cathedral-like buildings he called "phalansteries." Actually, that was the most realistic part, because he also believed the seas would turn to lemonade and lions would turn into an alternate creature called an "anti-lion." Needless to say, this did not happen.

Other utopias force us to ponder which aspects of our own society arise from human nature and which are social constructs that could one day disappear. There is a whole wonderful subgenre of nineteenth century utopian literature written by early feminists who conjured visions of a world in which gender roles were drastically different. Either women were in charge, and men had to wear dresses and do housework, or men had disappeared altogether after being discovered to be irrelevant.[5]

Science-fiction stories have given us windows into an endless number of possible civilizations, the best features of which we can adopt in our own time. Iain M. Banks, in his "culture" novels, envisaged a society where all of the problems of scarcity had been sorted out, and people had all of their needs satisfied. Ursula K. Le Guin's *The Dispossessed* features a functional egalitarian, anarchist society. As one of the society's members explains:

> We have no law but the single principle of mutual aid between individuals. We have no government but the single principle of free association. We have no states, no nations, no presidents, no premiers, no chiefs, no generals, no bosses, no bankers, no landlords, no wages, no charity, no police, no soldiers, no wars. Nor do we have much else. We are sharers, not owners. We are not prosperous. None of us is rich. None of us is powerful.[6]

Oscar Wilde once said, "A map without utopia on it is not worth looking at." I believe that strongly myself. Utopias can be dangerous, though, because if you treat them as literal blueprints you can get carried away (sometimes murderously) trying to socially engineer the perfect society. But they can stimulate the imagination in useful ways. When we ask what would an ideal society look like and sketch the result, the exercise can help us come up with ideas that might actually be practical in our own world. I actually think that *lacking* a utopia can be just as dangerous as having one, because if you don't have a guiding star for your journey, you won't know whether you're going in the right direction. Marx was famously an opponent of utopian socialism, and he and Friedrich Engels advocated a more "scientific" approach to thinking about future social transformation. But the lack of a clear vision of what a better world would look like is one of the reasons the Soviet Union successfully convinced many communists that it was what they had been asking for.

You've got to know what you're striving for, and I have a sense that many people on the left often have a fuzzy vision in part because they're wary of utopias. Once, I asked a liberal friend of mine to describe his dream world, to tell me what it would look like if *everything* he wanted had been accomplished. What did he see in the dream? "Full employment," he said. Now, I think everyone should have a job who wants one, but I have to say this is a pretty pitiful dream! It looks exactly like our current world, except we all have *jobs*. And jobs suck!

I was more pleased with the answer given when I asked the *Current Affairs* staff to come up with a utopia. They fleshed out a whole city, a place where people lived in wonderful, elaborate tree houses with rope bridges connecting them, where there were fountains and public pools everywhere. There was a place where kids could come and play with every Lego piece ever made—for free!—and a communal pickle barrel where anyone could stop and get a pickle. There were lots of public parks and benches, free shows, dogs and cats galore. It seemed like the sort of place I wouldn't mind living in.[7]

I also asked my friends and *Current Affairs* readers what they would put in their own utopias. Here are some of their answers:

- "A piano bar in every town."
- "Real-life Pokémon."
- "All restaurants' menus legally have to include at least one nutritious free dish, and all hotels with vacant rooms after 10 p.m. have to offer them to the homeless."
- "As many butterflies and parrots in the average city as there currently are pigeons."
- "Super high-tech cities and towns with all the comforts of modernity that also [have] spacious green public parks so people wouldn't have to travel too far to enjoy nature. Also, vast nature preserves where wilderness is allowed to do its own thing as much as possible."
- "24-hour diners with well-compensated staff."
- "So many cats . . . [F]ields and fields of free-range kittens."
- "Amusement parks with short lines."
- "An international government service that translates all newspapers and works of literature (and television/animation) around the world as quickly as possible after it comes out in that country into your prefer[ed] language."
- "Libraries for musical equipment."
- "Lots of palm trees."
- "Municipal gaming lounges."
- "Men are able to get pregnant and women's reproductive age can be extended indefinitely."
- "The cure for male pattern baldness."
- "Free, publicly funded ice rinks in every neighborhood."
- "Mid-rise (three- to six-story), multifamily housing complexes with common spaces allowing multiple families to live TOGETHER, rather than just close to each other."
- "Widespread scientific literacy."
- "Lots of public gardens and green spaces."
- "A network of pneumatic tubes for moving stuff around."
- "Candy corn that doesn't make me feel sick."

- "Way more public bathrooms . . . [B]athrooms so beautiful you feel honored to poop there."

- "Synthetic meat, dairy, and eggs that are indistinguishable from the real thing, so we can phase out animal agriculture."

- "Amazon pays taxes. Or maybe no Amazon at all . . . except the one with the iguanas."

- "There are free psychedelics and everyone gets a dog."

- "Three-day work week."

- "Musicians everywhere."

- "Schools would become smaller—qualified community members would have the time, energy, and competence to take turns as teachers in their local schools."

- "Lots of street cafes."

- "Broad swathes of the country left mostly untouched by urban sprawl, to be explored and available to the public for free."

- "Cat libraries, which would be like cat cafés but free and more hygienic."

- "There would be a corps of safety officers instead of police—more like fire fighters. Their mission would be to assist. Generally, if someone got dangerously unruly, they could be wrapped in a giant blanket and taken somewhere safe."

- "Huge herds of buffalo roaming across an ecologically restored Great Plains."

- "Return of megafauna."

- "Libraries would be bigger, multipurpose community centers, but more social. Need a power drill? Check one out from the library. Need to host a banquet? Do it there. They have everything."

- "High-speed, affordable trains to every major destination and many minor ones."

- "Pants that stay warm like they're fresh out the dryer and pillows that stay cold."

- "Complete control over your own time."

- "Acceptable to wear costumes every day."
- "Excellent strawberries."
- "Lots of local and regional holidays with their own traditions."
- "Large communal play spaces with board games and role-playing games."
- "Reliable, consistent, free public transit."
- "Polar ice caps."
- "Perfected medical science that can cure pretty much anything with non-invasive treatment."
- "Space travel."
- "All space used for advertising would be replaced by art."
- "The rhythm of life changes with the seasons."
- "Glass-bottomed airplanes."[8]
- "Public spaces with lots of flowers and fruit trees."
- "Public spaces that equal the magnificence and extravagance of private, wealthy-only spaces."
- "Flying beds are a must."
- "People speak a group of universal languages, which are familiar and diverse at the same time (but not in a top-down Esperanto way)."
- "Children and animals play together freely without fear of each other or others."
- "Books with pictures, words, and games [on] every block and bench[es] with a neat little cupboard to put them back in after."
- "Free canteens where people can be layabouts, make friends, be social, and argue with each other about every harebrained philosophical idea that comes to their mind."
- "All buildings would be beautiful; art would be everywhere."
- "Ice cream and hot fudge dispensers next to the water fountains."
- "More sousaphones."
- "All the Beatles would be back together."
- "Everyone has everything they need and most of what they want

and the only work that people do is the work they're passionate about."

An exercise: Imagine your own utopia. Tell us what you see in it.

You might think we're being *very* silly here. After all, the problems I described in Part I were deeply serious and in many cases horrifying. Now we're speculating about a world of sousaphones and palm trees. Is this the most detached and irrelevant kind of idle dreaming?

I don't think it is. In fact, I think it is profoundly important.

Utopias matter because they help us understand what we really want out of life. They enrich our political philosophy by showing what we should actually be aiming for. If the purpose of government is to secure life, liberty, and the pursuit of happiness, then what would people actually need to pursue that happiness? What would it mean for them to be free? If their every desire were fulfilled, what would the world look like?

My friends and our *Current Affairs* readers are obviously disproportionately young lefties. But I think their dream worlds are very appealing. There are some common themes: They want to be free of the stress of having to think about money all the time. They want to be able to choose what they do with their time. They want a vibrant culture, where art, music, and literature flourish. They want people to be able to satisfy their intellectual curiosities and understand science and the natural world, but also have plenty of time for play and leisure. They want plants and animals in their life. (One thing you will notice about capitalistic spaces is that they tend to be very "dead." From office blocks to suburbs, the plants are minimal and the only animals are personal pets. This is partly because the value of beautiful plants and wild animals is difficult to quantify, so they get destroyed, or developers don't see the point of wasting money on introducing them.)

You will also notice that the concept of public space and community comes up over and over. People in my generation often feel very alone. We are isolated and depressed, and we want a world where people don't just sit alone in their apartments watching Netflix, but have *places to go.* Places that are free and welcoming, where you don't have to worry about whether you can afford to stay. They want time for reading, discussion, physical activity, and adventure. They want to contribute to a community, to take care of others and be taken care of.

How utopian is any of this really, though? Some of the things on the list are fanciful, but not much of it is technically impossible. (The megafauna might be difficult.) Public gardens and street cafés, healthcare and good food, a soft bed for anyone who wants one and musicians playing on the corner—when we look at how far humanity has come in the last few hundred years, why should any of this seem impossible? Utopian thinking is valuable in part because it can make us realize just how *achievable* something very close to paradise really is. Oh, sure, we'll always bicker and hurt each other, we'll always strive for things and fail. But making sure everybody has a house? Not being tyrannized by your boss? Communal spaces with free coffee and games? Giant playgrounds the size of cities? I think we could do that.

To help you come up with your own utopia, try thinking about a perfect moment you had. There aren't too many of these nowadays, but they do happen. Moments when just about everything is right. The last perfect moment I had, I was sitting on a balcony in the quiet part of the French Quarter, eating a pistachio muffin and sipping an iced coffee. I was with an old friend, and we were talking excitedly about things we had read. There was a breeze, and we could see boats going by on the Mississippi River. In the distance, we heard the sound of a trumpeter playing on a street corner. I was wearing a comfortable shirt, it was spring, and there were flowers around. Music, food, sunshine, friendship, plants, old architecture, proximity to a body of water, and intelligent but unpretentious conversation: To me, these are all the elements needed for total peace and satisfaction.

When you think about what you'd need for a really perfect moment, you'll probably soon realize that it's not very demanding in terms of economic resources. Given the phenomenal productive powers that capitalism has unleashed, it shouldn't be difficult to create an awful lot more rest and satisfaction than we currently have. We may not know quite how to get to utopia yet. But if we think about our ideal and start to move toward it, we will not just have an abstract and empty "hope" but a set of real things to strive for.[9]

Of course, some lives have far fewer idyllic moments than others. Some lives are lived in constant, unimaginable agony. We shouldn't get onanistically lost in contemplation of our own bliss, because we also need to be angry at how unequally distributed that bliss is across the population. Our friends and neighbors may be suffering silently to a greater degree than we are aware. Utopian thinking is only possible if you have a certain amount of privilege—amid situations of extreme violence and deprivation, fantastical visions seem far more distant, and talking about how possible they are seems absurd. But it isn't *actually* absurd. As Orwell put it, "The world is a raft sailing through space with, potentially, plenty of provisions for everybody."[10] We use our resources in ways so unfair that it seems like it would take a colossal amount of change to get anywhere close to justice. There is no reason, however, why that colossal change cannot occur.

* * *

IF YOU THINK utopian thinking is unrealistic or pointless, let me ask you to consider libraries. Everyone knows that libraries are incredible places. Multiple people mentioned them in response to my utopia survey. But we don't often consider just how *radical* public libraries are. A library is a place where anyone can go and—for free!—explore a mountain of human knowledge. It has meeting spaces, computers, and research assistance. It's there for everyone, regardless of their means.

A library is a pretty socialist institution, honestly. It's owned by everyone, and there's no money involved. (Unless you keep your books too long!) There's no profit, no private ownership, no ulterior motive. It's a place we all pay for and can all visit. They're spaces of absolute equality, where anyone can go to study, learn, and hang out. You don't have to purchase anything in order to get to sit in them, you don't have to be means tested or background checked. They provide the same services to everybody, and there's something beautiful (and increasingly rare) about that.

Privatization generally involves the elimination of that kind of place. It makes us think constantly about how much we can afford.

Economist Noah Smith has explained what the results of that can be: when everything costs money, life becomes far more stressful (though that stress is distributed unequally). He discusses the situation in Japan:

> What would it really feel like to live in a society where almost every single thing is privately owned and priced? . . . In terms of the constituents of daily life being privately owned and marginally priced, [Japan] is a libertarian's dream world. [T]here are relatively few free city parks. Many green spaces are private and gated off (admission is usually around $5). On the streets, there are very few trashcans; people respond to this in the way libertarians would want, by exercising personal responsibility and carrying their trash home with them in little baggies. There are also very few public benches. In cafes, each customer must order something promptly or be kicked out; outside your house or office, there is basically nowhere to sit down that will not cost you a little bit of money. Public buildings generally have no drinking fountains; you must buy or bring your own water. Free wireless? Good luck finding that![11]

Smith says that all this privatization doesn't actually make him feel free. In fact, he says, it's the opposite: "The lack of a 'commons' makes me feel constrained." There is a "constant stream of mental effort" required, in which one has to determine whether it's worth it to pay a few dollars to sit and have rest or get a drink of water.

I get the same feeling walking around New York City, actually. Sitting down or using the restroom can cost money, because you have to do them in a café, where you likely need to buy something. I find this experience extremely taxing; I just wish there were lots of big, public restrooms and big, public places to sit, free for everyone to use. This is, first and foremost, because the poor deserve to be able to sit down or pee, and obviously those things should be basic human rights. But it's also because even non-poor people should be free to move around the world without constantly having to weigh their choices the way Smith discusses: Can I afford this extra 10 minutes? Do I want to sit down so badly that it's worth two dollars? The book comparison here is useful. When I'm doing research, I want to be able to access all books, to look through them without thinking, *Is this source so valuable that I am willing to pay X amount for it?* The privatization of knowledge, with lots of important information stored in academic journals or newspaper archives or legal documents that cost significant amounts of money to access, makes it difficult to do open-ended research.

Imagine the library model in other spheres of life. Say, for example, free medical clinics where anyone could go and get treatment. Free colleges, where people could go and take whatever classes they wanted, without being bankrupted by debt. Free bikes to borrow, a free water park.

Libraries are not full socialism, but they show what socialized institutions can look like and provide a model for the left way of satisfying human needs. The conservative argument against left policies is often some variation on "do you want your healthcare to run like the post office?" And everyone usually thinks *Oh God, no*, because the post office is slow and loses packages. (One time they literally sold my mail at auction instead of delivering it.[12]) Of course, that could be fixed if the elected federal government actually cared about improving the post office, which they don't. But more importantly, public libraries offer a clear counterpoint. Do you want your healthcare to be like the public library, where you can show up and get whatever you like for free? Where we'd pay a little more in taxes but get more than that back in services? Of course. People love libraries.

Now, I know, I know, nothing is actually free. ("That's *other people's* money!" I hear you shout, without remembering that property is theft.[13]) They're free *at the point of use*. But there is something very liberating about not having to think about money when you use a service, about having everything prepaid and accessible to all. It makes life less stressful and transactional. It means we don't have to constantly be conducting little mental calculations about value, and we can just go and enjoy our lives.

Lefties are often mocked for wanting "free stuff." Free college! My God, what's next, free ponies?[14] But libraries work. Everyone loves them. (They're most popular among millennials, actually.[15]) From a certain perspective, though, they seem just as crazy as anything dreamed up by Morris or Le Guin. Free books! What next?

In order to build these kinds of radical institutions, we need to dare to have those kinds of radical dreams.

A WORLD WITHOUT BORDERS

I want to give you one small example of a utopian vision that I find morally clarifying and politically useful: the dream of a world without borders between countries.

We can tell a little story about the existence of borders. Once upon a time, a small band of adventurers came across a sea and happened upon a continent. The continent was inhabited, but the inhabitants turned out to have vulnerable immune systems. The sicknesses brought by the band of adventurers wiped out a good portion of the inhabitants. The rest were pushed off their land, assimilated, or outright murdered. The band of adventurers built towns and cities, and when they needed more land, they stole it. After a few hundred years, they had the audacity to start talking about the importance of secure borders.

The United States is wealthy, in part, because it is rich in resources. It is as if we have happened upon the proverbial land of milk and honey, and instead of inviting people who desperately need milk and honey to come and join us, we have built a wall. Leftists are skeptical in principle of *all* immigration restrictions, which is why we are often accused of advocating "open borders." That isn't because we reject the idea of making sure the people in a country are safe from dangerous intruders. Rather, it's because the whole idea of borders strikes us as somewhat odd: fencing off stolen land and refusing to share its bounties with perfectly harmless people who want to come and share in them seems downright immoral.

If you go and look at ports of entry along the border, they are strange things. Gigantic barriers tearing human populations in two, where soldiers decide who gets to see who. The Berlin Wall strikes us as perverse because of the way it divided people, but the wall separating San Diego and Tijuana is not that much different. And in the span of human history, it's a very recent phenomenon. In the early part of the twentieth century, if you went to a border town, on one side of the street you would be in Mexico, and on the other side the United States. To go from one to the other, you'd simply step across. This is almost un-imaginable to us now, but we actually have lots of "borderless" politi-cal units. The states that comprise the United States have independent governments, but you can go from one to the other without getting permission. The idea of "open borders" is just the idea of having coun-tries operate more like states: you don't become a voting resident of one simply by crossing into it, but nobody is going to stop you from passing freely back and forth.

The Berlin Wall came down. In fact, most of the borders in Europe came down, and among the countries of the European Union there is now almost complete freedom of movement. Borders are artificial, and they can disappear. Take a moment to imagine a future in which there are no borders at all. The whole world is open to everybody. You don't need paperwork to leave your country; you just get up and go. Soldiers don't stop you, walls don't block you. You can wander the Earth at your leisure.

That's not the case now, and it's hard to think it will be the case any-time soon. There are endless pragmatic obstacles to a borderless world, and Republicans are horrified by anyone who even dares to suggest such a thing. But even though it may take us 50 years (or 200, or 1,000), I think it's a state of affairs worth fighting for. A quick anecdote about present-day borders: I know a man, a friend of a friend, who has not seen his mother in ten years. He was living in the United States illegally and was deported and barred from reentering for a decade. She was here illegally, too, and cannot cross the border. The existence of nation-states and laws determining who is allowed to go where keeps families apart and makes people far less free than they would be if we let nature make the borders rather than governments.

I don't know about you, but I think it's worth imagining a radical alternative in which anyone could go and see anyone whenever they wanted. In fact, it doesn't sound all that "radical" to me.

PRISON ABOLITION

The United States imprisons a hell of a lot of people. At any given time, it holds "almost 2.3 million people in 1,719 state prisons, 109 federal prisons, 1,772 juvenile correctional facilities, 3,163 local jails, and 80 Indian Country jails as well as in military prisons, immigration detention facilities, civil commitment centers, state psychiatric hospitals, and prisons in the U.S. territories."[16] This is like having an entire small country locked up. Prison America's population is larger than the entire state of New Mexico. It's an absolutely staggering number.

Prison conditions vary around the country. But at their worst, sending someone to prison means keeping them in a place where they will be tormented constantly by deprivation and violence. The Trump administration's Justice Department, which has generally been reluctant to enforce civil rights protections, released a disturbing report on the Alabama Department of Corrections (ADOC). It concluded that conditions in Alabama prisons fell beneath the bare minimum standard guaranteed by the Constitution.

> ADOC's overcrowding and understaffing results in prisons that are inadequately supervised, with inappropriate and unsafe housing designations, creating an environment rife with violence, extortion, drugs, and weapons. Prisoner-on-prisoner homicide and sexual abuse is common. Prisoners who are seriously injured or stabbed must find their way to security staff elsewhere in the facility or bang on the door of the dormitory to gain the attention of correctional officers. Prisoners have been tied up for days by other prisoners while unnoticed by security staff . . . Prisoners are being extorted by other prisoners without appropriate intervention of management.[17]

Because the ADOC doesn't bother to properly investigate sexual assault and violence, prisoners are constantly being victimized. The youngest and weakest are therefore extremely vulnerable to being brutalized, and the ADOC is "deliberately indifferent" to its obligation to investigate abuse.

Not only that, but the facility conditions are horrendous. The Justice Department reported that "decrepit conditions are common." Moldy showers without hot water, overflowing toilets, cockroaches and spiders in people's cells, rats and bugs in the kitchens, no heat or ventilation—ADOC simply neglects people.

This is at the extreme end of things. But what it means is that when some people are sentenced to prison, they are sentenced to being raped in a cage. They're not just being taken out of society for violating its rules, but are plunged into a miserable place where they are going to live in a combination of fear, stress, tedium, loneliness, and pain. I think you would have to be a sadist to believe anyone "deserved" this.

I'm going into some detail here about the hidden reality of mass incarceration because it helps us understand why some on the left consider themselves "prison abolitionists." They look at this mess and think, *This cannot be the way to keep social order. It's like having thousands of miniature totalitarian cities within the country.* It's even more disturbing, of course, when we add in the racial element: there are more black people in prisons than white people,[18] even though black people compose only 12.4 percent of the U.S. population.

Looking at the absurdity of caging people by the millions, some have dared to imagine a world that didn't have these places at all. Angela Davis, in *Are Prisons Obsolete?*, argued that prisons are a convenient way to avoid confronting social problems.

> The prison . . . functions ideologically as an abstract site into which undesirables are deposited, relieving us of the responsibility of thinking about the real issues afflicting those communities from which prisoners are drawn in such disproportionate numbers. This is the ideological work that the prison performs—it relieves us of the responsibility of seriously engaging with the problems of our society, especially those produced by racism and, increasingly, global capitalism.[19]

Instead of wrestling with the extremely difficult task of figuring out how to prevent people from becoming criminals, we simply dump the problem people in a container and forget about them. This, Davis and the prison abolitionists say, is not really solving the underlying problem. There has to be a better way.

Prison abolitionists can be quite pragmatic, pushing to give prisoners humane conditions and educational programs, encouraging the greater use of alternate punishments like house arrest and community service. But they are also proud utopians: they are imagining a whole different kind of society, one where a "prison" simply isn't a thing at all. It shouldn't be *that* difficult to conceive of such a situation. Iceland, for example, has a population of 340,000, and about 130 people total in its prisons. Many of those prisoners live in "open" prisons where there isn't anything to stop them from leaving. Inmates have comfortable rooms, are on friendly terms with staff, and engage in productive pastimes. Couldn't we at *least* go from Alabama prisons to Icelandic prisons? And couldn't Iceland someday go from 130 to 20, then from 20 to 0?

Many people hear the phrase "prison abolition" and think it means letting everyone currently in prison go free tomorrow, from purse snatchers to serial killers. That is not how I think about it. Instead, I think it is a demand to be more utopian in our thinking. Let's say we're trying to eliminate crime, but we don't consider prison an option. What would we do? Don't say it's impossible. The value of utopianism is that it says impossible is not acceptable, you can't know until you try.

Socialism, Democracy, Social Democracy

Sorting Out Words & Terms

"The capitalist ideal is that government plays very little role in the economy—and the socialist ideal is that government plays the leading role in the economy."

—Bryan Caplan, "Capitalism vs. Socialism"

"There's incredible amounts of slippage in DSA messaging between 'we should have an integrated national health care system like all other rich democracies' and 'we should eliminate profit unlike any other rich democracy.'"

—Matthew Yglesias

"In most economic issues . . . the new socialist movement doesn't look that different from a standard progressive Democratic agenda."

—Noah Smith, "Worried About Socialism Coming to America? Calm Down," *Bloomberg Opinion*

LET ME ASK YOU A question: What is love? How about these: What is justice? What is beauty? What is perfection? Abstract words are often difficult to pin down because they mean different things to different people. That does not mean, however, that they are meaningless. They may describe a bundle of real tendencies, the precise boundaries of which people disagree over.

Political terms are no different. It can be difficult to define *liberalism, conservatism, nations,* or *democracy. Fascism* is a particularly tricky one. (Everything I loathe is fascism.) *Socialism,* then, while often vague, is not much worse than a lot of other terms that we frequently use. People use the term differently and then bicker endlessly about which one of them is using it correctly. Yet these disputes do not make the word meaningless. As G. D. H. Cole notes in his *A History of Socialist Thought*:

> The impossibility of defining Socialism has often been emphasized, and sometimes regarded as reproach. But neither in Politics nor in Morals is any important idea or system ever capable of being exactly defined. Who can satisfactorily define democracy, or liberty, or virtue, or happiness, or the State, or, for that matter, individualism any more than Socialism?[1]

As a new democratic socialist tendency has arisen in the United States, much of the debate has focused on what exactly that term should be understood to mean. Is it simply a way of describing old-fashioned New Deal social democracy, of the kind many Democrats have historically endorsed? Or is it a call for the total abolition of private industry and complete government control of the economy?

Interestingly, this debate has actually been occurring since the word *socialism* was coined, with communistic and revolutionary socialists arguing that the only "true" socialism involved swift seizure of the means of production by the state, and reformist socialists arguing that socialism was a set of egalitarian ideals that could be implemented bit by bit on a gradual road to utopia. Sometimes these debates have torn apart socialist movements and made it impossible for multiple groups of people who call themselves socialists to work together. The famous split between Bolsheviks and Mensheviks during the Russian Revolution, for instance, was a schism between two different groups of socialists who all nominally shared the same principles but couldn't agree on what socialism required.

What is democratic socialism? is an impossible question to answer in a satisfactory way, then, because people who use this term disagree with one another. I can, however, explain how *I* use the term, and how I *think* some other people mean it.

Is this socialism or just social democracy? is a frustrating question. It is often used as a retort to Bernie Sanders: "Ah, you say you're a socialist, but you're just talking about *Scandinavian social democracy,* which is really just *regulated capitalism.*" I think there's a key distinction we can draw, though, between socialism and social democracy. The socialist is a utopian. They might believe that small reforms over a period of centuries are the best way of getting to the utopia, but they're fundamentally unsatisfied by the idea that the highest human ambition is simply to turn the United States into circa 2019 Scandinavia. It might be that we should borrow Scandinavian social policies, such as generous paid parental leave and universal healthcare. But this is not the dream. The dream is transformative. The dream is to see a total elimination of exploitation and hierarchy and a change in the structure of *who owns capital.* The dream is a decommodified life, where people have ownership over their work and cooperate for the common good.

The difference between a socialist and a social democrat is that a socialist is constantly thinking about the dream, taking into consideration whether every action gets us closer to the dream. The social democrat, on the other hand, is mostly content with the achievement of a robust welfare state. Socialists want that, too. But they won't be satisfied with it.

At the same time, it's important to not pooh-pooh social democracy. In the United States, at least, a real social democracy would be considerably different from what we have now. Parts of Scandinavia are actually much more socialistic than the phrase *regulated capitalism* assumes. In Norway, for instance, over 60 percent of the non-home wealth is controlled by the government, and the government owns and operates large-scale industries in a variety of sectors.[2] Now, mere state ownership doesn't itself make an enterprise socialistic, because socialism also depends on having robust democratic control. But vast government intervention in the economy does not sound like what *regulated capitalism* calls to mind.

Not all socialists are revolutionaries. Historically, there have always been "Fabian" socialists like Bernie Sanders, who try to work within existing institutions. (The Fabian Society, formed in Britain in 1884, aimed to bring about radical socialist ends through gradual change. Its logo, the tortoise, reflected its desired pace.) To a great extent, this was what the British Labour Party was. The Labour Party was founded by a socialist, Keir Hardie, and for most of its history it was officially a socialist party. The National Health Service, the crown jewel of Labour's social democratic policies, exists in part because the Socialist Medical Association helped make it a viable idea, and because a democratic socialist, Nye Bevan, made it a reality.[3]

What do I mean when I say that Labour was "officially a socialist party"? I mean that until neoliberal war criminal Tony Blair took it out and replaced it with mushy pap about "realizing our true potential," there had always been a clause in the Labour Party constitution calling for popular control of industry.

> To secure for the workers by hand or by brain the full fruits of their industry and the most equitable distribution thereof that may be possible upon the basis of the common ownership of the means of production, distribution and exchange, and the best obtainable system of popular administration and control of each industry or service.[4]

This clause, Clause IV, caused strong internal division between those who thought the party was taking progressive steps toward this radical end and those, like Blair, who did not have radical ends in mind in the short- *or* long-term. In this division, you can see the stark difference between a democratic socialist and a social democrat. Even though they can look identical in their policy platforms, there's a difference between believing that your policies are a small step toward a utopian endpoint and believing that your policies are the endpoint. That difference is well captured in the debate over Clause IV: a democratic socialist believes in Clause IV, a social democrat does not.

I want to be careful not to reinforce the conflation of socialism with government. Many people, even some intelligent ones, think socialism means more government intervention in the economy and capitalism means less government intervention in the economy.

First, as we have seen, in *every* system the government plays a strong role in the economy. In Hong Kong, for example, supposedly one of the most "economically free" political territories on indexes of capitalist policies, the government owns nearly every square inch of land.[5] A country like China, in which the state heavily controls industry but operates capitalistically and without any economic democracy, blurs the easy distinction between capitalism and socialism. Things we think of as products of the free market are anything but. In *The Entrepreneurial State,* Mariana Mazzucato shows that many innovations that we think are the products of brilliant entrepreneurs are in fact the result of massive investments by the U.S. government.[6] You can have a society that looks "capitalistic"—because it allows corporations to trample and exploit people—but in fact has a vast state apparatus. You could also theoretically have a society that looks socialistic but has a small government (for example, if the government kept to peace-keeping and wealth-redistribution functions and a network of private, worker-owned cooperatives were far more important institutions in people's lives). The distinction between public and private is something of a fiction, and we should probably focus less on the question of whether something is in one category or the other than on questions about who gets the benefits and who holds decision-making power. A country with a great deal of state intervention in the economy can be authoritarian or democratic, and a country with a smaller degree of state intervention can also be authoritarian or democratic. (Recall that some libertarians are quite open about their opposition to democracy, believing that philosopher-kings should govern in a capitalist utopia.)

There's a further complication, in that a large number of socialists have historically been *outright anarchists.* People like Mikhail Bakunin, Emma Goldman, and Peter Kropotkin considered themselves libertarian socialists. They despised government and capitalism equally, and believed that the ideal society was one in which workers managed their own affairs without bosses or rulers. Those who believe socialism is intrinsically a system based on government authority and coercion have to reckon with the existence of a substantial socialist contingent that has rejected government authority entirely, that says, as Bakunin did, that the state "has hitherto only enslaved, persecuted, exploited and corrupted" human beings and must be abolished *in order to create socialism.*[7] Bakunin believed that freedom from the state and freedom from the rich went hand in hand.

Other socialists, however, *have* suggested that government action to manage the economy is socialism, and that the measures we call "social democratic" should actually be considered partial steps toward a more fully socialized society. Socialist writer Robert Blatchford claimed in 1895 that England's various attempts to regulate industry over the years should all be attributed to socialists.

> The abolition of toll bars and bridge tolls was Socialistic action, for it made the roads and bridges common property . . . The Factory Acts are Socialistic, for they deny the employer the power to work women and children to death. The Compulsory and Free Education Acts are Socialistic. The Acts which compel the inspection of mines and factories, the inspection of boilers, the placing of a loadline on ships, and the granting of relief to paupers are all Socialistic Acts, for they all interfere with the "freedom of contract" and the "rights of the individual."[8]

Some socialists argue that the U.S. Postal Service and our public schools are socialistic, because they operate on a principle of common ownership and control. Other socialists argue that these socialists are delusional. It can all get very confusing! But if you think socialists are confused about their own ideology, you should see the debates between religious conservatives and libertarian conservatives about whether conservatism means that the state should respect individual sexual liberty.[9]

For contemporary socialists like myself, it is difficult to give a clear answer to the question of whether socialism is a radical call for the total transformation of society or a push for social democratic reforms like those already existing in many European countries. That's because it's not necessarily either/or. For us, the answer is *both*: there's a utopian and pragmatic element. While in the long term I'd like to live in a stateless society in which the means of production are democratically controlled, in the immediate future I think socialists have to devise and pursue attainable, useful goals like guaranteeing healthcare, demilitarizing the police, and creating a humane immigration policy.

There are important common elements among nearly all socialist ideologies, just as there are among conservative or liberal ideologies. One is a deep dissatisfaction with the existing state of economic life and a rejection of standard arguments for why it's acceptable to have capital concentrated in the hands of a small number of rich people.

Socialists believe that there ought to be a radically different distribution of wealth and power across society. This already sets them apart from the political mainstream. Socialists also believe that there should be greater "collective" rather than "private" ownership, and that assets that rightfully belong to everybody should be part of the "commons." But there are many differences of opinion among socialists about the scope and structure of these new forms of ownership.

Personally, I consider myself both a radical and a pragmatist. I think there should be no borders, no prisons, and no bosses. That makes me a utopian socialist. But I also think that the job of a moral human being is to actually accomplish things that help people, and to understand political reality *while* trying to alter it. (These are essentially the political principles of Noam Chomsky, who nobody doubts is a socialist.[10]) It's perfectly possible to believe that the most viable political causes in the twenty-first-century United States are paid family leave, single-payer healthcare, debt forgiveness, and prison reform and still hold out hope that someday our descendants will live in blissful *Star Trek* communism.

* * *

> "You keep using that word. I do not think it means what you think it means."
>
> —Inigo Montoya, *The Princess Bride*

Perhaps, however, you are a bit unsatisfied by my approach to terminology. You may crave a bit more specificity. I hesitate to offer precise definitions, for fear of triggering needless arguments that distract us from the underlying issues, but here are my own starting points for thinking about what a few highly contentious terms mean. These are personal definitions, not dictionary definitions, and I recognize that there are legitimate differences of opinion.

- **Socialism:** An egalitarian political tradition characterized by its skepticism of wealth inequality and private, for-profit ownership. There are many strands of socialist philosophy, including Marxism, anarchism, and the less radical "Fabian" socialisms. Some are in favor of centralized states, some are against the state entirely. Some are revolutionary and some are reformist. Some believe that markets, money, and some private ownership will be necessary, while others believe the world should be held in common and shared by all. But each has a radical vision for a more fair and equal social/economic landscape, and is trying to shift control of the production of goods and services from rich owners to ordinary workers. You are not a socialist if you do not aspire to drastic changes in the existing arrangement of economic power, meaning it is not enough simply to affirm vague rhetorical support for "equality."

- **Democratic Socialism:** A strand of socialist thinking that emphasizes the role of popular participation in governance. The "democratic" modifier is used to distinguish this kind of socialism from the kind in which unelected central planners make decisions on people's behalf. Democratic socialists strongly believe that people themselves should be the arbiters of their needs and desires.

- **Marxism:** A body of social and economic thought that draws from the writings of Karl Marx and Friedrich Engels. There are as many varieties of Marxism as there are varieties of socialism itself.[11] While Marxists often subscribe to the same kind of broad egalitarian vision that socialists generally do, they use particular analytical tools refined by Marx, such as class struggle and the materialist conception of history.

- **Capitalism:** An economic system characterized by the existence of a large number of people who work for wages and a small number of people who privately own the country's economic resources. Capitalism and a "market economy" are not the same thing; market economies have existed for thousands of years, while modern capitalism came about in the last few hundred years. The existence of class differences, wages, and profits are key characteristics of capitalism. A market economy in which all of the factories were owned collectively and there was no class of rich profiteers would not be considered capitalist.

- **Democracy:** The belief that people ought to be able to participate directly in decisions that affect them. Democracy means that people themselves, rather than oligarchs or aristocrats, are allowed to decide how political power is used. Democratic socialists believe that democracy means more than just being allowed to vote for your government representative. It also means having a meaningful voice at work, and in your family, and at your school. Many conservatives are distrustful of democracy because they believe that it leads to a "tyranny of the majority," by which they generally mean "poor people being fed up with being dictated to by rich people." Some liberals distrust democracy, too, believing that ordinary working people are too uneducated to know how to exercise power responsibly.

- **Social Democracy:** A contested term. Some believe that one could maintain the basic structure of capitalism—the division between a few rich owners and many poorer laborers—and have a "social democracy," if the government provided substantial welfare benefits to members of the working classes. Under this definition, it wouldn't matter who owned the factories, if there was a national health program and free childcare provided by the state. Others, like Bernie Sanders, reject this idea of social democracy as limited, and see "social democracy" and "democratic socialism" as relatively synonymous aspirations. This is because they believe anything with the word "democracy" or "democratic" in it requires making sure small groups of wealthy people do not have colossal amounts of power.

* * *

LABELS ARE FRUSTRATING. Every moment spent discussing what socialism *means* or whether someone does or does not qualify as a socialist is not being spent discussing their actual proposals. The right does not have good arguments against what socialists are advocating today. Ted Cruz, a champion debater, was bested when he went up against Bernie Sanders.[12] Why? Because, fundamentally, the right has no plausible answers to the questions of how we can ensure that people don't need to use GoFundMe to pay for insulin, or why someone bleeding on a train platform would beg people not to call an ambulance because they couldn't afford it.[13] In Brazil, the Amazon rainforest—which is not only one of the great wonders of the natural world, but is critical to the fight against climate change—is being destroyed at a stunning rate (nearly three football fields per minute)[14] thanks to a far-right president committed to deregulation. Conservatives are not thinking about this problem. They will not stop this problem. Regardless of what you think the term means, the socialists are the only ones who take the problem seriously and stand a chance of solving it.

We can no more hope for a perfect definition of what socialism is than we can ask for a definitive answer on what love or democracy is. But like those other terms, socialism is a value worth pursuing—a valuable orienting principle.

One Long Struggle

The Grand Libertarian Left Tradition

"Arise ye workers from your slumbers
Arise ye prisoners of want
For reason in revolt now thunders
And at last ends the age of cant.
Away with all your superstitions
Servile masses arise, arise
We'll change henceforth the old tradition
And spurn the dust to win the prize.
So comrades, come rally
And the last fight let us face
The Internationale unites the human race."

—Eugène Pottier, "The Internationale"

SOCIALISM IS OFTEN CONSIDERED TO have a dreary pedigree. This could not be more false. The radical left has a beautiful tradition, one that has long been buried but is worth excavating and celebrating.

Some of the greatest minds in history have been radical socialists: Albert Einstein,[1] Bertrand Russell, Helen Keller, Martin Luther King Jr. All of them dreamed of a far more equal world, one where the demands of profit didn't cause widespread exploitation and predatory behavior. And while *socialism* as a word dates back only to the early nineteenth century, history has been full of thinkers who sought to restructure society among fairer lines.

Consider Thomas Paine, the most radical (and by far the most interesting) of the Founding Fathers. Paine is much neglected today, even though his popular treatise *Common Sense* laid the intellectual groundwork for the American Revolution. Paine was a freethinker and a humanist, and he alienated himself from many of his peers through his persistent questioning of religious dogma and his frank challenge to the legitimacy of Christian scripture. But Paine also advocated the redistribution of wealth, and his *Agrarian Justice* is known as one of the earliest texts to push for strong social welfare programs and the taxation of the rich. *Agrarian Justice* also explains how wealth is socially rather than individually produced:

> Separate an individual from society, and give him an island or a continent to possess, and he cannot acquire personal property. He cannot be rich . . . [All accumulation] beyond what a man's own hands produce, is derived to him by living in society; and he owes on every principle of justice, of gratitude, and of civilization, a part of that accumulation back again to society from whence the whole came.[2]

There are all sorts of inspiring left figures to be found in the annals of history. John Ball, one of the leading English peasant revolutionaries, gave a famous oration in 1381 making a case for the rights of working people: "From the beginning all men by nature were created alike, and our bondage or servitude came in by the unjust oppression of naughty men."[3] People remember 1216's Magna Carta, but they forget another document from 1217 called the Charter of the Forest, which reasserted the claim of the people to share in the commons. The forest charter was radical, because it granted an affirmative right of people to a share in collectively owned wealth, and it's unsurprising that the political right would prefer to forget it. As the American Bar Association described it:

> The Charter has 17 articles, which assert the eternal right of free men and women to work on their own volition in ways that would yield all elements of subsistence on the commons, including such basics as the right to pick fruit, the right to gather wood for buildings and other purposes, the right to dig and use clay for utensils and housing, the right to pasture animals, the right to fish, the right to take peat

for fuel, the right to water, and even the right to take honey. The Charter should be regarded as one of the most radical in our history, since it asserted the right of commoners to obtain raw materials and the means of production, and gave specific meaning to the right to work.[4]

In 1600s Britain, the Diggers tried to form an agricultural communal lifestyle, while the Levellers made demands for "a secular republic, abolition of the House of Lords, equality before the law, the right to vote for all, free trade, the abolition of censorship, freedom of speech and the absolute right for people to worship whatever religion [or none] that they chose."[5] The Chartists of the 1800s, "the first mass movement driven by the working classes," pushed for the political rights of working people, including universal suffrage.[6]

In the nineteenth century, both pre- and post-Marx, there were dozens of fascinating socialist philosophers developing potent critiques of existing economic structures. Robert Owen, in England, tried to think of ways to redesign the factory system, and even inspired "Owenite" utopian communities in North America.[7] Charles Fourier, of lemonade seas infamy, also led people to set up communes, which, you will not be shocked to find out, petered out rather quickly. Leo Tolstoy was a socialistic anarchist, and George Bernard Shaw, when he wasn't writing classic plays, was putting out books like *The Intelligent Woman's Guide to Socialism and Capitalism*. (Shaw thought women would be a far more receptive audience for radical ideas, though the result now looks insufferably patronizing.)

In Europe, socialist statesmen formed a substantial part of many national governments. They helped set up social welfare programs, opposed militarism and colonialism, and regulated industry to make workplaces safer and less exploitative. The French Socialist Party in the early twentieth century was an impressive force for reform and produced great statesmen who made their country a more humane place. In the decades prior to being outlawed by the Nazi government, the German Social Democratic Party (SDP) had produced an impressive record of egalitarian reforms, expanding the role of women in politics, improving working conditions and workplace safety, offering educational and cultural programs, eliminating child labor, and expanding social security, as well as producing the great revolutionary socialist Rosa Luxemburg and the great reformist socialist Eduard Bernstein.[8] If we think of Europe today as social democratic, it is not because it was that way naturally, but because generations of socialists fought to make it that way and succeeded.

LESSONS FROM MARX

Karl Marx is the most famous historical socialist, and can't be ignored. While not all socialists are Marxists, and there are vigorous disputes between Marxist and non-Marxist socialists, there is a great deal of value in his writings. You may have been told that Marx is "discredited," or that the records of twentieth-century communist regimes are proof that Marx was wrong. But serious sociological and economic thinkers recognize that he was an intellectual force to be reckoned with. Joseph Schumpeter, the great exponent of capitalism, called Marx an important prophet, teacher, and sociologist, and recognized that Marx's magnum opus, *Das Kapital,* while "partly unfinished, partly battered by successful attack, still stretches its mighty skyline before us."[9]

Marx was prolific, and his thinking has many dimensions. Some are less applicable today than others, understandable given that he was writing about nineteenth-century industrial capitalism. The core reason to appreciate him, however, is that he had a better understanding than almost anyone else of the way that economics determines the fabric of the social world, and the way our economic system operates according to rules of its own that produce outcomes nobody wants. He brilliantly explained the conflict between capitalists and workers, and the way that changes in how goods are produced can affect the entire character of our relations with one another. Jim Sidanius and Felicia Pratto, in *Social Dominance*, offer a useful summary of his doctrine:

> Marxist theory argues that capitalist societies are hierarchically organized social systems in which the economic surplus that technology and productive instruments produce is unequally distributed between the owners of this technology and those who actual produce the wealth . . . Marxism argues that those with the power and control

over the means of production will exploit those with little power and control . . . These owners are able to structure economic transactions in ways that almost always benefit themselves at the cost of workers. Furthermore, the owners own not only the means of economic production (e.g, manufacturing), but the means of intellectual and cultural production as well (e.g., mass media, the universities). Because this ruling class controls the major venues of intellectual production, this gives [it] great power over the kinds of ideas available for public discourse and how this discourse is framed. Finally, this economic and intellectual power also translates itself into political power and control over the organs of the state. For Marxists, the ruling class's control over the state is considered so complete that the state is regarded as the "executive committee of the ruling class."[10]

This certainly rings true, as we've seen in previous chapters. Marx saw the way capitalism destroyed workers' humanity, turned them into fungible mechanical parts who existed to generate profits for their bosses. As he wrote:

The worker's existence is thus brought under the same condition as the existence of every other commodity. The worker has become a commodity, and it is a bit of luck for him if he can find a buyer. And the demand on which the life of the worker depends, depends on the whim of the rich and the capitalists.[11]

Marx had a profound understanding of the way people's labor was exploited, with workers giving far more in production than they got back in compensation. He also showed how people were "alienated" from their labor, alienation being the difference between building a bookshelf for your own house for pleasure and building a bookshelf because you work at a bookshelf factory. An alienated worker:

. . . does not affirm himself but denies himself, does not feel well but unhappy, does not freely develop his physical and mental energy but mortifies his body and ruins his mind. The worker, therefore, feels himself only outside his work, and feels beside himself in his work.

He is at home when he is not working, and when he is working he is
not at home. His work therefore is not voluntary, but coerced; it is
forced labor. It is therefore not the satisfaction of a need, but only a
means for satisfying needs external to it. Its alien character emerges
clearly in the fact that labor is shunned like the plague as soon as
there is no physical or other compulsion.[12]

Marx describes facts about the economic world that should be obvious, but that often go unnoticed. He shows how we are caught up
in systems, and why having "good" people on corporate boards can't
fundamentally change the actions of corporations. He shows how we
come to see the world as consisting of commodities, and lose sight of
the labor that goes into producing them. Some of Marx's writings are
difficult to penetrate. Others, however, are poetic and clarifying. Marx
has a way of showing things as they really are, of getting to the heart
of the matter using powerful and original language. Take, for example,
this famous passage from *The Eighteenth Brumaire of Louis Bonaparte*:

> Men make their own history, but they do not make it as they please;
> they do not make it under self-selected circumstances, but under cir-
> cumstances existing already, given and transmitted from the past.
> The tradition of all dead generations weighs like a nightmare on the
> brains of the living.[13]

There is great insight packed into these sentences; one can ruminate
on them for hours. How does the past constrain our actions in the present? What power do we have to "make our own history" given that the
circumstances are not of our own choosing?

Or take Marx's famous passage about religion as an opiate. In its
full version it reads:

> Religious suffering is, at one and the same time, the expression of
> real suffering and a protest against real suffering. Religion is the sigh
> of the oppressed creature, the heart of a heartless world, and the soul
> of soulless conditions. It is the opium of the people. The abolition
> of religion as the illusory happiness of the people is the demand for

their real happiness. To call on them to give up their illusions about their condition is to call on them to give up a condition that requires illusions. The criticism of religion is, therefore, in embryo, the criticism of that vale of tears of which religion is the halo.[14]

That's not some snarky dismissal of religion as a kind of stupefying drug. Rather, it's a deep observation about the way that religion offers something powerfully important to people who desperately need it. His problem is not with religion, but with the conditions that make religion necessary. Throughout Marx's writing one finds staggeringly original descriptions of everyday phenomena that cause us to examine them anew.

Yet while Marx's sociological and economic analyses have value for all leftists, Marx offers only a limited guide to political action. Even in Marx's own day, anarchists like Proudhon and Bakunin were sharply criticizing what they saw as authoritarian tendencies in Marx's actual programmatic beliefs. Proudhon wrote to Marx and warned: "For God's sake . . . do not let us think of indoctrinating the people . . . Let us not set ourselves up as the apostles of a new religion."[15] Proudhon said that communists of his time were becoming "fanatics of state power,"[16] who held the "doctrinaire, authoritarian, dictatorial, governmental" belief that "the individual is essentially subordinate to the collective."[17] The historical record shows that Proudhon was right to worry. Marx's followers frequently had too little regard for the importance of individual liberty, and were too inflexibly committed to their doctrine. The libertarian socialist Murray Bookchin, in his scathing essay "Listen, Marxist!," cautioned that despite Marx's "lasting contributions to revolutionary thought . . . a theoretical corpus which was liberating a century ago is turned into a straitjacket today," and we should remember "the idea that a man whose greatest theoretical contributions were made between 1840 and 1880 could 'foresee' the entire dialectic of capitalism is, on the face of it, utterly preposterous."[18] Ultimately, this is why it's important not to be a "Marxist," but an independent thinker who takes what is valuable in Marx and discards what isn't.

I know some socialists who believe that nobody can really be a socialist unless they have read Karl Marx. I don't agree with them. To me, this is like saying that nobody can be a physicist unless they have read Isaac Newton, or that nobody can talk about triangles unless they have read Euclid. Karl Marx is the single most dominant figure in the history of socialist thought, and his ideas have influenced the course of left movements and thinking. But while any historical account of the development of socialism necessarily has to deal with Marx, socialist conclusions are fairly easily deduced through ordinary reasoning. It is worth knowing why Karl Marx is important and influential, but one need not crack open the dense text of *Das Kapital* to pursue the project of human liberation.

THE LIBERTARIAN SOCIALIST

In 1920, Emma Goldman arrived in the Soviet Union filled with hope. The Bolshevik revolution had swept away the oppressive Tsarist regime, and like many leftists, Goldman was thrilled at the idea of a revolutionary workers' state. But when she saw how the country was run under Lenin's government, Goldman's excitement quickly turned to disgust. In Petrograd, she said, "the people walked about like living corpses; the shortage of food and fuel was slowly sapping the city; grim death was clutching at its heart."[19] This couldn't entirely be blamed on the communist government—after all, the country was in the midst of a civil war. But she soon noticed concerning tendencies: police brutality and corruption, restrictions on basic freedoms. The bureaucracy was stifling: "To get a pound of nails one had to file applications in about ten or fifteen bureaus; to secure some bed linen or ordinary dishes one wasted days."[20] It certainly did not seem as if the workers were in charge. Goldman's interactions with the Bolsheviks convinced her that they were not fighting for the same kind of freedom that she was.

> On a certain occasion, when I passed criticism on the brutal way delicate women were driven into the streets to shovel snow, insisting that even if they had belonged to the bourgeoisie they were human, and that physical fitness should be taken into consideration, a Communist said to me: "You should be ashamed of yourself; you, an old revolutionist, and yet so sentimental." In short, I had come to see that

the Bolsheviki were social puritans who sincerely believed that they alone were ordained to save mankind.[21]

Goldman, never quiet in the face of injustice, took her concerns to Vladimir Lenin. She asked him why he was imprisoning her fellow anarchists and demanded to know what had happened to free speech. "Free speech," Lenin replied, "is, of course, a bourgeois notion . . . There can be no free speech in a revolutionary period." Goldman was appalled.

Philosopher Bertrand Russell had a similar experience when he met Lenin. Russell was impressed with Lenin's personal humility but disturbed by his dogmatism. Remarking on his time in the Soviet state, Russell said, "I went to Russia a Communist; but contact with those who have no doubts has intensified a thousandfold my own doubts, not as to Communism in itself, but as to the wisdom of holding a creed so firmly that for its sake men are willing to inflict widespread misery."[22]

Neither Russell nor Goldman abandoned their leftist politics. Near the end of Goldman's life, she traveled to Spain to support the anarchists in the Spanish Civil War. And Russell was leading antiwar protests into his 90s. But each valued freedom as much as they valued equality, and they could not tolerate a socialism that involved restricting the liberties of the very people they were fighting for. Goldman and Russell were, in other words, libertarian socialists.

In the United States, libertarian socialism strikes people as oxymoronic. Libertarians hate government and love capitalism; socialists love government and hate capitalism. Surely these two things are opposites. But they aren't: libertarian socialists hate government and capitalism alike! More specifically, libertarian socialists have rejected the false dichotomy between capitalism and communism. They recognize that the freedom promised by libertarian capitalists is illusory, that where there is economic and social hierarchy the people at the bottom are not free. But they also recognize that nobody wants to live in an oppressive bureaucracy, and that you don't fix the problem of inequality by making everyone equally unhappy.

Libertarian socialists are often left out of discussions about socialism, because Marxist socialists are uncomfortable with their critique of Marxism, and both capitalists and mushy centrists want to pretend that all socialists are Stalinists. But during the time of Marx himself, there were vigorous debates about the relationship between socialism and freedom. Anarchist Mikhail Bakunin frequently sparred with Marx, saying that if a "dictatorship of the proletariat" ever arose, it would still beat the people with the same stick, but would call it "the people's stick." Bakunin issued a prophetic warning about what could happen if one's commitment to socialism wasn't coupled with a distaste for bureaucracy and centralized authority:

> There will be a new class, a new hierarchy of real and pretended scientists and scholars, and the world will be divided into a minority ruling in the name of knowledge and an immense ignorant majority. And then, woe betide the mass of ignorant ones! . . . You can see quite well that behind all the democratic and socialistic phrases and promises of Marx's program, there is to be found in his State all that constitutes the true despotic and brutal nature of all States.[23]

Bakunin had a simple formula that captures the ethos of libertarian socialists:

> We are convinced that liberty without socialism is privilege, injustice; and that socialism without liberty is slavery and brutality.

Liberty without socialism means rule by CEOs, socialism without liberty means rule by bureaucrats. This is not a particularly difficult idea to grasp, but thanks to their willingness to condemn *all* unjust rule consistently, libertarian socialists are usually the ones who end up facing the firing squad when the new regime takes power.

The spirit of the libertarian socialist is consistent attachment to principle. Thomas Paine, for example, traveled to France to support the 1789 revolution. But Paine protested the execution of the French king because of his consistent opposition to the death penalty. He won himself no friends this way, and landed in the Bastille. Paine would die penniless and despised, having alienated nearly everyone with his commitment to his principles and consistency.

Libertarian socialism has long been a minority tendency, but it is an admirable and humane one. It forces us to ask difficult questions about when the use of power is and isn't justified, what kinds of liberties matter, and what democracy really means. It does not offer simple clichés like "you have to break a few eggs to make an omelet" or "that government is best which governs least." It commits itself unwaveringly to a set of respectable principles and compromises neither its radical socialism nor its radical libertarianism.

LOVE THY NEIGHBOR: THE CHRISTIAN LEFT

> "Jesus answered, 'If you want to be perfect, go, sell your possessions and give to the poor, and you will have treasure in heaven. Then come, follow me.'"
>
> —Matthew 19:21

> "You cannot serve both God and money."
>
> —Matthew 6:24

Jesus was not big on material possessions, and there has long been a socialist tradition that takes seriously the words of the Beatitudes ("Blessed are you who are poor, for yours is the kingdom of God" and "Woe to you who are rich, for you have already received your comfort") and sees egalitarianism as a Christian imperative. Left Christian writer Elizabeth Bruenig has said that because the faith teaches that, in the words of St. Augustine, "God made the rich and poor from the one clay," there has long been religious skepticism of dividing up into private property a world originally held by all in common, and the Church has often "urged vigilance against the tendency of the wealthy to amass more than their due, to the detriment of the poor."[24]

The socialist theologian David Bentley Hart has said that the Bible lends itself toward leftist or even communist conclusions, and that "while there are always clergy members and theologians swift to assure us that the New Testament condemns not wealth but its abuse, not a single verse (unless subjected to absurdly forced readings) confirms the claim."[25] Many Christians, of course, are right-wing rather than left-wing, and it is possible to use Biblical teaching to justify amassing colossal wealth (see the "prosperity gospel" and America's rich tradition of huckster televangelists). But it would be a mistake to overlook the leftist currents in Christian thinking.

Take, for instance, Dorothy Day (1897–1980). She is a legendary figure among social justice Catholics, organizing the Catholic Worker Movement and advocating pacifism, economic equality, and civil rights from a Christian anarchist perspective.[26] Arrested numerous times for her civil disobedience, Day often took Biblical teaching more seriously than the Church did. She was the kind of Christian who defers to the Sermon on the Mount rather than the prejudices of local priests and bishops, and as such has been long admired for her moral courage. Predictably, there have been attempts to sanitize her legacy and minimize her radicalism. The Catholic *Crisis* magazine has suggested she was a conservative, because she "lamented the encroachment of the state and the perils of the welfare system."[27] She did so, however, because she was an anarchist, not a conservative. It's true that her economics were not purely socialistic, but her words made clear how she felt about capitalism:

> I am sure that God did not intend that there be so many poor. The class structure is of our making and our consent, not His. It is the way we have arranged it, and it is up to us to change it. So we are urging revolutionary change . . . We need to change the system. We need to overthrow, not the government, as the authorities are always accusing the Communists "of conspiring to teach [us] to do," but this rotten, decadent, putrid industrial capitalist system which breeds such suffering in the whited sepulcher of New York.[28]

There are other fascinating Christian socialists in history. Francis Bellamy, the author of the original Pledge of Allegiance, was one. Ammon Hennacy, a member of both the Industrial Workers of the World and the Catholic Worker Movement, established the "Joe Hill House of Hospitality," a social service center in Salt Lake City, philosophically based on a mixture of radical leftist labor politics and Christian theology.[29] Leo Tolstoy, in *The Kingdom of God Is Within You*, used a radical religious message to condemn "this social order with its pauperism, famines, prisons, gallows, armies, and wars" and urged the embrace of pacifism.[30] The liberation theologians, most famously Gustavo Gutiérrez of Peru,[31] mixed traditional Catholic values with Marxist analysis, developing the "preferential option for the poor" as a Christian imperative. The tradition flourished in Latin America, but also developed into Black Liberation Theology in the United States and even a variant unique to Palestinian Christians. Echoes of it can still be heard in Pope Francis' critiques of capitalism and statements like "Human rights are not only violated by terrorism, repression or assassination, but also by unfair economic structures that creates huge inequalities."[32]

GOOD OLD-FASHIONED, HOMEGROWN AMERICAN SOCIALISM

It is often claimed that the United States differs from Europe in that it lacks a socialist tradition. The title question of Werner Sombart's 1906 book *Why Is There No Socialism in the United States?* was answered nearly a century later by Seymour Martin Lipset and Gary Wolfe Marks' *It Didn't Happen Here: Why Socialism Failed in the United States*. It is common to say that socialism "failed" here. This is true insofar as socialists never became a substantial force in American politics. But it overlooks the fact that we *did*, for a short time, have a socialist movement that positively thrived.

A century ago, when socialism was at its peak in this country, the Socialist Party held 1,200 offices in 340 cities.[33] There were two Socialist members of Congress, dozens of Socialist state legislators, and more than 130 Socialist mayors in over half of the U.S. states. (The University of Washington has maps showing just how impressive socialism's spread across the country was.[34]) Socialist Party successes were especially concentrated in the Midwest, which makes Senator Tammy Duckworth's comment that you can't "go too far left and still win the Midwest"[35] somewhat ironic.

Many people are taught, mostly as a curious historical footnote, that Eugene Debs received more than a million votes when he ran for president, even when forced to campaign from a prison cell. But the socialists who actually did hold public office are rarely discussed. That's a shame, because it could help us answer one of the most serious critical questions facing socialism: Would socialism be a disaster if socialists were actually put in charge? Are socialists impractical utopians whose ideology would crush freedom and destroy our fragile institutions? What would socialist political power look like in the United States?

In fact, we *had* a taste of socialist political power in the United States, albeit only on the local level. Three mayors of Milwaukee were socialists! And during their tenure, did Milwaukee turn into a bleak and bloody revolutionary nightmare?

Turns out, it did not.

> Under the Socialists, Milwaukee gained a reputation as a well-managed municipality. They believed that government had a responsibility to promote the common good, but particularly to serve the needs of the city's working class. They built community parks, including beautiful green spaces and recreation areas along the lakefront that are still widely-used. They increased the citywide minimum wage (28 years before the federal government adopted the idea) and established an eight-hour day standard for municipal workers. They championed public education for the city's children, built excellent libraries and sponsored vibrant recreation programs. The city municipalized street lighting, the stone quarry, garbage disposal and water purification.[36]

Daniel Hoan, the longest serving of the three socialist mayors, was so popular among the city's residents that he served in office for *24 years*. In 1936, Hoan was featured on the cover of *TIME* magazine, which said that under his administration, "Milwaukee has become perhaps the best governed city in the U.S."[37] The city "won many awards for being among the safest and healthiest cities in the country," and "regularly had among the lowest rates of infant mortality and epidemic diseases of any American city." Hoan "experimented with the municipal marketing of food, backed city-built housing, and in providing public markets, city harbor improvements, and purging graft from Milwaukee politics."[38]

We've even had a more recent example of a socialist mayor, a person many more people have heard of. Bernie Sanders served as mayor of

Burlington, Vermont, for eight years, being reelected three times. How did it go? Did he create a little Leningrad on Lake Champlain?

No, it was fine. Sanders was regarded as "a hardworking, pragmatic, effective mayor who helped transform Vermont's largest city (population: 38,000) into a thriving town."[39] And furthermore,

> Burlington is now widely heralded as an environmentally friendly, lively, and livable city with a thriving economy, including one of the lowest jobless rates in the country. Burlingtonians give Sanders credit for steering the city in a new direction that, despite early skepticism, proved to be broadly popular with voters.

During the heyday of the Socialist Party, Socialist state legislators were always in the minority and usually outvoted. The party's 1914 report on its legislative activities makes for fascinating reading, and documents a series of low-key socialist policy successes across different states. In Wisconsin, for example, "both major parties had adopted parts of the Socialist platform, and the legislature was passing bills that a decade before would never have been reported out of committee."[40] What sort of measures were these?

> In 1907, the socialist measures were typical and serve to illustrate the nature and extent of the work. The socialists introduced 72 different bills during one session. Fifteen were finally carried. Among the successful measures were the following: (1) A bill which provided for the erection of guards and railings over dangerous machinery in factories. (2) A bill which provided that all metal polishing machines shall be equipped with blowers and sufficient draft to remove the metallic dust. (3) A bill requiring railway companies to equip all trains with sufficient men to handle the work without overburdening the train men, known as the Full Crew Bill. (4) An eight-hour telegraphers' law. (5) A greatly improved child labor law. (6) Certain measures securing a greater degree of justice to labor through court processes. Thus it will be seen that as early as 1907 the socialist legislatures were beginning to force considerable concessions from the legislatures. By

the time the 1911 legislature closed its session, the number of successful socialist measures had increased rapidly.[41]

Alright, but here I'm going to encounter the inevitable objection: this isn't socialism! Sanders did not govern Burlington "as a socialist," therefore his tenure tells us nothing about socialism. I think this is mistaken, for a simple reason: there is nothing inherent in the basic principles of socialism that precludes pragmatic governance. There is a distinction between "a socialized economy" and "socialist values," and Sanders *did* govern in accordance with his socialist values. He took on developers, fighting to ensure that the Lake Champlain waterfront would be a "people's waterfront" that everyone could enjoy rather than containing nothing but luxury condos for the rich. The bills passed by Socialists in the Wisconsin legislature may not have been particularly radical, since they had to have support of non-socialists. But they flowed directly from the socialists' fundamental conviction that the way economic life functions is deeply dysfunctional and harms ordinary workers. So they advocated for an eight-hour workday, ending child labor, workplace safety regulations, etcetera. Today, these may seem standard-issue liberal policies, but it was radicals who made those issues mainstream. Today's capitalists like to give Henry Ford credit for creating the eight-hour workday and the two-day weekend. But remember that Ford adopted them after labor radicals had been campaigning for *sixty years* to get the length of the workday reduced.[42] Socialists' job is to put radical ideas in people's heads. After a while, they become mainstream, then they get taken for granted, and finally everybody insists they believed in them all along.

In other countries, the great socialists are legendary. In the United Kingdom, for instance, the contemporary welfare state wouldn't have been possible without the diligent efforts of socialist statesmen like Keir Hardie and Aneurin Bevan. In the United States, however, we forget all sorts of extraordinary people from our past. People like Helen Keller.

Keller herself is, of course, well remembered. But her radical socialist politics are too frequently neglected. She was a member of the Industrial Workers of the World (IWW), a supporter of Debs, and an anti-militarist feminist trade unionist who was staunchly committed to the rights of working people. If you read her socialist writings, it's a little surprising to realize just how firm her conviction was. Here she is describing the IWW and why she supports it:

> The creators of wealth are entitled to all they create. Thus they find themselves pitted against the whole profit-making system. They declare that there can be no compromise so long as the majority of the working class lives in want while the master class lives in luxury. They insist that there can be no peace until the workers organize as a class, take possession of the resources of the earth and the machinery of production and distribution and abolish the wage system.[43]

I don't remember hearing that when we watched *The Miracle Worker* in middle school! In her essay "How I Became A Socialist," Keller says she is pleased that people seem so interested in her inspiring life story, particularly because it will help get the word *socialism* into more newspapers! (Ah, how she underestimated the power of the whitewashing machine!) She also amusingly recounted how the *New York Times* asked her to write an article, then soon after printed an editorial condemning the "contemptible red flag." This would not do, Keller said.

> I love the red flag and what it symbolizes to me and other Socialists. I have a red flag hanging in my study, and if I could I should gladly march with it past the office of the *Times* and let all the reporters and photographers make the most of the spectacle. According to the inclusive condemnation of the *Times* I have forfeited all right to respect and sympathy, and I am to be regarded with suspicion. Yet the editor of the *Times* wants me to write him an article![44]

Nor did Keller think much of the *Brooklyn Eagle* when they suggested that her left-wing politics were a product of her physical disabilities. Keller's reply is so deliciously scathing that it's worth quoting at length.

> The *Brooklyn Eagle* says, apropos of me, and socialism, that Helen Keller's "mistakes spring out of the manifest limitations of her development." Some years ago I met a gentleman who was introduced

to me as Mr. McKelway, editor of the *Brooklyn Eagle*. It was after a meeting that we had in New York in behalf of the blind. At that time the compliments he paid me were so generous that I blush to remember them. But now that I have come out for socialism he reminds me and the public that I am blind and deaf and especially liable to error. I must have shrunk in intelligence during the years since I met him. Surely it is his turn to blush . . . Oh, ridiculous *Brooklyn Eagle*! What an ungallant bird it is! . . . *The Eagle* is willing to help us prevent misery provided, always provided, that we do not attack the industrial tyranny which supports it and stops its ears and clouds its vision. *The Eagle* and I are at war. I hate the system which it represents, apologizes for and upholds. When it fights back, let it fight fair. Let it attack my ideas and oppose the aims and arguments of Socialism. It is not fair fighting or good argument to remind me and others that I cannot see or hear. I can read. I can read all the socialist books I have time for in English, German and French. If the editor of the *Brooklyn Eagle* should read some of them, he might be a wiser man and make a better newspaper. If I ever contribute to the Socialist movement the book that I sometimes dream of, I know what I shall name it: Industrial Blindness and Social Deafness.[45]

The United States has produced other exceptional socialist women, like the rabble-rousing labor agitator Mary Harris "Mother" Jones, who once led a march of hundreds of child laborers to Theodore Roosevelt's summer home, where she demanded to see the president to protest child labor.[46] (She was refused admission.) Nor should one neglect the countless socialists of color, many of whom have been unjustly forgotten. Peter Clark, known as the first African American socialist, was an abolitionist, labor organizer, schoolteacher, and newspaper editor who was once fired from his teaching post for daring to mention Thomas Paine to his students. (Clark: "Whatever Socialism may bring about, it can present nothing more anarchical than is found in Grafton, Baltimore and Pittsburgh today."[47]) Hubert Harrison, known to his peers as the "Black Socrates," was a key figure in the Harlem Renaissance, known for combining radical race consciousness with radical class consciousness.[48] Paul Robeson, the legendary singer-actor-lawyer-football player,

was infamously blacklisted over his left politics. Robeson felt true solidarity with the "workers of the world," and when he was in Britain he
developed a lasting bond with the striking Welsh miners.[49] Ella Baker
brought radical democracy to the civil rights movement,[50] and Black
Panther Fred Hampton tried to politicize and broker peace between
Chicago street gangs before being shot to death in his bed by the FBI.[51]
Angela Davis, the legendary black leftist scholar, has now spent over
50 years fighting against racism and capitalism, and was famously removed from her UCLA teaching post on orders from Ronald Reagan.
Each of these figures merits a book-length biography of their own.

* * *

PEOPLE LIKE KELLER and Clark and Davis are just individuals, though.
Just as important are the anonymous members of groups like the
IWW, the thousands and thousands of radical labor organizers who
waged small-scale campaigns to secure slightly better conditions. Social movements are mostly made up of devoted ordinary people who
work tirelessly to try to improve the lives of those around them. In the
Seattle General Strike of 1919, for instance, thousands of workers in all
industries left work at once in protest.[52]

These people accomplished so much. They brought us the eight-
hour day. It's them we have to thank for the existence of social insurance, workplace safety standards, and minimum wages. If you want
to read about just one of these "ordinary" lives, I recommend Matilda
Rabinowitz's *Immigrant Girl, Radical Woman*.[53] Rabinowitz came here
from the Ukraine as a teenager in 1900 and went to work in a shirt-
waist factory. She had a difficult life, but she did everything she could
to further the cause of women's equality and workers' rights. She did
the thankless work that doesn't end up being written about: coordinat-
ing a kitchen to make food for striking workers, collecting money for
their legal representation, running strike offices, and getting arrested
plenty in the process. Rabinowitz, and the hundreds of thousands of
others like her, have bequeathed to us both an example and a responsibility.

A look through socialist history can yield all kinds of useful lessons
for contemporary politics. The 10-point program of the Black Panther

Party, dated as it is, still resonates: calling for decent housing, full employment, and an end to police brutality. (The program even borrows the language of the Declaration of Independence: "We hold these truths to be self-evident: that all men are created equal.") Instructive models can be found all over the world, from the postwar Labour government of Britain that introduced the National Health Service and achieved massive popular support to the Zapatistas who built authentic libertarian socialism among the indigenous people of Chiapas, Mexico. One does not have to look only at those explicitly labeled "socialist"; nobody should forget the record of courageous dissidents and rebels, from abolitionist John Brown to Chelsea Manning.[54] History is replete with figures we can contemplate and take counsel from whenever we are feeling hopeless or dejected.

* * *

THE SOCIALIST LEFT has a great heritage, both in the United States and everywhere else. The historical record of socialism is not, as some would have it, merely a long string of authoritarian regimes. It is also the record of labor agitators and intellectuals who crafted ideas that later became public policy, who built schools and libraries, who developed the idea that everyone was equally entitled to a dignified life. This idea is commonplace now, but we wouldn't have it if it weren't for our dedicated socialist forebears. To be a socialist is to take part in a tradition that is intelligent, humane, and honorable.

Those who treat socialism as synonymous with the Soviet Union are being selective in their presentation of history. If we are going to inquire about history's lessons honestly, we have to look at all of it rather than the bits that suit our ideological purposes, and it's strange to talk about what history can teach us about whether socialism would be good for the United States without looking at the history of socialism in the United States itself. We have had socialists, and they have been good for the country. They have not been corrupt autocrats. They have been good people, trying to readjust the balance of power to make their country fairer.

Ultimately, one can only treat socialism as synonymous with the USSR or Venezuela if one deletes countless socialists from the pages of history. What about Kropotkin or Goldman or Rosa Luxemburg or Fred Hampton or Tony Benn? What about the great European socialists like August Bebel or Jean Jaurès? These individuals were not moderates, they were radical dissidents who stood up against the consensus of the day. Bebel led the only political faction to oppose Germany's brutal genocide in West Africa and abhorred racism. Jaurès was murdered for his anti-militarist stance against a pointless war that killed millions. In our own country, what about Debs, who bravely defied the law in order to oppose that same war and was sent to prison for it? What about Victor Berger, the first Socialist congressman, who was denied his seat in the House of Representatives because he dared to oppose needless nationalistic slaughter? What about the socialists who fought the Nazis in the streets of Berlin, who died trying to prevent Francoism from rising in Spain, and who tried desperately to stop the Vietnam War? Some of the greatest humanitarians of the twentieth century, like King and Mahatma Gandhi, and the strongest opponents of state repression and totalitarianism, like George Orwell, were staunch critics of capitalism. If we're going to discuss socialism's "record," we can't limit ourselves to the brutal dictators who have claimed to rule in the name of the people and waved the word *socialism* around to justify whatever brutality they cared to pursue. We have to give credit to those who have consistently been humane voices for the downtrodden and improved the world by expanding our moral imagination.

Making Our Plans

Sensible Agendas

"I am convinced Socialism is the only answer and I urge all comrades to take this struggle to a victorious conclusion."

—Malala Yousafzai, Statement to the
32nd congress of Pakistani Marxists

WE HAVE, SO FAR, A set of basic principles, an instinct toward utopia, a clearer understanding of the term *socialism*, and a sense of the great tradition that today's left continues. But this doesn't tell us much about the practical side of politics. Hooray, yes, we have sound moral instincts and a good philosophy and some fine guidance from our forebears. But do socialists have a *plan*?

In fact, we have lots of plans, and they're very good. Today's socialists are generally avoiding getting wrapped up in disputes between utopianism and pragmatism, reform or revolution. They understand that you have to have both. You have to dream of a very different world, but also look closely at the world you actually live in and be realistic in setting short-term political goals.

Some socialists are still skeptical about anyone who talks about pragmatism or "being realistic." This is a healthy reaction, because for a long time "be realistic" was code for "do very little" or "take baby steps." Martin Luther King Jr. was constantly told by white liberals that he needed to go slow—his "Letter from Birmingham Jail" is written to supposedly well-meaning moderates who caution radicals that they need to go slow.[1] Everyone who has tried to bring about major social change has been told that their agenda is unrealistic. Part of the core socialist commitment involves insisting on pressing forward even when you're being told your goals are unachievable. When members of the British Labour Party selected a socialist leader, Jeremy Corbyn, the consensus in the press was that the move was political suicide. It wasn't: in the next election, Labour increased its vote total by unprecedented numbers. As it turned out, an explicitly socialist agenda was far more appealing than the milquetoast "New Labour" liberalism of Corbyn's unpopular predecessors.[2]

In fact, nearly every ambitious endeavor to *some* degree involves a defiant unwillingness to be pragmatic, to accept the consensus opinion on what's possible. Those who want you to fail (because they don't share your commitments) will try to convince you that you're doomed. And even those who do share your commitments may be risk-averse and miss opportunities due to excessive skepticism. I don't, therefore, mind those who are defiantly unrealistic. Most people who claim to understand what *can* and *can't* be accomplished politically are just speculating. Expert political scientists, statisticians, and pundits were convinced Donald Trump could never be president. They were wrong. The truth is: political reality changes quickly, so it's best to pick the things you want to see happen, and do your best to try to make them happen. The old anarchist slogan rings true to me: "Demand the Impossible."[3]

> We live in capitalism. Its power seems inescapable. So did the divine right of kings. Any human power can be resisted and changed by human beings.
>
> —Ursula K. Le Guin

But while your long-term demands should be ambitious in the extreme, your short-term goals should be carefully grounded in an understanding of the needs of a particular time and place. You've got to actually get stuff done and materially improve the lives of people in the here and now.

To see an example of how pragmatism and utopianism can be

successfully combined, we can look at the approach of the Democratic Socialists of America (DSA). The DSA states, "Many structures of our government and economy must be radically transformed,"[4] and believes in a society without profit, exploitation, racism, sexism, or social hierarchy. That's extremely ambitious, to say the least. But the DSA also admits, "We are unlikely to see an immediate end to capitalism tomorrow," and so it "fights for reforms today that will weaken the power of corporations and increase the power of working people." "In the short term," it says, "we can't eliminate private corporations, but we can bring them under greater democratic control." There won't be perfect democratic socialism anytime soon, but we can make the world more socialistic and democratic. The Medicare for All fight is a clear example of this kind of rational radicalism.

First, the problem: Everyone knows that American healthcare is dysfunctional. People pay obscene amounts of money for basic medical services, to the point where they have to fear calling an ambulance because it might cost $900 or more for a five-minute ride.[5] By now, we have all heard that "despite having the most expensive health care system, the United States ranks last overall among 11 industrialized countries on measures of health system quality, efficiency, access to care, equity, and healthy lives."[6] Even after the Affordable Care Act, one-fourth of Americans have to refuse needed medical care because they can't afford it. Americans borrow an astonishing $88 billion every year to pay for healthcare.[7] Health insurance companies not only profit from denying people adequate care, they create vast bureaucracies that are almost impossible for ordinary people to navigate. We live in a country where people can be *terrified* of getting an illness, not because of the consequences of the illness itself, but because they know the bill will inevitably ruin their life.

The left has an elegant and efficient solution to this: instead of private health insurance systems, put everyone under the publicly run Medicare system.[8] Make healthcare "free at the point of service," meaning that it's paid for by tax revenue rather than premiums and co-pays. This kind of single-payer system, in which one entity (Medicare) coordinates healthcare payments rather than a patchwork of for-profit companies, is used successfully around the world. The developed countries that employ it have better health outcomes, and they save money by removing the profit motive and giving the government greater capacity to negotiate costs. A Medicare for All system would make medicine more fair and less costly. As public health scholars Abdul El-Sayed and Micah Johnson write, it's simple: "Too many of us don't have health-care. We spend too much on healthcare. And we hate our healthcare experience. Medicare-for-All solves all three of those problems."[9]

Medicare for All is not what we might call "fully socialistic," in that it does not eliminate the profit motive from medicine or bring hospitals under public ownership. It's not a system of socialized *medicine*, it's a system of socialized *insurance*—that is, the government isn't managing treatment, it's managing the payment system. In Great Britain, they do have actual socialized hospitals run by the government's National Health Service (NHS). Its model is very popular. Even though budget cuts by neoliberal governments have devastated the quality of care the NHS can offer, over three-quarters of Britons still want to keep the service in its current form, and its core principles are supported by a staggering 91 percent of British people. The Commonwealth Fund has ranked Great Britain's NHS as the best healthcare system out of 11 developed countries based on efficiency and performance (the United States was dead last at number 11).[10]

A group like the DSA would, naturally, prefer a system like the NHS (albeit a properly funded one that didn't have outrageous wait times and service cuts). But it so happens that in the United States, there is an obvious next step for creating a socialized healthcare system: expanding Medicare. Medicare, which covers seniors, is already the largest insurer in the country. It is also *very* popular. Among Americans over 65, nearly 90 percent have a positive opinion of the program and say it is "very important" for them and their families.[11] And there's no good reason why this sort of program should be limited to older people.

Medicare for All is not a radical or utopian proposition. It brings the United States roughly in line with contemporary Canada (a country not known for political radicalism). It alters the way healthcare is paid for (premiums become taxes, insurance is public rather than private) but nothing about the way it is delivered. It's not much more than an accounting tweak: instead of funds flowing through unnecessary profit-maximizing insurance corporations, they flow through a public institution. It's designed to save people money.[12] The Nobel Prize–winning economist Kenneth Arrow, no leftist, said that in healthcare markets it was simply obvious that "the government is better than the private sector at keeping costs down for insurance purposes."[13] Yet Medicare for All embodies the core socialist principle that everyone should be cared for equally well, and that we all have mutual obligations to support one another. This is why it's now one of the DSA's core campaigns.

DSA is pushing for Medicare for All by pressuring existing congresspeople to sign on to a Medicare for All bill introduced by Representative Pramila Jayapal (D-WA). Here in New Orleans, the local DSA chapter has several hundred members, and they regularly canvass local neighborhoods to talk to voters about healthcare and encourage them to call their representatives and ask them to support the bill. Local DSA organizers also hold regular "health fairs," where people can get blood pressure and blood sugar screenings and receive information about ways to receive free and low-cost medical care. People are also offered assistance in trying to clear medical debt. Through the fairs, the DSA not only helps people directly, but builds a wider understanding about the problem and the proposed solution.

It's not clear yet whether the Medicare for All campaign will succeed. Expanding Medicare to cover everyone would eliminate much of the private insurance companies' business, meaning that they will lobby ferociously to stop the law from going through. But Medicare for All represents an example of a practical solution to a social inequity, one that is within the realm of realistic possibility in the here and now (after all, if lots of other industrialized countries have such systems, and they work, there's no reason it can't work in ours).

* * *

IT'S FUNNY, PEOPLE often talk about leftists as impractical dreamers. But in the last few years, the most concrete solutions to social and economic problems have been coming from the left. Medicare for All is a real fix for healthcare, one that actually makes sure everyone can get treatment. It's based on a sound empirical understanding of how countries finance universal healthcare successfully. But it's far from the only solid left-wing plan.

In fact, if you look at the Bernie Sanders' 2016 agenda, what's striking is how direct it is: a $15 minimum wage and free college tuition were not vague promises of "change," but specific promises of particular outcomes. There's no ability to fudge if you don't deliver: either you raise the minimum wage or you don't. Sanders' book *Our Revolution* is worth looking at closely. Less than half the pages are taken up by typical campaign memoir material. Most of the book is dedicated to his Agenda for a New America. That agenda is clear as can be. It includes:

- **Passing the College for All Act:** This act would provide two dollars in federal funding to states for every dollar they spend making their public college tuitions free.

- **Cutting interest rates on federal student loans.** Sanders has since proposed an even more sweeping plan to cancel *all* outstanding student loan debt.

- **Tightening regulation of for-profit schools:** The U.S. would crack down on for-profit schools that make grandiose promises, charge large sums of money, and then deliver degrees that are essentially worthless.

- **Ending federal subsidies for the fossil fuel industry:** The U.S. government provides billions in support to oil and gas companies annually, even though their activities are directly causing catastrophic climate change.

- **Passing the Climate Protection and Justice Act:** The act would tax carbon emissions and give the money to Americans. Sanders has since gone even further and introduced a comprehensive $16 trillion plan to fight climate change.

- **Ending new federal leases for oil, gas, and coal extraction on public land.**

- **Passing the Justice Is Not for Sale Act:** The act would bar the federal government from contracting with private prisons.

- **Having the U.S. Department of Justice investigate every death that occurs in police custody.**

- **Passing a series of financial reforms:** Financial reforms would include new regulations on derivatives, separating commercial and investment banks, taxing speculation, capping ATM fees, and offering low-cost banking services through the post office.

- **Passing the FAMILY Act:** The act would guarantee workers twelve weeks of paid family and medical leave
- **Introducing a universal childcare program.**
- **Creating an Employee Ownership Bank:** The bank would provide loans to help workers collectively purchase their companies and turn them into cooperatives.

The list goes on (and on, and on). Bernie's book is not exactly a page-turner, but it contains lengthy, statistic-laden descriptions of the various ways inequality harms people and a series of very clear steps that the federal government could take to make life better for people.

Paid family leave is a clear example. At the moment, many workers are guaranteed unpaid leave, but that means that only those who have accumulated savings can take any meaningful time off. Parents who live paycheck to paycheck, on the other hand, have to return to work almost *immediately* after the birth of a child. This is downright cruel to both the parents and the child. Obviously, families need to be able to spend time together! The United States really is an outlier in declining to guarantee any leave. Some other countries provide *well over a year.*

This really isn't complicated. It's a law that could be passed, a law that *has* been passed nearly everywhere else, but not in the Richest Country on Earth. What's remarkable is that in the United States, only those on the left seem to feel any urgency about this. If you want to understand why so many young people are calling themselves socialists, one answer is that they can't afford to have children, and Bernie Sanders is one of the sole politicians who seems to be presenting real-world solutions to that problem.

Socialists are the ones thinking of the most ambitious fixes. Matt Bruenig, of the left-wing People's Policy Project, has come up with a comprehensive set of policies that would end child poverty and make sure families had what they needed in order to raise a child well. Bruenig proposes providing 36 weeks of paid leave, free public childcare centers, free pre-K from ages 3 to 5, free school lunch, Medicare coverage for everyone under 26, and a $300-a-month child allowance for

Mandatory Paid Parental Leave Across 41 Nations

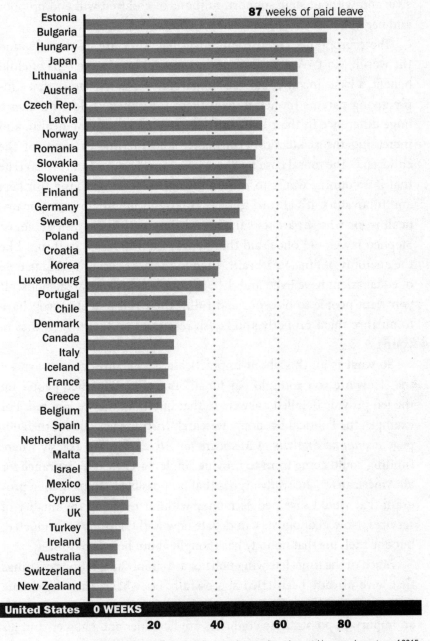

87 weeks of paid leave

Estonia
Bulgaria
Hungary
Japan
Lithuania
Austria
Czech Rep.
Latvia
Norway
Romania
Slovakia
Slovenia
Finland
Germany
Sweden
Poland
Croatia
Korea
Luxembourg
Portugal
Chile
Denmark
Canada
Italy
Iceland
France
Greece
Belgium
Spain
Netherlands
Malta
Israel
Mexico
Cyprus
UK
Turkey
Ireland
Australia
Switzerland
New Zealand

United States   0 WEEKS

20   40   60   80

Source: Pew Research Center. Includes maternity, paternity, and parental leave requirements as of 2015.
https://www.pewresearch.org/fact-tank/2016/09/26/u-s-lacks-mandated-paid-parental-leave/

parents.[14] The difference these programs would make in people's lives is astronomical—raising a child is terrifyingly expensive and labor intensive, and without state support, millions of children will end up poor and neglected.

These programs are also quite feasible. They are in place around the world. Most Western European countries have some type of child benefit, a basic income that goes to parents. Research shows that simply giving parents money to help them raise their children makes a huge difference in their lives: cutting poverty, improving health, and increasing the academic performance and lifetime earnings of the children.[15] The moral case for these programs is clear. But it's also true that if a country wants to raise a new generation of young thinkers and innovators, it's absurd to have children that are homeless or unhealthy, or whose parents can't spend time with them. The biologist Stephen Jay Gould once said that he was less interested in things like the anatomy of Einstein's brain "than in the near certainty that people of equal talent have lived and died in cotton fields and sweatshops." If you want people to blossom and fulfill their full potential, you have to nurture them properly and lavish resources on them when they're young.

So what is all this about impracticality? Oh, sure, you always get the "How are you going to pay for it?" question. But when people on the left provide detailed answers to that question, they're ignored. For example, the Political Economy Research Institute has put out the 200-page *Economic Analysis of Medicare for All*, explaining exactly where funding could come from to provide single-payer health insurance for all Americans.[16] The study argues that it's possible to implement a program that would save people money without reducing the quality of services. Now, economists can debate how well the study is conducted, but don't tell me that nobody has thought about how to pay for it.

Much of the time, left-wing policies are simply adaptations of things that have already been tried successfully elsewhere. The silly debate over whether this or that European country is socialist or not obscures an important point: these countries are healthier and happier, and it's in part because the government has programs that make people's lives easier. Britons don't want to give up NHS and Swedes love their family-friendly leave policies. It doesn't matter if it's socialism, it matters that it helps create something slightly closer to an equitable society.

A SLEW OF GOOD IDEAS

Leftists are constantly working on good and useful ideas. The Green New Deal, for instance, is an attempt to get serious about solving climate change. For decades, both Democrats and Republicans dithered on this. Republicans mostly denied that climate change was a problem at all, while Democrats acknowledged it was an important problem but didn't seem to feel compelled to actually do anything about it. The Intergovernmental Panel on Climate Change (IPCC) kept churning out increasingly dire reports, and tens of thousands of scientists were warning us to get off our failing trajectory before it was too late. Nobody in Congress seemed interested.

The Green New Deal is the result of the most pragmatic kind of thinking. It is, first off, a statement of goals. As introduced in a House resolution by Representative Alexandria Ocasio-Cortez, those goals are pretty straightforward:

- To achieve net-zero greenhouse gas emissions through a fair and just transition for all communities and workers.
- To create millions of good, high-wage jobs and ensure prosperity and economic security for all people of the United States.
- To invest in the infrastructure and industry of the United States to sustainably meet the challenges of the 21st century.
- To secure for all people of the United States for generations to come—clean air and water; climate and community resiliency; healthy food; access to nature; and a sustainable environment.
- To promote justice and equity by stopping current, preventing future, and repairing historic oppression of indigenous peoples, communities of color, migrant communities, deindustrialized communities, depopulated rural communities, the poor, low-income workers, women, the elderly, the unhoused, people with disabilities, and youth.[17]

To me, this sounds like an excellent place to begin. Now, granted, it's a statement of goals. But net-zero greenhouse gas emissions is an extremely clear target, and setting the aim is a precondition of developing a plan. You've got to understand what you're trying to do before you begin figuring out how to do it. As Steve Cohen of Columbia University's Earth Institute wrote, FDR's original New Deal "was a series of improvisations in response to specific problems that were stalling economic development . . . [T]here was no master plan, many ideas failed, and some were ended after a period of experimentation," while others, "like social security and the Security and Exchange Commission's regulation of the stock market, became permanent American institutions."[18] It's okay if the plan starts off vague, because the path to zero emissions is unpredictable, and we'll only know what works once we experiment.

The IPCC has given us some guidance here. We'll need to switch all of our power generation to be low or zero emission, change our food systems, electrify transport, plant a hell of a lot of new trees, and use sensible urban planning to make everyday life as energy efficient as possible. Sensible how? Well, in Los Angeles many people spend hours each day sitting in traffic, engines running. It's a colossal waste of both people's time and of the planet's capacity to absorb new carbon emissions. In a well-designed city, that wouldn't happen.

The Green New Deal is only at the beginning of its development, a fact that is important to understand.[19] There has to be a strong public debate about what the most technologically feasible and cost-effective ways of getting to zero emissions are. Some proposals are no-brainers: taxing carbon emissions is an excellent way to account for their real cost to the planet, and the United States is the only large industrialized country without a carbon tax. (This is both colossally irresponsible and yet another reason for the rest of the world to think we are a bunch of selfish assholes.[20]) But most importantly, this debate should take place within the context of a political consensus. In other words, we all know we've got to undertake this project, now let's figure out how to do it.

*   *   *

INTERESTING POLICY IDEAS are all coming from the left these days. Republicans spent years talking about their great plan to repeal

Obamacare, but had no serious policy for replacing it. I once publicly challenged an economist from the libertarian Cato Institute on how capitalism could deal with climate change. He could not come up with an answer, instead dismissing the problem and saying that he knew a lot of people who thought the warnings were "Chicken Little stuff."[21] Same with fixing poverty: when Ben Shapiro is asked about poverty, he says that if people graduate high school, have a full-time job, and get married they won't be poor.[22] This is true, of course: anyone with a full-time, minimum-wage job is technically above the poverty line. But the bulk of the poor are children, old people, sick people, and those who care for children, old people, and sick people. Fully one-third of the poor are children, and unless we want to bring back child labor and underage marriage, it's almost comically stupid to tell children to go get married and start working.[23]

On the other hand, you can look at the policy plans of 2020 presidential candidate Elizabeth Warren and see someone honestly committed to fixing injustices rather than rationalizing them. Warren is no socialist, but she has proposed specific criminal laws for Wall Street and vowed to break up giant tech monopolies using antitrust law; to provide universal, federally funded childcare for parents who can't afford it; to invest billions in new affordable housing; and to have the federal government support small farmers instead of giant agribusiness conglomerates.[24] When Warren talks about poverty, she follows it up by talking about her plans to fix it.

It's exciting to have people on the left putting forward proposals, even when they're flawed and need work. If you look at the current state of affairs I described in Part I, you may find yourself wanting to hide under a very soft blanket for a very long time. Many of these problems seem insoluble, and it's impossible to know where to start. Once we have a set of ideas on the table, we can perhaps feel a little less helpless and hopeless. We can begin the process of having vigorous arguments over whether idea A or B is superior (and hopefully *not* vigorous arguments over whether idea A or B is "true socialism").

Let me present, then, a few of the specific political and economic changes that various parts of the left are putting forward. There is no single left agenda, and some of these aren't at all radical, but they show that the left is beginning to think concretely about how to turn our values into action.

THE "STRUCTURAL" CHANGES

If democracy is participation in power by the governed, the United States is not terribly democratic. We have lots of elections, it's true, but there are all sorts of obstacles keeping the average citizen from having a meaningful say in how things are run. There are ways of making this better, however. There is a whole category of reform we might call "structural" because it rearranges the processes by which government power is exercised.

- **Give statehood to Washington, D.C.:** Most people have a representative and two senators. Not the residents of Washington, D.C., who have "taxation without representation." Not allowing Washingtonians to have a voting congressperson tramples on the very basic principles of representational democracy.

- **Make voting much easier:** Why do we even have "voter registration"? If you're eligible to vote, you should just be able to vote. Several states have now implemented automatic voter registration, and it makes perfect sense. As it stands, people are often denied the vote simply because they've failed to fill out a form months in advance. There are other sensible reforms: Election Day should be a holiday so that people who have jobs can vote easily. And at the very least, voting rights should be automatically restored to felons when they've finished serving their sentences (it's supposed to be the end of their punishment, after all). But a serious commitment to democracy would mean that everyone could vote, even current prisoners and noncitizens. "Universal adult suffrage" should mean exactly that: everyone gets a say no matter what, without classes of voters and nonvoters. (And perhaps we should even question the "adult" part and consider lowering the voting age so that teenagers are allowed to have a say.)

- **Make Elections Fairer:** It's absurd that political candidates have to spend so much of their time begging people for money. I get a "Can you give us 27 more dollars?" email from Sanders once every other day. Fundraising is like a nuclear arms race, and it has escalated absurdly. In one Georgia House district in 2017, the Republican and Democratic candidates each spent over $25 million to try to win. A voter from the district showed me the stack of glossy campaign mailers she had received from both candidates—there were dozens upon dozens.[25] If each candidate was granted a fixed sum by the government to spend on their campaign, with outside contributions prohibited, not only would it be easier for less-rich candidates to be viable contenders, but the whole mad scramble for your money would cease. What should matter is votes, not dollars, and if you want a candidate to win, you shouldn't have to give up your money to help them print signs.

- **Scrap the Electoral College:** The principle that the candidate with the most votes should win is a fairly elementary one, but it doesn't hold in U.S. presidential elections. In six out of the last seven presidential elections, the Democratic candidate has gotten more votes than the Republican. Between 1992 and today, the only time the Republican candidate received more votes was George W. Bush's defeat of John Kerry in 2004. Democrats are right to complain about this—if the rules of the game are rigged against them, those rules should change.

- **Expand the Supreme Court:** Everyone knows the Supreme Court is political.[26] This means that one branch of the government, the branch passing judgment on executive and legislative actions, can be captured by one party or another. Because justices have life tenure, this can mean that a panel of jurists representing the popular will of 30 years ago is deciding whether to keep or throw out laws made today. Putting term limits on justices and expanding the size of the court to ensure it at least approximately represents the political allegiances of the population would make one of our least democratic institutions slightly more defensible.[27]

- **Implement Ranked-Choice Voting:** One reason third parties aren't viable in the United States is that people don't want to vote for a "spoiler" candidate. But if, in a three-person race, people could rank their preferences from one to three, a person's vote would go to the voter's second-choice candidate if their first choice wasn't going to win. This way, a progressive could vote for Ralph Nader, giving Ralph a bump in votes, but when Ralph lost, the vote would go to Al Gore. Yet another way in which the 2000 election could have been saved and the Iraq War prevented.

- **Preserve legal rights:** Theoretically, the courts exist to uphold the laws. In reality, however, plenty of valid legal claims get tossed out on technicalities. Companies use their bargaining power to get people to sign contracts waiving all of their rights and agree to have disputes resolved by a private arbitrator selected by the company rather than in a court of law.[28] Courts find all kinds of utterly silly reasons to deny perfectly valid claims. In *Connick v. Thompson*, a Louisiana man who was wrongfully convicted and spent 14 years on death row won a $14 million jury verdict against the prosecutors who had manipulated the evidence against him. The Supreme Court (5–4, on predictable lines) threw out the verdict, effectively declaring the prosecutors' office immune from accountability for serious misconduct.[29] Or look at *Wal-Mart v. Dukes*, in which the Supreme Court threw out a class action on behalf of women who worked at Walmart and had allegedly been subjected to widespread sex discrimination.[30] The Court (5–4 again) set up a series of barriers that make it as difficult as possible for groups that have been harmed to file class actions. Because the American court system is such a web of tangled bureaucracy and formalistic rules, even when people have the legal right to something, they are often unable to get it. This explains why wage theft is so rampant in the United States. Every year, employers withhold $50 billion from employees that the employees have earned, but the workers have no realistic way to enforce their rights.

It will be argued that these "structural reforms" are actually partisan, that they clearly favor the interests of the political left. Of course they do! The bulk of the people in the United States lean left. As we make the political system fairer and more inclusive, it's going to become less conservative. A democratic system will end up being very Democratic.

It's also worth responding to those who give undue weight to the text of the Constitution and object to structural reforms that would involve altering it. It's funny how much reverence the U.S. Constitution gets, considering that it's a wholly illegitimate document. Women, African Americans, and Native Americans, despite together comprising the majority of the population at the time of the country's founding, did not get to participate in the document's drafting and ratification. If the basic rules of government were set up without consulting "we the people," then what respect do those people owe to those rules? Of course, we all abide by laws we did not make, but laws should not be treated as anything other than useful tools, to be updated and altered as necessary.

ECONOMIC, SOCIAL, AND POLITICAL CHANGES

Moving away from reforms to government processes, thrilling as those are, let's look at some more substantive changes to politics and the economy that left-wing people favor.

- **Expanding Union Membership:** Unions are crucial.[31] They give workers much more power in negotiating to make life at their jobs better. Not only do unionized jobs pay better and have better benefits, but a union can push for a contract containing the kinds of rights that you don't get under the law. (For instance, with a union contract, your boss might only be able to fire you if you actually do something wrong, whereas under the law they can fire you if they decide they don't like your face.) Currently, it's extremely complicated to form a union, but there is a proposed bill called the Employee Free Choice Act (EFCA) that would make the process simple: if the majority of workers signed cards indicating they wanted a union, they'd have one. (Barack Obama promised to pass the EFCA, but forgot about it when he was elected president.[32]) This would be extremely useful, especially since employers use ruthless tactics to prevent their workers from unionizing.[33] (The fact that they work so hard to prevent it shows you that unions really can redistribute power at a company.) Anti-union laws need to be gotten rid of. For example, right-to-work laws should be repealed, and there should be no ban on secondary strikes (in which union workers at one company go on strike to support union workers at a different company).[34] While some union leadership is bureaucratic and hierarchical, this isn't an argument against having a union, it's an argument for having a democratic union whose leaders represent the will of the members.[35]

- **Making Better Workplaces:** Socialists talk a lot about what happens in workplaces because we realize that a lot of the "politics" of people's day-to-day lives happens at work. Many left proposals aim to give people more power at their jobs. For example, Warren has proposed legislation that would require companies to have workers on their boards of directors. Germany already requires this, and the research shows it "leads to less short-termism in corporate decision-making and much higher levels of pay equality, [and] positive results on productivity and innovation."[36] Economist Richard Wolff has devised a model of Worker Self-Directed Enterprises that would radically restructure corporate management.[37] We can also look to large worker-owned companies around the world, from the John Lewis department store chain in the United Kingdom to the Mondragon co-op federation in Spain.[38]

- **Guaranteeing a Job or Universal Basic Income:** There is a vibrant debate on the left right now about two different kinds of schemes that aim to make sure every single person has a reliable income. The first is a jobs guarantee: Anyone who wants a job could always go to the federal government and ask for one. They might send you to deliver meals to old people, or keep the state parks tidy, or hose down the megafauna. But you'd always have work available. Some people have proposed a different scheme: just give people an income no matter what. Advocates of a Universal Basic Income (UBI) think there's no need to require work. UBI advocate and 2020 Democratic presidential candidate Andrew Yang has advocated giving every person $12,000 a year, arguing that the money would provide a massive stimulus to low-income areas, reduce stress, improve health, allow for more creativity and innovation, and eliminate a lot of month-to-month financial scarcity.[39]

- **Making the Wealthy Pay Their Taxes:** We know that the American tax code favors the wealthy in many ways, more so thanks to the Trump administration's generous tax cuts. There have been serious proposals from left-leaning economists for wealth taxes and financial transaction taxes that could slow down the growth of inequality. A heavy estate tax could prevent the accumulation of intergenerational dynasties, and while Republicans call estate taxes "death taxes," they're actually among the fairest possible taxes. They tax a person who quite literally no longer exists, and there's very little reason why anyone "deserves" a large inheritance they have done nothing to build. But it's also important to enforce the tax laws we actually have. A global tax enforcement agency may sound a bit Orwellian, but it is actually necessary to prevent capitalists from stashing money overseas to avoid having to contribute a portion of their income to the collective good. Financial journalists Jesse Eisinger and Paul Kiel write that the Internal Revenue Service is outmatched when it comes to actually getting the wealthy to pay what they owe, since the rich "can devote seemingly limitless resources to hiring the best legal and accounting talent" and "employ complex, highly refined strategies that seek to stretch the tax code to their advantage," to the point where "it can take years for IRS investigators just to understand a transaction and deem it a violation."[40] Sometimes the IRS just gives up entirely and accepts payments in the millions when billions are actually owed. Needless to say, the laws need to be properly enforced.

- **Forming Community Land Trusts:** These are a neat idea. A community organization would buy up houses and then sell the houses *without* selling the land. Because homeowners are only leasing the land from the community land trust (CLT), they are able to afford a house, and the CLT's ownership of the land means that it can bind the homeowner to an agreement to make sure the houses always remain affordable. Though the legal structure is a bit quirky, and the concept a bit hard to grasp at first, these have been tried successfully in various places—there are now 225 CLTs around the country.

- **Making Schools Equal:** There's no reason that poor neighborhoods should get poor schools and rich neighborhoods should get rich schools. If anything, it should be the other way around; the students with the most disadvantages outside of school need the most investment within it. At the very least, school funding needs to be equal. The imbalance in what children receive depending on who their parents are and where they live is revoltingly unfair.

We can begin here, but there's far, far more to think about. There are proposals like the People's Policy Project's Social Wealth Fund, in which the government would buy up assets and distribute the returns on those assets to everyone equally in the form of a dividend. There are large public investment plans that would fund research on unprofitable medicines or build the kind of high-speed rail networks found in China and Europe. Tenant associations can help protect people's rights against unscrupulous landlords, and consumer-purchasing cooperatives can counter the power of corporate monopolies. Experiments like Wikipedia can create genuine democratic platforms where people make decisions together and all contribute equally to a community project.

THE BLACK LIVES MATTER AGENDA

People who do not know much about Black Lives Matter (BLM) may assume it is mainly concerned with police violence and misconduct. Indeed, many of the most visible BLM actions have occurred after the deaths of people like Eric Garner, Sandra Bland, and Philando Castile. But BLM's agenda goes beyond better policing. The Movement for Black Lives organization has put out a comprehensive platform to tackle racial injustice in America, across many different domains and in all areas of life. In its criminal justice section alone, some examples include:

- An end to money bail, mandatory fines, fees, court surcharges and "defendant funded" court proceedings.
- An end to capital punishment.

- An end to zero-tolerance school policies and arrests of students, the removal of police from schools, and the reallocation of funds from police and punitive school discipline practices.

- A reallocation of funds at the federal, state and local level from policing and incarceration . . . to long-term safety strategies such as education, local restorative justice services, and employment programs.

- The retroactive decriminalization, immediate release and record expungement of all drug related offenses and prostitution, and reparations for the devastating impact of the "war on drugs" and criminalization of prostitution, including a reinvestment of the resulting savings and revenue into restorative services, mental health services, job programs and other programs supporting those impacted by the sex and drug trade.

- Direct democratic community control of local, state, and federal law enforcement agencies, ensuring that communities most harmed by destructive policing have the power to hire and fire officers, determine disciplinary action, control budgets and policies, and subpoena relevant agency information.[41]

The Movement for Black Lives platform is worth reading in its entirety. It lays out the well-known statistics on racial imbalances in the United States, then proposes bold, concrete steps that need to be taken in order to achieve something that a reasonable person might believe resembles justice.

IDENTITY AND THE "INTERSECTIONAL" APPROACH

Different groups of people have distinct needs. This should be quite obvious. Older people face the difficulties that come with being old in a society that rewards people based on the sale of labor. Transgender people face ostracism, bullying, violence, and employment discrimination. Disabled people have to navigate a world designed for the able-bodied, in which the needs of those with differing capacities are invisible. It's irresponsible, then, to ignore "group interests" when designing policies. Public policy doesn't affect everyone in the same way.

It's vital to have an agenda that considers everybody's actual needs, not just the needs of some abstract median person. And when talking about "what to do," it's very easy to overlook the interests of groups you are not personally a member of. The reason people use the term *marginalized*, abstract as it is, is that some people always seem to end up on the margins of discussions. Here are some important subgroups to keep in mind:

- **Transgender People:** In the mainstream press, the only transgender issue you hear about is bathrooms. But there's a lot of other important issues. Transgender people are discriminated against when seeking housing and employment, and many end up homeless. Transgender people face an alarmingly high risk of suicide and live in a society that is openly hostile to them. The National Center for Transgender Equality has put forth a set of policy proposals that can protect and support transgender people, from bans on discrimination to support for young transgender people in school. No leftist who takes everybody's rights seriously can treat transgender people's political issues as secondary.

- **Indigenous People:** Native issues nearly always get left out of policy discussions. Yet indigenous concerns are urgent. The *Los Angeles Times* reports that "under the Trump administration, tribal leaders [have been] shocked by how little regard this administration has shown [for Native Americans], particularly as its agenda of advancing fossil fuel interests collides with efforts to restore Native American lands and rights."[42] Tribal lands and sovereignty are under threat from government regulatory rollbacks, and as we saw with the Dakota Access Pipeline protests, Native people have to fight hard to preserve control over what little is left of their historic territory. And this doesn't even begin to touch on the issue of long-standing underinvestment in Native communities, which has kept poverty rates high and life expectancies low.

- **Immigrants:** To be an immigrant, whether authorized or unauthorized, is worse than being a second-class citizen, because at least a second-class citizen would be a citizen. Immigrants cannot vote, meaning that they have "taxation without representation," even though the laws apply to them. As my colleague Brianna Rennix has documented in her commentary for *Current Affairs*, the immigration system in the United States is arbitrary and cruel in ways most people don't know about, splitting up families and disrupting lives to enforce absurd rules.[43] Both Democrats and Republicans talk about the need for "border security," but neither party is very serious about making immigrant lives less mired in exploitation, fear, and bureaucracy. The left, on the other hand, calls for actual humane plans like ending expedited removal, guaranteeing access to lawyers in immigration proceedings, easing the strict procedural rules for filing asylum claims, eliminating detention altogether, beefing up labor rights and employment protections, and decriminalizing immigration offenses. Immigrant advocates have recently taken up the call to "Abolish ICE [Immigration and Customs Enforcement]," which can be taken to mean "stop deporting people." But so much more is necessary before we have anything approaching a fair immigration system.[44]

- **The Entire Rest of the World, Actually:** It's strange; in the United States, nationalism is pervasive even among those on the left. We often talk about the loss of U.S. jobs and the interests of American workers, but not much about the interests of workers in China, Bangladesh, Russia, or Honduras. When people on the left talk about the human consequences of American drug laws, they point to those housed in U.S. prisons, but not to the tens of thousands of people in Mexico killed each year in violence caused by the drug trade (and, therefore, by our country's insatiable appetite for drugs).[45] Opponents of the Iraq War talk about the deaths of U.S. soldiers far more than the deaths of Iraqis, and even liberal immigration advocates often talk about what immigrants can do for *us* and our economy rather than the immigrants themselves. For years, Saudi Arabia was bombing Yemen with U.S. support, creating the worst humanitarian crisis in the world, but there was little discussion domestically.[46] This kind of provincial thinking makes little moral sense: if every person is of equal moral weight, that is true no matter which country they are from. Global poverty matters just as much as U.S. poverty, global labor rights as much as U.S. labor rights.[47] Socialists that take our core principles seriously reject nationalism and recognize the shared interests of working people everywhere. Not for nothing did we come up with the slogan "Workers of the World Unite." Ultimately, to prevent capitalists from simply exploiting whichever country has the most desperate workers, there will need to be a unified global socialist movement rather than one confined to a single country.[48]

- **Non-Human Animals:** The killing and eating of animals, especially on a gigantic industrial scale, presents deep moral problems, one few people want to confront. As Glenn Greenwald said in a recent interview with *Current Affairs*, "You can tell yourself that there are moral distinctions between the animals that you value and the animals that you don't. But none of them are sustainable upon any kind of minimal scrutiny."[49] The mass torture and killing of dogs would be a national scandal, but the same acts inflicted on pigs are an accepted part of the food system. Anyone who accepts that animal welfare is compelling and urgent (as I do) should want to make sure it becomes a political priority. Candidates should be asked about it. We're actually at a very promising moment right now; as Jacy Reese writes in *The End of Animal Farming*, even though slaughter is being conducted on a historically unprecedented scale, it is also finally conceivable that someday no meat will be from live animals.[50] (The off-putting phrase "lab-grown" is misleading; it's more like "factory-made.") In exciting news, Burger King is starting to serve the "Impossible Burger," which gets us closer than ever before to replicating the taste of meat without the accompanying torture and death. It's imperative that political candidates be pressured to commit to a pro-animal agenda, and then held to that commitment.[51]

* * *

WE'VE SEEN HOW particularistic thinking about group interests can be important. But isn't this "identity politics"?

I am not always sure what identity politics is, though there is criticism of it from both right and left. David French of *National Review* describes it as a politics in which "skin color [is] a stand-in for virtue" and it is "impossible for a black person to be racist."[52] Ben Shapiro has talked about those who think "the value of your opinion depends on how many victim groups you belong to," with straight white men "at the bottom of the totem pole."[53] "Identity politics," libertarian Dave Rubin said, "only works if you believe the most important quality about each of us are the attributes we are born with, rather than the ideas which we come to learn."[54]

I think it's clear that you don't have to believe natural-born attributes are our "most" important quality to understand that they can matter quite a lot. Though skin color is obviously not synonymous with virtue (there are plenty of conservatives of color whose beliefs I find nauseating), a color-blind politics will be oblivious to the consequences that group identity has on people's lives.

There is a left-wing criticism of identity politics that deserves to be taken more seriously. They argue that when groups form exclusive political alliances, moving away from traditional, broad-based party politics, it ultimately makes it harder to fight politically for people's common interests and produces a fragmented left. Political scientist Adolph Reed Jr. has strongly criticized how looking through the prism of identity can prevent recognition of economic causes responsible for multiple problems. If our politics are *solely* "antiracist," he says, we will miss the fact that "the struggle against racial health disparities . . . has no real chance of success apart from a struggle to eliminate for-profit health care."[55]

Ironically, the solution to this problem of identity politics comes from a concept long associated with the identity politics left: intersectionality. It's a bit of a jargonistic term, but it describes a very sensible concept, namely the importance of understanding how different kinds of oppression can intersect, overlap, and diverge. So, for instance, a middle-class white woman may find herself subjected to harassment in the workplace because she is a woman, a wealthy black man may find himself constantly scrutinized by the police, and a homeless white man will have the privilege that comes from being white and male (meaning he's not going to be racially profiled and is less likely to have a #MeToo story), but he still won't be able to afford basic medical care. Kimberlé Williams Crenshaw, who devised the concept, also wanted to emphasize that when you belong to more than one oppressed group, your difficulties multiply, and for black women, "the intersectional experience is greater than the sum of racism and sexism," and you're often neglected by movements that treat the interests of each group separately.[56] If black civil rights groups are dominated by black men (because of patriarchy) and feminist groups are dominated by wealthy white women (because of racism), then who is going to advocate for black women?

* * *

SHAPIRO, IN A Prager University video called "What Is Intersectionality?," dismisses the concept as "nonsense."[57] Interestingly enough, though, he also explains why it's useful for overcoming identity-based division. "By focusing on the place where various victim identities intersect," he says, "intersectionality creates a united 'us' versus 'them' paradigm," that is, the oppressed together against the oppressors. This, he says, is why you might see lesbian activists at a Palestinian solidarity march these days. But his example shows that intersectionality is actually a *solution* to the problems of identity politics. Intersectionality encourages people to see what they have in common and view oppression as something that affects different people of every race and gender in different ways.

Rhiana Gunn-Wright, who served as policy director for Abdul El-Sayed's gubernatorial campaign in Michigan, has said that intersectionality can actually help policy-makers create policies that address both race and class issues: "The analysis of intersectionality was all about how systems are designed with either a deep inattention to all identities or attention to one identity at a time, and therefore ignoring people who lived at the intersections of those identities . . . We think that race, in particular, is a purely social issue and not connected to economics or reproductive justice or criminal justice."[58] Intersectionality has informed Gunn-Wright's work on the Green New Deal, which she says tries to solve environmental problems *and* problems of racial justice by planning green investment in ways that benefit people who have long been denied their share of American prosperity. Intersectionality can therefore help us reject false dichotomies: we don't need to look at either particular interests *or* universal interests, but can and should understand both.

*   *   *

THERE ARE SO many things to be done, and progressive minds are overflowing with ideas and proposals. As we consider real-world actions, though, there's one thing worth remembering above all: the future can't be planned by a group of socialist intellectuals designing bullet-pointed lists of what's best for the rest of humanity. Democracy means that people make choices *themselves*, and good ideas emerge from healthy, collective deliberation. Technocracy, in which a group of wonkish experts sort everything out, is a horrible idea, in part because if they don't consult with the people affected by their decisions, the experts don't have the necessary data to make those decisions well. Personally, I'd like to see a thriving culture of political discussion, where the cafés are full of people passionately hashing out their disagreements about What Must Be Done. Not everyone has to participate in political life, but everyone should at least feel like someone would listen to them if they came up with a solution to a problem.

Getting It Done

Effective Strategies

"The fact is that a reformer can't last in politics. He can make a show for a while, but he always comes down like a rocket. Politics is as much a regular business as the grocery or the dry-goods or the drug business. You've got to be trained up to it or you're sure to fail. Do you understand now, why it is that a reformer goes down and out in the first or second round, while a politician answers to the gong every time? It is because the one has gone into the fight without trainin', while the other trains all the time and knows every fine point of the game."

—William L. Riordon, *Plunkitt of Tammany Hall*

YOU CAN HAVE THE MOST marvelous blueprints for a sparkling tomorrow, but without a plan for political action, it will come to nothing. Policy comes after politics, meaning that you can only make laws after you've built power. As veteran Tammany Hall machine politician William L. Riordon pointed out in 1905, you will get nowhere in politics as a mere "reformer." The reforms might be good ideas, but good ideas don't get implemented simply because they're good. People have to fight for them.

This means that people on the left need to think hard about what it actually takes to shift political and economic power. (And ask themselves frustrating questions like, What is "power" anyway? And from whence does it spring?) Putting Bernie Sanders in the White House isn't going to change the world, though it would be a remarkable thing indeed.

Labor organizer Jane McAlevey speaks regularly about how a "structural analysis of power" is necessary for developing sound strategy. McAlevey thinks the left has frequently been doing things all wrong; they've focused on mobilizing rather than organizing.[1] What's the difference? Well, mobilizing is when a bunch of committed activists show up to a protest. It's getting people who are already on your side to go out and support a cause. Organizing is somewhat different: it means building a structure that didn't exist before.

When people want to "organize" their workplaces, they have to start from scratch. Labor organizers make lists of everyone they are trying to convince to join a union. They write the names on a big wall chart, and then go out and start talking to each of them one by one. They start with the aim of getting every single person to join them. It's a staggeringly time-consuming process, involving hours upon hours of conversations with fellow workers, trying to explain the benefits of joining together as a unit.

Organizing involves persuading people who *aren't* on your side to join you. You think about the entire universe of people who could theoretically want to share your goals, and you think hard about what it would take for those people to go from indifferent or hostile to supportive. This does not involve compromising your values or meeting the other side halfway. It may, however, involve a lot of uncomfortable conversations with people who are highly doubtful and reluctant.

For a long time, Democrats haven't appeared to think much about how to convert people. In fact, there seems to be a prevailing idea that political beliefs are fixed—that everyone in the country has a certain ideology and your job in politics is to get the ones who agree with you to go to the polls. That's certainly one of your jobs, but political reality isn't really fixed—people change their minds constantly as they see new things and in response to conversations with trusted friends and colleagues. One question to ask is, How do we move forward given the existing political landscape? Another, however, is, How do we change what that landscape looks like entirely?

Here's what I mean: for a long time, centrists have made the argument that democratic socialist ideas are too radical for the American electorate. The theory is that if you run a candidate who is on the left

wing of the Democratic Party, they will lose badly, as George McGovern did in 1972. So you must present an agenda that appeals to the
mainstream. Bill Clinton had tremendous political success and became
extremely popular by adopting large parts of the Republican agenda:
cracking down on crime, ending the existing welfare system, speeding
up the death penalty, and signing the Defense of Marriage Act. Clinton
raised taxes on the wealthy, but it was argued that he could only do so
because he was willing to be "pragmatic" on other things.

If you look at Clinton's success and McGovern's failure, it's easy to see
how you could conclude that being "too far to the left" is politically damag-
ing. But perhaps the world is not so simple—Donald Trump was openly
extreme in his positions and found his way to the White House. When
New Deal liberalism was in its heyday, it was so popular that Franklin
Roosevelt might possibly have gotten reelected indefinitely had he not
passed away. The idea that you simply find the median voter and target your messaging at them certainly makes politics easy, but it keeps us
from looking at how voters' beliefs are formed in the first place.

Conservatives have long understood the need to shape public opinion. Because the right's positions are abhorrent (see Chapter 10), and
most people reject them, it has taken a very deliberate effort to keep
the country from enacting economically leftist policies. In an infamous
1971 memo to the Chamber of Commerce, future Supreme Court justice
Lewis Powell wrote, "The assault on the enterprise system . . . is gaining
converts," and asked, "What Can Be Done About the Public?"[2] Powell
stated that the American businessman was the "forgotten man," and that
corporate America should aggressively fight back against its critics. It
should install pro-business professors on college campuses, turn out a
stream of books, "press vigorously in all political arenas for support of
the enterprise system," and "penalize politically all who oppose it."

The direct influence of Powell's memo is debated, but it certainly re-
flects the thinking of capitalists who were increasingly disturbed by the
vibrant leftist politics that had come out the 1960s.[3] In the years after,
conservatives built an extraordinary network of think tanks, legal
organizations, and lobbying groups that pushed their ideas. Today,
endless papers in favor of laissez-faire economic policies are churned

out by institutions like the American Enterprise Institute, Heritage Foundation, Cato Institute, Mercatus Center, Hoover Institution, Competitive Enterprise Institute, and Foundation for Economic Education. There are the campus groups, like Turning Point USA and the Young Americans for Freedom, which pay giant speaking fees for conservative pundits to go to small colleges, and which even funnel "dark money" into student government elections.[4] The American Legislative Exchange Counsel writes model pro-business bills and gives them to Republican state legislatures to pass, while the Federalist Society trains and supports new generations of conservative legal scholars, attorneys, and jurists. There are no real left analogues to these groups, and thousands of legislators and public officials around the country are affiliated with them.[5]

The "scholarship" put out by these think tanks is often shoddy, but it allows the *Wall Street Journal* to report that "a new study" shows X or Y.[6] The standards at Fox News are even lower.[7] But there is good reason to believe that all of this is effective. We know that just reading an argument, any argument, can make people more likely to agree with it, meaning that swamping people with right-wing talking points can drag public opinion in the desired direction.[8] Several studies claim to show empirically that the presence of Fox News in a town can actually shift residents' views rightward.[9] Millions upon millions of people have watched the conservative YouTube videos put out by "Prager University," with titles like "The Left Ruins Everything," "Government Can't Fix Healthcare," "Build the Wall," and "Why You Should Love Fossil Fuel."[10] The videos have over two billion views collectively, and on the Prager website counter, you can watch that number tick up second by second.

In part, these projects succeed because they are backed by giant piles of money. It's no conspiracy to point out that the Koch brothers enjoy spending large portions of their fortune funding things with "Enterprise" and "Freedom" in the name. But while it's true that the left has fewer billions of dollars sitting around to put to use, there also hasn't been much of an *attempt* made to get serious about tugging the ideological direction of the country leftward.

Consider YouTube. It is crawling with fascists.[11] Thanks to the company's generally permissive approach to speech (which I do not mind), and its algorithms' tendency to recommend increasingly extreme and bigoted political content to teenagers (which I very much do mind), the far right has a strong presence on the platform and has radicalized a lot of young people.[12] In a report on the influence of young YouTubers in Brazil, *BuzzFeed* concluded that they are a political force to be reckoned with, as a generation of right-wing teenagers has had its ideology forged on YouTube.[13] The report suggests alarming consequences that may occur as the politics of YouTube become the politics of the real world.

The left's response has not been too encouraging. We have *The Young Turks*, an online news show now over 15 years old, but there are only a few notable left-leaning YouTube channels. The most prominent and successful is ContraPoints, a channel put out by Natalie Wynn. Wynn uses colorful costumes and luxurious sets, plus wit, verve, and a dash of surrealism to debunk conservative arguments on race, gender, and economics (her videos frequently feature her sparring with bizarrely dressed alternate versions of herself).[14] It's notable, however, that ContraPoints is made by Wynn alone in her house. Her work is beginning to successfully lure impressionable teens away from right-wing ideas, but she's doing it on her own without any institutional support. And even as the *top* left YouTuber, her most popular videos receive fewer views than even middling PragerU videos.[15]

Still, left media today is more vibrant than it has been in a long time. *Jacobin*'s readership is growing every year, and it has branched into books and podcasts. It now runs two additional periodicals, the academic *Catalyst* and the U.K.-based *Tribune*. The number one podcast on crowdfunding site Patreon is *Chapo Trap House*, which is angry, sharp, often hilarious, and uncompromisingly leftist. Left publishers like OR Books, Verso, Haymarket, AK Press, and Zero Books publish both scholarly works and primers on left politics. Socialists are even beginning to infiltrate mainstream publications: the *Washington Post* now has an openly socialist opinion columnist, Elizabeth Bruenig, and leftists have gone on Fox News shows and successfully defended their position against incredulous interviewers.[16] The left agenda is getting an airing everywhere, not just in tiny radical zines or Marxist reading groups. CNN is running profiles of the Democratic Socialists of America, *Vox* is running articles by socialists, Alexandria Ocasio-Cortez is appearing on *The Tonight Show*, and NBC is asking, "What's on [the DSA] agenda?"[17]

* * *

SPREADING IDEAS IS not enough; we need political organization. But the political advancement of left candidates shows that there has been more than just a change in discourse. There are now two DSA members in Congress, and the organization itself has grown to over 50,000 dues-paying members. In the 2018 midterms, DSA-backed candidates were elected to two congressional seats, eight state legislative seats, and several dozen seats on city councils, party committees, education boards, and neighborhood advisory committees. Around 40 DSA-supported ballot initiatives won across the country, from a Colorado cap on payday loans to a raise in the minimum wage in Anaheim, California.

During Occupy Wall Street, there was a strong reluctance on the part of many activists to get involved in electoral politics. Protesters even deliberately adopted "no demands," in defiance of Frederick Douglass' famous dictum that "power concedes nothing without a demand." Thanks to the encouraging campaigns of Sanders, Ocasio-Cortez, and other socialists, electoral politics now seems far more viable than it once did. The institutional Democratic Party looks weak and ripe for overthrow by a new generation of left activists.

In the future, socialists should probably try to run candidates in every election in the country. Not just the ones in "blue" districts, but *every* House and Senate seat. Everything down to the election for municipal dogcatcher in Duxbury, Vermont.[18] Everywhere a position of power is democratically contested, socialists should offer someone up.

Why not just run in the places they think they can win? Well, for a few reasons. First, if people don't always have a socialist option, we won't know how many people are socialists and how many people are just settling for the lesser of two evils. Left ideas are popular everywhere—remember, even many Republican voters say they support Medicare for All. But people can only choose from among the options they have available on the ballot. Second, elections are not just about winning: they also exist to build political infrastructure. When you campaign, you bring people who otherwise would not have met together. Those people make connections, they hatch plots, they form groups. Eugene Debs did not run for president so many times because he thought he was going to win, he ran because his presidential campaign was an opportunity to educate the public about what socialism was. And even when you're in it to win it, you're not always running to win *this* time around. Sometimes it's about getting your name and ideas out there and organizing a support network, so that when the opportune political moment does arrive, it will be possible to take advantage of it. Bernie Sanders ran for statewide office several times in the 1970s and received well under 10 percent of the vote. But he was slowly building his political network and eventually won a Senate seat.

During campaigns, people who never thought of becoming involved in politics suddenly find their inner organizer. And that initial politicization can lead them to organizing beyond elections. Indeed, this is exactly what happened with Sanders' run in 2016: after getting excited and activated by Sanders' campaign, large numbers of people around the country joined DSA and other grassroots groups, and they now organize around a wide variety of issues beyond elections, like union organizing, affordable housing, and immigrant rights.

Building a grassroots infrastructure that isn't solely tied to elections will be critically important if the Sanders presidential agenda is to have any chance of succeeding against the inevitable propaganda blitz by corporate interests.

Campaigns provide the opportunity to present democratic socialist ideas to people who have never heard them. Every conversation the candidate has with a voter will leave them with an impression: the socialists care enough to talk to me. Vaughn Stewart, a DSA member newly elected to the Maryland House of Delegates, has said that the most important factor for voters considering him was the fact that he showed up to talk to them.[19] Stewart actually thinks the ideas matter less to voters than the personal connection: if the DSA candidate is the one who came to your house and talked to you about your needs, the DSA candidate will often get your vote. On the other hand, if nobody from the DSA ever shows up, the DSA candidate most likely will not.

Besides, we often can't predict ahead of time which districts are actually winnable. A democratic socialist judge was elected in Houston, part of a clean sweep of the local judiciary by Democrats. Houston, let's remember, was not too long ago "the capital of capital punishment," sending more people to death row than almost anywhere else.[20] Even if DSA candidates only win 10 percent of the races, or even if their wins were just a handful of flukes, they will have significantly improved left representation in government.

* * *

RUNNING IN ELECTIONS and winning them is very, very important. But that's impossible without a strong network of left organizations. Fortunately, there are currently many excellent groups, comprised of caring, energetic, and committed people, all doing superb work. So that we do not get lost in abstraction, and to see what is actually meant by "doing the work," let's very briefly look at a number of organizations that are advancing the left's cause.

- **Justice Democrats:** Justice Democrats are trying to get more progressive Democrats who refuse corporate PAC/lobbyist money and support Medicare for All and the Green New Deal elected to office. They are becoming a formidable force challenging existing Democrats from the left.
- **California Nurses Association:** The California Nurses Association was the first major union to endorse Sanders in 2016. They're more radical than many other unions, and in addition to organizing, these nurses are deeply involved with electoral advocacy and are leading the push for Medicare for All.
- **DiEM25:** In Europe, many people have become skeptical of the European Union, seeing it as a distant bureaucracy trampling on local rights. Distaste for the E.U. led to the radical measure of "Brexit" in

the U.K. DiEM25 was founded to offer another way: instead of re-acting to the E.U.'s problems by leaving it, it is trying to democratize it—to maintain the advantages of a multinational union while re-forming its governing structure. DiEM25 has produced an agenda for how to address the primary problems facing Europe and is de-veloping campaigns, issuing policy papers, and cultivating political candidates.

- **Dream Defenders:** The Dream Defenders were founded in Florida after the murder of Trayvon Martin. They're working on issues faced by young people of color. They register people to vote, lobby legislators, promote prison and police abolition, and have drafted papers outlining a new vision of freedom.[21]

- **Cooperation Jackson:** Cooperation Jackson is an attempt to build the first major cooperative network in the South. It's associated with Jackson mayor Chokwe Lumumba's movement, which is attempt-ing to create "the most radical city in the country" by combining sound municipal governance with the expansion of cooperatives and antipoverty policies.

- **Assata's Daughters:** Assata's Daughters, founded in 2015, is a col-lective in Chicago of young black women, femmes, and gender-nonconforming people fighting for black liberation, prison, and police abolition. The organization provides political education for young black people (in addition to meals, toiletries, mentor-ship, help with job placement, etc.), intensive organizing training, and additional services, like targeted support plans and weekly stipends.

- **Southern Center for Human Rights:** The Southern Center for Human Rights, founded in 1976 by ministers and activists, works to improve the abysmal conditions in jails and prisons; represents people facing the death penalty; ensures everyone's right to quality legal representation is realized; combats illegal, unconstitutional, and inhumane criminal justice practices; and works to stop the criminalization of poverty. The organization has won five death penalty cases argued before the Supreme Court, won important prison and jail reforms, publicized the shortcomings of the criminal justice system (including by testifying before Congress), and much more.

- **Moral Mondays:** Led by Reverend William Barber, the Moral Mondays movement is bringing a grassroots left politics to North Carolina in order to combat the state's conservative government. They have been so successful that they are credited with ousting the state's Republican governor and ending the Republicans' legislative supermajority.

- **Our Revolution:** Our Revolution is a PAC established following Sanders' impressive presidential campaign in an effort to continue building power and support for progressive policies and candidates. They have done remarkably well, supporting numerous candidates around the country—from city councils on up—including Ocasio-Cortez, Rashida Tlaib, and Pramila Jayapal.

- **Sunrise Movement:** Established in 2017, the Sunrise Movement is an organization advocating action on climate change, using tactics ranging from protest to lobbying members of Congress and endorsing individual candidates. The Sunrise Movement has received national attention over their willingness to challenge Democratic congresspeople, having staged a sit-in in Nancy Pelosi's office and had a public exchange with Dianne Feinstein in which Feinstein was widely seen as dismissive and out of touch.

- **Coalition of Immokalee Workers:** The Coalition of Immokalee Workers (CIW), which began in 1993, is a human rights organization fighting gender-based violence and human trafficking in the workplace. The CIW has established worker education programs and third-party workplace monitoring; uncovered, investigated, and assisted in the prosecution of many farm slavery operations in the southeastern United States; and in the process helped free over 1,200 workers since the 1990s. They have also negotiated agreements with large food companies to pay decent wages.

- **Providence Student Union:** Formed in 2010, the Providence Student Union runs campaigns around student rights in the city of Providence, Rhode Island. They are impressive for two reasons: first, they are a union led by high school students, and second, they have achieved significant victories. They have prevented school closures and curriculum changes and altered graduation requirements. High school students everywhere can learn from their campaign for a "Student Bill of Rights."

- **Causa Justa:** Based in Oakland, Causa Justa has won legislative and legal victories around tenant and immigrant rights and has also organized around the issues facing black people, including the racist criminal justice system.

STAYING FOCUSED ON WHAT MATTERS

The above groups have the right idea. But what should the rest of us be thinking about as we act politically?

First, at a time when it's easier than ever to get distracted, we need to stay focused on what matters. Each second on Earth, many trillions of things happen all at once. One's attention span and energy are finite, meaning that everyone has to make decisions about what they're going to spend time thinking about and what they're going to ignore. Anyone who *doesn't* make such decisions will end up thinking about whatever the press and cable news decide are important on any given day. It will probably be something trivial.

So, focus on the things that matter the most. It may be interesting, even important, that Donald Trump has refused to release his tax returns, or has retweeted a white nationalist, or has falsely claimed his father was born in Germany, or has repeatedly mispronounced the word *origins* as "oranges."[22] But the administration's actions on climate change, student debt, drone strikes, and immigration are far more consequential. Like him or hate him (I like him), Sanders is very good at zeroing in on things that materially affect lives: Can you afford to go to the hospital? Are you being mistreated at work? Are you struggling with debt? He's a broken record, it's true, but that's a good thing; it's called effective messaging. If you never shut up about healthcare and debt and militarism, everyone will know those are things you care about.

Politics is not supposed to be a soap opera. It may be tempting to see it as entertainment, especially when it is filled with comically detest-

able characters such as Ted Cruz and Betsy DeVos. But getting too ab-
sorbed in watching the "Trump show" and tuning in daily to see what
new conspiratorial tidbit about Russia has emerged is to have one's attention drawn away from the purpose of politics, which is to use the
government's resources to improve the condition of the world.

There are a few things that a successful left needs to do. Leftists
should think self-critically about what they are aiming for and why,
and then think strategically about how to get there. Everyone will
have to try to get along, to form a "big tent" and avoid being riven by
the kind of internal fights that have destroyed so many promising left
movements. Dogma should be shunned, and ideas should be straightforward. There needs to be a clear agenda that will help people, one
that everyone can understand and explain. Leftists should make sure
groups operate democratically, that unions are run by their workers
and not taken over by calcified and inept bureaucracies. The left should
not just focus on national politics, but on state and local issues. It's easier to win at the local level, as the successes of DSA candidates have
shown, and the failure of Democrats to build infrastructure outside of
Washington resulted in catastrophic losses during the Obama years.

Adolph Reed Jr. has usefully encouraged the left to watch out for
"cargo cult" politics.[23] Famously, the Pacific island cargo cults believed
that by building makeshift runways and bamboo control towers, they
would cause planes to land, bringing cargo. But there is a difference
between building something that looks like an airport and building
something that functions as one. Similarly, in politics, we have to make
sure we are not doing things that simply look like political action, but
aren't. We might be making symbolic gains without making material
ones. We might be waving a lot of signs, and gathering large numbers
of people in public places, without actually changing the conditions in
which most people live. To make sure we're not practicing something
that looks like politics, but isn't, we have to constantly ask the questions: What is this actually getting for people? How will this change the
balance of who has power and who doesn't? Is this what matters most
and are we pursuing our objectives wisely?

The left is in a more promising position than it has been for a long time. Gains are leading to more gains, organizations are being built, and new people are being brought into the fold. People are excited and optimistic. Just a few socialist elected officials (Sanders and Ocasio-Cortez) have managed to shift the entire national political discourse to the left. Now imagine a hundred Sanderses, a hundred Ocasio-Cortezes. The next generation has its work cut out for it.

PART III

WHAT ARE THE OTHER POLITICAL IDEOLOGIES AND WHY ARE THEY BAD?

————————

Our path so far: We've discovered that outrage is morally necessary. We've looked inside prisons and workplaces and war zones and realized it would be monstrous not to be sincerely committed to the radical improvement of the human condition. We've seen how certain features of contemporary political and economic systems are irreparably dysfunctional. We were introduced to socialism, which provides a set of principles and aspirations that can guide us in the right direction. We've learned how socialism has an honorable tradition despite the shameful history of dictatorial states that have called themselves "socialist." We've seen that there is no contradiction between loving liberty and loving equality, and that libertarian socialists have always realized that people are more free in the absence of hierarchy. We've realized that there is nothing wrong with utopian thinking, because it can stimulate the imagination and give us a better understanding of what we truly want. We've also realized, however, that left-wingers are not detached fantasists. They are serious about developing institutions that improve people's lives and strategies for how to get from the nasty neoliberal present to a bright socialist future.

Because you are a reasonable person, I am sure you are now basically sold on becoming a leftist. You've joined the Democratic Socialists of America, you're unionizing your workplace, you're practicing mutual aid, and you have subscriptions to *Jacobin*, *Dissent*, and *Current Affairs*. But leftism is not the only way of looking at the world, and it's worth examining conservatism and liberalism. Why do leftists reject the prevailing ideologies? What's wrong with them? Can't people of all political stripes live in harmony without attacking one another? Whatever happened to bipartisanship, unity, etcetera?

Socialists are not much for unity, I'll admit. We libertarian socialists believe strongly in free speech and open discussion, but ultimately we want to bring everyone around to seeing as we do, at least on the basics. That is not because we are intolerant, but because there are fundamental flaws in both the conservative and liberal approaches to politics, and everyone will be better off once we get past them.

In this final part, then, let me explain what socialists consider irredeemable about the dominant political tendencies and why we can't really compromise in the long run. Then, to close us out, I'll address the complaints that conservatives and liberals make about *us* and give some rapid responses to the usual anti-socialist talking points.

Mean, False, and Hopeless

The Ugliness of Conservatism

"What are your masses but mud to be ground under foot, fuel to be burned for those who deserve it? What is the people but millions of puny, shriveled, helpless souls that have no thoughts of their own, no dreams of their own, no will of their own, who eat and sleep and chew helplessly the words others put into their mildewed brains? . . . I know no worse injustice than justice for all. Because men are not born equal and I don't see why one should want to make them equal. And because I loathe most of them."

—Ayn Rand, *We the Living* (first edition)[1]

"The egalitarian ideal of contemporary political theory under-estimates the importance of the differences that separate human beings. It has become objectionable to say that some people are superior to other people in any way that is relevant to life in society . . . Discrimination, once a useful word with a praiseworthy meaning, is now almost always used in a pejorative sense."

—Charles Murray and Richard J. Herrnstein, *The Bell Curve*

"Nobody, by and large, cares enough about you to stop you from achieving your dreams . . . I don't care about you; no one cares about you . . . That means, in a free country, if you fail, it's probably your own fault."

—Ben Shapiro, speech at University of California, Berkeley

BY INSTINCT, I AM "CONSERVATIVE." The British conservative philosopher Michael Oakeshott said that, for him, the word referred to a sort of temperamental preference. To be conservative, he said, is "to prefer the familiar to the unknown, to prefer the tried to the untried, fact to mystery."[2] I admit, I like familiar things. I like old buildings and daily rituals and Louis Armstrong records. I get upset when my morning routine is disrupted, and my greatest pleasures come from experiences that are tied to tradition or history: going to Mardi Gras, sitting under oak trees, leafing through old books, marveling at the ocean. Likewise, I share Oakeshott's suspicion of the "untried." I am cautious and unadventurous by nature. I worry that any experiment will end in disaster. When it comes to my life and my environment, I don't like change.

If this were all there was to conservative thinking, it would fit me nicely. Unfortunately, there's more. In its devotion to the familiar, Oakeshott-type conservatism also has a certain myopia, a certain reluctance to question old arguments and prescriptions. We leftists like to interrogate the authority of the past, to decide for ourselves whether an existing practice is right rather than deferring to what is generously called "ancient wisdom," but is often properly regarded as ancient prejudice. At its worst, the left's "ruthless criticism of all that exists," to use Karl Marx's phrase, can result in tearing down institutions without appreciating why they were important. But elementary moral principles demand that we scrutinize our societies and figure out whether existing ways of doing things can be justified.

This is how moral progress is made. At every point in history, there have been atrocities and injustices. There were people who defended those injustices, who suggested that slavery was the natural order of things, or a woman's "proper" place was in the home, or "separate but equal" was fair and sensible. In each era, there were social justice warriors who loudly voiced their outrage, and there were those made uncomfortable by calls for radical change. The social justice warriors were right, and the ones who deferred to tradition and authority were wrong.

Some on the left think all this language about skepticism of the unfamiliar and deference to tried-and-true methods are not really what conservatism is actually about. In *The Reactionary Mind*, political scientist Corey Robin argues that conservatism is a response to the threat of having power taken away. There are moments in history, Robin says, when

> the subordinates of this world contest their fates. They protest their
> conditions, write letters and petitions, join movements, and make

demands. Their goals may be minimal and discrete—better safety guards on factory machines, an end to marital rape—but in voicing them, they raise the specter of a more fundamental change in power.[3]

At those moments, when the conservative "looks upon a democratic movement from below, this (and the exercise of agency) is what he sees: a terrible disturbance in the private life of power."[4] Conservatism is "the felt experience of having power, seeing it threatened, and trying to win it back."[5] Conservatism is a reaction to when the poor try to get a bit of the collective wealth, or blacks try to achieve equal status with whites, or women try to win the vote.

I am not quite this cynical. While political conservatism does protect the interests of the powerful, many of those who subscribe to conservative beliefs do not actually have power themselves. Conservatism is not simply a bad-faith rationalization of the status quo.

I do, however, find it morally rotten.

At the heart of my objection to conservatism, in all its forms, is its fundamental *meanness*. I think it's very telling that conservatives tend to criticize liberals as "bleeding hearts." When you see bad things, your heart *should* bleed, unless you're some kind of monster. Yet throughout conservative writings, I see minds that are unmoved by the pain of others.

Consider this piece from the *National Review*'s Kevin D. Williamson, who was commenting on the small postindustrial towns that have been ravaged by the opioid epidemic:

> The truth about these dysfunctional, downscale communities is that they deserve to die. Economically, they are negative assets. Morally, they are indefensible. Forget all your cheap theatrical Bruce Springsteen crap. Forget your sanctimony about struggling Rust Belt factory towns and your conspiracy theories about the wily Orientals stealing our jobs . . . The white American underclass is in thrall to a vicious, selfish culture whose main products are misery and used heroin needles.[6]

This lack of empathy is particularly evident when it comes to people who are different. In her book *¡Adios America!*, Ann Coulter does not only give an argument for strict border controls, she's also just down-right nasty about immigrants, showing an indifference to their pain that should make any decent person feel sick. This may not be obvious to some of her readers, because Coulter suggests that she operates from a position of compassion—she simply cares about the good Americans who are victimized by criminal immigrants. But she writes about people's pain with such glibness that it's impossible to think she has an ounce of genuine feeling. For instance, she writes:

> The defendant in a story [by] the *Chattanooga Times Free Press*...
> was thirty-six-year-old German Rolando Vicente Sapon, an illegal
> alien from Guatemala. He had persuaded his sixteen-year-old first
> cousin, Yuria Vicente Calel, to join him in the United States, where
> he immediately began raping her, got her pregnant, and then began
> sexually abusing their infant daughter. So the good news is: They
> have an anchor baby![7]

I mean, really, what kind of person talks like this? How can you tell a *joke* about something like that?

When it comes to immigration, those who advocate for tighter restrictions often insist that they value human well-being. But it's clear that they only value the well-being of American citizens, and believe everyone else essentially doesn't matter. Here is Coulter complaining that the NYPD had to investigate a crime committed by an unauthorized immigrant:

> The NYPD spent twenty-two years and a small fortune trying to
> solve a case that never should have taken place in this country in
> the first place. How many other crimes went unsolved because, for
> two decades, the police were pouring resources into a manhunt for
> a Mexican illegally in this country, who committed child rape and
> murder in New York City?[8]

"Never should have taken place *in this country*." Coulter isn't really upset that a child was raped and murdered. She's upset that *we* had to waste *our* resources trying to punish the perpetrator, when it should have been some *other* country's problem. You see this a lot in discussions about immigration. Every time someone talks about how a crime committed by an immigrant "should never have happened" because the person shouldn't have been in the United States, what they're really saying is that it should never have happened *here*. After all, if you deport someone with murderous proclivities, they're not going to be any less murderous; they're just going to be somewhere else, murdering people we happen to care about less. In fact, it's even worse than that: many developing countries have much less reliable criminal justice systems than we do, meaning that if a woman is killed in, say, Honduras, her killer is less likely to successfully be prosecuted. But people like Coulter don't care what the real-world consequences of their immigration policies are for those who live in other countries. That's because they place a higher value on American lives than other lives, seeing no problem with adopting policies that save "our" people at the expense of "their" people. This kind of national chauvinism is born out of a lack of empathy, one that condones inflicting horrendous harms on other people so long as we end up better off. That, to me, is sociopathic.

You notice this meanness or indifference everywhere in conservative writing. Of course, I'm sure no conservative intellectual would accept my characterization. Usually, what they say is something like, "Ah, when I was young and naive, I used to feel the same; I thought conservatism meant greed and indifference, that the right simply lacked compassion. But then I grew wiser, and I realized that it was not a lack of caring, but a realization that left politics hurt the very people they are trying to help." Now, whether left policies end up hurting people is an empirical question, and this line of argument is plausible on its face. However, I've always noticed that even as they protest that they're not un-empathetic, just realistic, conservatives never seem to actually spend much *time* empathizing and are prone to dismissive and insulting remarks about other people's perspectives.

For example, in the 2007 book *Why I Turned Right*, a number of prominent conservatives explain how they developed their beliefs. The Manhattan Institute's Heather Mac Donald says that she started off as a liberal, "the inevitable condition of those who do not bother to educate themselves about social facts." She discovered, however, that leftist talk about oppression was empirically false: homeless people were irresponsible, cops weren't bigots, and welfare made people dependent. She met a real-life "welfare queen" who wore "leopardskin pants, stiletto heels, and fashionable sunglasses" to collect her Supplemental Security Income. These were cold, hard facts, not a lack of feeling.

Mac Donald is correct that these are empirical questions (though they are shot through with value judgments about what our responsibilities are and why it's bad for some people to depend on being supported by others). And yet, there is an underlying lack of generosity. Mac Donald talks about the "facile . . . idiocy" of the left, and like many conservatives enjoys poking fun at silly academic excesses (such as the more inscrutable pronouncements of Jacques Derrida). But this replicates the very tendency she castigates the left for: it shows a lack of curiosity about others' perspectives. She doesn't care to investigate the *life* of the woman in leopard-skin pants. For Mac Donald, the pants are enough for her to conclude that the woman is defrauding the government and falsely claiming to need a disability check. So much conservative thinking is like this: a quickness to judge people for their bad choices without taking the time to understand where they're coming from and why they do what they do.

It's also the case that every time I see a conservative insisting that they are not unsympathetic, just rational, I see another being quite obviously unsympathetic. A few pages before Mac Donald's testimony in *Why I Turned Right*, there is another testimonial from Dinesh D'Souza. D'Souza writes gleefully and unrepentantly about his undergraduate years, when he edited the conservative *Dartmouth Review*. In D'Souza's time, the *Dartmouth Review* became infamous for its tasteless provocations, including publishing an editorial mocking Ebonics called "Dis Sho' Ain't No Jive, Bro." A *Review* reporter also secretly taped a meeting of the Gay Student Association and outed several of its members in the paper. The *New York Times* reported:

> One [gay] student named [by the *Review*], according to his friends, became severely depressed and talked repeatedly of suicide. The grandfather of another who had not found the courage to tell his

family of his homosexuality learned about his grandson when he got his copy of the *Review* in the mail.

D'Souza looks back fondly on all of this, saying that "feminists and homosexuals were regular targets," and cheerfully unearthing the "jokes" they told, such as suggesting Jesse Jackson's "grandmother has been posing nude in *National Geographic*." What disturbs me here is the sheer pleasure D'Souza seems to take in upsetting people, seeing their reactions as confirmation that they are oversensitive, liberal snowflakes. Years later, Milo Yiannopoulos would do the same thing, making "terrorist" jokes about students in hijabs and mocking the appearance of transgender and overweight people.[9] At no point is there any attempt to understand *why* the offended parties are such "snowflakes," what it *feels* like to be a gay person outed in the press, or a Muslim constantly subjected to nasty, hateful taunts.

There is an undercurrent of nastiness to so much of right-wing thinking. Even William F. Buckley, the refined and debonair representative of conservatism at its most intellectual, famously called Gore Vidal a "queer" and threatened to "sock [him] in the goddamn face." (Buckley's *National Review*, which is credited with reviving the American right, also defended segregation, with Buckley himself penning an editorial called "Why the South Must Prevail," arguing that white people were the more "advanced" race and therefore deserved to be politically dominant.[10]) Of course, there's plenty of nastiness on the left, too. But, at least on the humanistic, anti-authoritarian left, we are not nearly as quick to trivialize or rationalize suffering and misery or tell people that their problems are *their own fault* and they should take responsibility for their pain.

A certain kind of thinking on the right goes like this: if you're sad, it's because you're weak; if you're poor, it's because you're stupid; if you're marginalized, it's because you're culturally dysfunctional; if you're being screwed over, you shouldn't have signed the contract; if you did something horrible, it's because you're evil; if you don't understand, it's because you haven't paid attention; if you're angry, it's because you're resentful; if you're sentimental, it's because you're not a man.

I have to admit, I hate that kind of thinking, in part because all my life I have had to resist it in order to maintain my self-confidence. When you start to believe that all of your problems are your own fault, you can begin to hate yourself. As important as it is to take responsibility for our actions, it's also important to acknowledge that many things are beyond our control: we don't choose our parents, genes, physical abilities, economic environments, social class, or opportunities. We can decide how to make use of what we are given, but it's not an "ideology of victimhood" to say that many people are, well, victims. Some people are destined to try their hardest and still fail, and suggesting that they didn't is adding insult to injury, tormenting them by making them feel not only the pain of deprivation but *guilt* and *shame*. (And they say the left likes shaming people!)

At its worst, conservatism exudes a kind of bitter loathing of humanity for its stupidity and self-pity. You can see this in the writings of H. L. Mencken and Ayn Rand, who both saw the masses as ignorant and selfish beneficiaries of the generosity of brilliant capitalists. (A representative Mencken quote: "When a candidate for public office faces the voters he does not face men of sense; he faces a mob of men whose chief distinguishing mark is the fact that they are quite incapable of weighing ideas, or even of comprehending any save the most elemental."[11]) Rand's *Atlas Shrugged* so dripped with bitterness that it horrified even the *National Review* when it was released in 1957. Reviewer Whittaker Chambers said that from every page of the book one could hear the command: "To a gas chamber—go!" Yet even to this day, Rand's work is admired by top Republicans, like former House Speaker Paul Ryan.

* * *

IN *THE RHETORIC OF REACTION,* Albert O. Hirschman famously categorized conservative arguments into three broad categories: perversity, futility, and jeopardy.[12] Nearly all of the right's rhetoric relied on one or more of these concepts. You shouldn't do X because it is *perverse*, that is, contrary to the natural moral order. You shouldn't do Y because it's *futile*, that is, you're wasting your time trying to fix the unfixable. Or you shouldn't do Z because it puts existing progress in *jeopardy*, that is, poses a threat to our fragile institutions. Hirschman's classifications usefully capture the fundamentals of nearly all conservative appeals.

They also show why conservatism tends to be a deeply limiting philosophy. It's true that counseling caution and restraint is useful, since attempts at social engineering have frequently gone (to understate matters somewhat) rather badly. But it also means that conservatism always ends up counseling us to accept the world as it is. It tells us that, in Margaret Thatcher's famous formulation, *there is no alternative.*[13] It becomes a philosophy of hopelessness, one that counsels us to accept the patently unacceptable. In a time of slavery, it will tell us that the ownership of human beings is the natural order and that struggling against it is futile and threatens our civilization. Nowadays, we are told that there's nothing we can do about social classes, racial and wealth inequality, climate change, militarized borders, and war. Any hope of progress requires us to reject this idea.

Sometimes it seems like all I hear from the right are excuses for why bad things are fine and just and everyone who disagrees is a whiny, weepy snowflake who can't handle the Facts. I refuse to accept that position. Is the left easily offended? Perhaps. But that's in part because we take serious things seriously, because we can't hear about the 500,000 deaths caused by the Iraq War without thinking about the Iraqi mothers who watched their children die in front of them. And when I hear someone like Thomas Sowell scoff that the left says we have a "duty to support people who refuse to support themselves," I think to myself, *I'm sorry, but we do have a duty. It's not a pleasant duty, and in many ways not a fair one, but that's what being a* better *person requires.* The bitterness and futility of conservative thinking has little to offer us.

* * *

THERE IS STILL some value in the conservative instinct described by Oakeshott at the beginning of this chapter. But this positive version is probably better referred to as "conservationism." A conservationist often sounds like a conservative: they don't want to squander the treasures we have been bequeathed by prior generations, they are cautious about tearing down and replacing traditions, they are skeptical of sudden, vast changes demanded in the name of rational or inevitable progress.

John Muir, the famous naturalist and founder of the Sierra Club, thought, "None of Nature's landscapes are ugly, so long as they are wild."[14] Because nature is so beautiful, it ought to be loved and nourished. Theodore Roosevelt, equally fond of the wilderness, believed preservation of our natural resources was a duty owed to our children, and warned us not "to let selfish men or greedy interests skin your country of its beauty, its riches, or its romance."[15]

Conserving, in this sense, must inherently involve a skepticism of capitalism, because of capitalism's tendency toward "creative destruction." True conservatism means stubbornly resisting the free-market paperclip maximizer as it gobbles up the Earth, which is one reason why the staunchly capitalist economist Friedrich Hayek wrote an essay called "Why I Am Not a Conservative."[16] The conservatives, he thought, were insufficiently committed to expanding the liberty of the market to do as it pleased. Hayek wanted to unleash the market's full transformative power and see what happened.

Roosevelt and Muir offer a lesson in the kind of conservatism we can have some respect for. The valuable lesson I have taken from this philosophy is expressed in G. K. Chesterton's famous "fence."[17] Chesterton spoke of a fence across a road, and the person who thinks, *I don't see why this is here, let's clear it away.* A more intelligent person, he says, would think, *I don't see why this is here, let's not clear it away until we know why.* It's a philosophy of caution: until you understand why things are the way they are, be very careful about assuming you know better. Importantly, it does not actually inhibit change, if applied rationally. It just counsels humility, which is something we could all benefit from.

Polishing Turds

The Inadequacy of Liberalism

"We are all capable of believing things which we know to be un-
true, and then, when we are finally proved wrong, impudently
twisting the facts so as to show that we were right. Intellectually, it
is possible to carry on this process for an indefinite time: the only
check on it is that *sooner or later a false belief bumps up against
solid reality*, usually on a battlefield."

—George Orwell, "In Front of Your Nose," *The Tribune*

THE FALSE BELIEF OF LIBERAL complacency "bumped up against solid
reality" at around 9 or 10 p.m. on the night of November 8, 2016. It didn't
happen on a battlefield, though. It happened on cable news. "It looked like
we would all get to bed early," the *New York Times* said the next day.[1] The
outcome, it had been agreed, was a foregone conclusion. The only reason
to stay up was to enjoy a bit of schadenfreude at the loser's expense.

The consensus opinion was not only that Donald Trump would
not win the 2016 presidential election, but that he could not win. For
months, pundits had been reassuring the public that the math simply
didn't add up. Chris Cillizza of the *Washington Post* said a few weeks
before the election that Trump's chances were "approaching zero."[2] Jonathan Chait of *New York* magazine said he was "frankly offended" that
anyone was even speculating on the possibility of Trump winning Michigan.[3] Statistician Sam Wang of the Princeton Election Consortium gave
Hillary Clinton a 99 percent chance of winning.[4] By October, Clinton

was so certain of victory that she ditched swing states like Wisconsin and instead began campaigning in deep red states like Arizona and Utah, a move that the press said showed "extraordinary confidence in Mrs. Clinton's electoral position."[5] Nobody seemed scared. Even among the more cautious, nobody actually showed real panic. The risk of a Trump victory was assumed to be fairly low.[6]

On Election Night itself, 200 pounds of celebratory confetti would be loaded into cannons at the Javits Center in Manhattan, where the Clinton campaign awaited the news of their victory. Democrats looked forward to watching Trump's humiliation—the man who had spent his life ridiculing "losers" finally becoming one himself. At last, the country could be rid of a figure whose candidacy was seen as so comically unserious that the *Huffington Post* initially refused to cover it in their "Politics" section, relegating Trump news to "Entertainment."[7] Election Night was going to be a cathartic moment, when the nation could finally say "good riddance" to the odious con man whose doomed and laughable reality-show candidacy had taken up far too much of our collective time and attention.

Things did not work out this way.

The night unraveled slowly at first. But by 9 or 10, as the state-by-state map began to look disconcertingly reddish, liberals around the country began to feel their stomachs drop into their trousers. Stephen Colbert articulated the inner thoughts of millions when he asked on live television, "What the fuck is happening?"[8]

Clinton did not give a concession speech that night. She hadn't even drafted one; the prospect of losing was inconceivable.[9] The Javits Center confetti cannons would go unfired.[10] The next day, phrases like "shocking" and "stunning upset" filled the papers. The international reaction was far more blunt: "What have they done?" ran the main headline in Britain's *Mirror* newspaper.[11] "OH MY GOD" was the lead in the *Journal de Québec*.[12] Australia's *Daily Telegraph* filled its front page with just three letters: "W.T.F.?"[13]

*   *   *

CLINTON'S BRANCH OF the Democratic Party received a nasty shock. Barack Obama's 2008 campaign manager David Plouffe said he had

"never been as wrong on anything [in his] life."[14] Democrats had believed that with the economy having recovered from its 2008 low and
Trump being so manifestly inferior to Clinton in experience and tem-
perament, it was impossible to lose. They had misread the signs badly.

It wasn't impossible to predict what was going to happen. I had
even written it myself, in February of 2016, when I warned Democrats
that nominating Clinton would assure a Trump presidency.[15] In July,
Michael Moore warned America that it was stumbling blindly toward
a Trump White House.[16] Giving "5 Reasons Why Trump Will Win,"
Moore said that complacent Democrats were failing to take a few key
factors into account: the Rust Belt's economic frustration, the anger
of white men, the unpopularity of Clinton, the disaffection of former
Sanders voters, and the "Jesse Ventura effect," that is, voters' willingness to lob a hand grenade at the establishment just to see what would
happen. Moore's analysis turned out to be correct.

Many on the left, including the Clinton campaign, did not appreciate these factors until Election Night. Afterward, there would be
plenty of public reflection about the widespread "anger and anxiety"
that had been ignored, and what living in a liberal "bubble" could
do to one's worldview. But none of this was understood until it was
too late.

This was much more than a failure of analysis and punditry. Democrats failed to predict and stop Trump because they fundamentally did
not understand the nature of the political moment we were in. They had
not noticed as public opinion about the Democratic Party had slowly
soured.[17] Obama, usually a highly empathetic observer of popular tem-
perament, was blindsided by the rise of Trump. In February 2016, I
had a somewhat stunning debate with a Clinton-supporting political
science professor on the *Democracy Now!* radio show.[18] He cited statistics showing that over 60 percent of the public was dissatisfied with the
country's direction, but then said the idea that "the electorate is angry"
was exaggerated by the media in order to create a "horse race" for popular consumption. I pointed out that if 60 percent of the country was upset with life under the existing Democratic president, and Democrats
ran a candidate who represented continuity instead of change, that
candidate was "going to lose." The professor dismissed this, saying that

elections were always presented as revolts against the establishment, and there was nothing different about this one.

But it was strange talking to Democrats at that time: very obvious facts were routinely ignored and dismissed. For example, if you pointed out that Trump's surprise victory over other Republican candidates could translate into a surprise victory over a Democrat, you would be told all the reasons why polling showed this was impossible. If you pointed out that it was an electoral risk to run a candidate who was under active investigation by the FBI, you would be told why the infamous email scandal was a fuss over nothing and the FBI investigation was bogus.[19]

The "bubble" effect was quite real. Something had been happening in the media over the last several decades that was not adequately appreciated. As media organizations had slowly consolidated in large coastal cities, and local newspapers were sold and shut down, prominent journalists were increasingly concentrated in major liberal cities.[20] This distorted their understanding of what was going on in America. Importantly, the growth of economic inequality exacerbated this problem: because affluent people in coastal cities are actually doing very well economically, from their perspective it looked like all of America was doing well.[21]

Obama himself shared this blindness. In October 2016, when he guest-edited an issue of *Wired* magazine, instead of stumping for Clinton, Obama called his lead editorial "Now Is the Greatest Time to Be Alive," boasting that "once-quiet factories are alive again, with assembly lines churning out the components of a clean-energy age."[22] This upbeat tone, focusing on the positive rather than the negative, was reflected in a lot of Democratic 2016 messaging, which was intended to highlight all the successful achievements of the Obama administration. It was thought that through a combination of attacking Trump and pointing out all of the great things about Obama's America, voters would see just how clear the right decision was and keep the Democratic Party in power.

This was misguided. "Now Is the Greatest Time to Be Alive" may well be true in the statistical aggregate. On average, people are getting healthier and more prosperous, and compared to the bloody nightmares that unfolded during the twentieth century, the twenty-first century is indeed a glorious time to be alive. But what's true on average isn't necessarily true for everyone. The optimistic message only resonated with people who were doing well. To an unemployed person or someone struggling with debt and poor health, it sounded oblivious and out of touch.

Democrats even went so far as to start selling hats that read "America Is Already Great," in an effort to counter Trump's promise to restore some former greatness that had been lost.[23] Just think about how this slogan came across to someone in Detroit or Ferguson or West Virginia. It seemed to say, "*My* America Is Already Great," and it reinforced Trump's message that Democrats in Washington were clueless about the lives of ordinary people. Trump promised to fix people's problems, and instead of responding with better solutions, Democrats replied, "What problems?"

* * *

AMERICA IN 2016 was a troubled place. The list is a familiar and depressing one: Drug deaths and suicides were at their highest point in decades. Student and household debt was climbing. Many families who'd seen their wealth wiped out during the Great Recession never saw it return.[24] While the Affordable Care Act had improved people's access to health insurance, it hadn't changed the fundamental brokenness of the costly and convoluted U.S. healthcare system. Labor unions had continued to disappear, with workers losing pensions and protection against abusive practices by employers. Many people felt hopeless and pessimistic.[25]

Trump was able to exploit those feelings of hopelessness. Just as his fraudulent Trump University had promised aspiring businesspeople the secrets of endless wealth, Trump promised America that if he was elected, all of the country's problems would be solved. He even had a secret plan to defeat ISIS. (He couldn't reveal it, though, because after all, it was a secret.) Trump knew how to speak to populations that felt alienated and underserved by Washington. He frightened them and played on their prejudices, telling them they were under threat from Islamic jihadists and sexually predatory Mexican immigrants. And he lambasted the institutions and people who had supposedly failed the country, from CNN to Obama and Clinton.

Democrats were powerless to respond to this, because much of it was true. While Trump drastically exaggerated the scale of various problems, dealt in bigoted caricatures, and lied about everything under the sun, he correctly identified areas where the Democratic Party was vulnerable. It was true that Democratic presidents had gotten the country involved in international trade deals that workers associated, rightly or not, with the disappearance of manufacturing.[26] It was true that Clinton bore at least partial responsibility for the disastrous American interventions in Iraq and Libya.[27] And it was true that deadly violence was a problem in Chicago and on the Mexican border. Trump made the situation sound far more dire and apocalyptic than it actually was, and one Trump adviser absurdly compared Americans to passengers on the planes during 9/11, whose only remaining option was to storm the cockpit.[28] But the message that America had lost its mojo was far more in tune with the feelings of the 2016 electorate than "America Is Already Great."

To be sure, Clinton still managed to win the popular vote. But this only revealed the nature of the problem. You could theoretically win the popular vote without leaving the coasts; California and New York alone have 60 million people between them, and Hillary Clinton ended up with 65 million votes. Winning the electoral college requires appealing to voters across the country. Nobody doubts that Democrats can do very well in liberal strongholds. But even as blue states were becoming bluer, Democrats were hemorrhaging support in the rest of the country. Moore was right: "Rust Belt math" would do them in.

Clinton's calamitous and unexpected defeat was the last in a series of Democratic political failures that had occurred since 2008, when Obama was elected on grandiose promises of fundamental political change. Over the course of the following eight years, Democratic political power had been slowly eroding without anyone taking notice. Governorships, seats in state legislatures, Congress—all were slowly turning red, even as Obama's occupancy of the White House made it appear as if Democrats were in a position of power.[29] In fact, their political efficacy had weakened to the point where they were unable to prevent a serial sexual harasser and fraudster from ascending to the presidency. The rude awakening in November 2016 left many Democrats asking the question that would ultimately become the title of Clinton's campaign memoir: "What happened?"

What had happened was that liberalism had fallen apart, slowly, without anybody noticing.

* * *

> "We're capitalists, and that's just the way it is."
> —Nancy Pelosi, CNN Town Hall

> "It is very, very disturbing when I hear the *millionaire* or *billionaire* word . . . And I've told [the Democratic politicians] to stop it. Knock it off . . . I've talked to Schumer, I've talked to Wyden, I've talked to Pelosi and I've said if you use the term *billionaire* again, I'm done."
> —Stephen Cloobeck, CEO of Diamond Resorts and major Democratic Party donor

When Clinton began her campaign, her staff faced a problem: their candidate could not come up with a reason why she was running. In *Shattered: Inside Hillary Clinton's Doomed Campaign*, Jonathan Allen and Amie Parnes write that, internally, "there wasn't a real clear sense of why she was in" the race, and Clinton was "unable to prove to many voters that she was running for the presidency because she had a vision for the country rather than visions of power."[30] Persistent efforts to get Clinton to come up with a justification for her candidacy all failed. Staffers even floated the idea of using "It's Her Turn" as a slogan.[31]

It wasn't surprising that Clinton couldn't come up with a vision. Clinton shared the worldview of many contemporary liberals, who don't actually have a real sense, beyond vague abstractions about "change," of the kind of transformations they want to effect. This kind of politics is far more interested in whether an individual is "qualified" for office than in what they're actually going to *do* once elected. Clinton didn't need a plan because she was so clearly the "best" person for the job.

My colleague Luke Savage has described this as the "*West Wing* view" of politics: the idea that credentials are more important than substantive vision.[32] In Aaron Sorkin's *The West Wing*, bright people who went to good schools walk through hallways taking their jobs very seriously. But it's often not quite clear what they're trying to *do*—in seven seasons of the show, the fictional Bartlet administration seems to accomplish very little in the way of real policy change that would impact American lives. (Though, as Luke points out, Bartlet "warmly embraces the military-industrial complex, cuts Social Security, and puts a hard-right justice on the Supreme Court in the interest of bipartisan 'balance.'") It has always struck me as funny that Sorkin's signature *West Wing* shot is the "walk and talk," in which characters strut down hallways having intense conversations but do not actually appear to be going anywhere. What better metaphor could there be for a politics that consists of looking knowledgeable and committed without any sense of what you're aiming for? It perfectly captures liberalism.

The political left, of which I am a member, often voices disdain for "liberals." The radical musician Phil Ochs, in his 1966 song "Love Me, I'm a Liberal," sang disdainfully of whites who loved people of other races, "as long as they don't move next door." Ochs addressed those who thought Mississippians "should all hang their heads in shame" but would want a police investigation of anyone who thought they should bus their children. The song has held up well, even referring to those who read the "*New Republic* and *Nation*." But what actually separates a liberal from a leftist? And why is the distinction important?

This can be argued about, but one of the core differences is the amount of faith in the system that each has. A leftist is cynical and skeptical. A liberal thinks that American institutions are fundamentally good and that capitalism is fundamentally fine but needs a few tweaks and regulations. A liberal is not a class warrior or a firebrand. Ochs' fictitious liberal says, "Don't talk about revolution / that's going a little bit too far," and this kind of resistance to large-scale change is characteristic of the liberal mindset. The liberal wonders why we can't all just put aside our differences, unify, and get along, while the leftist thinks conflict between people is inevitable until we've established a fair social and economic system.

Obama is the prototypical liberal. In his famous 2004 Democratic

National Committee address, Obama said that there wasn't a "red" or "blue" America, but one United States of America. Obama always tried to find "common ground." He invited congressional Republicans to a screening of *Lincoln* at the White House, hoping they would see in it how people of differing views can come together and reach productive compromises. Obama was surprised and disappointed when none of them showed up.[33]

To the leftist, this is a naive view of politics, one that misunderstands how political interests and power operate. Republicans play the political game to win, and if they can destroy the left outright, they will. They do not want reasonable bipartisan compromise, they want outright victory. Jim Messina, Obama's deputy chief of staff and re-election campaign manager, was shocked when a Republican staffer told him after the 2008 election, "We're not going to compromise with you on anything. We're going to fight Obama on everything." Messina replied, "That's not what we did for Bush." The Republican said, "We don't care."[34]

On *The West Wing*, Republicans are not political enemies in a zero-sum competition. They are foolish, misguided, but mostly well intentioned. In Washington, D.C., there are mere "disagreements" rather than fights, but everyone can get along. You can see this in the Obama family's warm relations with George W. Bush. Bush is responsible for the deaths of 500,000 Iraqis, but Michelle Obama has said she "loves him," and that he is her "partner in crime."[35] (What crime specifically, she does not say.) You can see the same chumminess in Joe Biden's warm relationship with Strom Thurmond, an unrepentant Dixiecrat racist who once promised to keep the "n*gger race" out of the South's swimming pools and diners. At Thurmond's funeral, Biden gave a tribute to Thurmond's "truth and genius and virtue," though Thurmond had never expressed contrition and remained on the hard right until he died.[36]

But there is something even more insidious about liberal politics: it is the politics of wealthy people who want to appear virtuous without actually making personal sacrifices. Ochs said the liberal was a person who was "ten degrees to the left of center in good times, ten degrees to the right of center if it affects them personally." He sang about the liberal reluctance to bus children, but today we see it in the way wealthy liberals take their children out of poor public schools and put them in private schools, where they can get ahead of other kids. If you want to see the true face of liberal politics, look at news stories about local proposals to equalize the educations of black and white children. Even in "progressive" coastal areas, you will see quotes from parents like, "It's not our fault those children don't have opportunities. You can't put that burden on us."[37] Nikole Hannah-Jones, who reports on educational segregation for the *New York Times*, has said that regardless of political leanings, "white communities want neighborhood schools if their neighborhood school is white," but "if their neighborhood school is black, they want choice." Hannah-Jones says, "People who say they believe in equality and integration" persistently "act in ways that maintain inequality and segregation," and the "most segregated parts of the country are all in the progressive North," where "white liberals" don't "live their values."[38]

Adolph Reed Jr. has been scathingly critical of liberalism for its lack of real commitment to its proclaimed values. He condemns

> their capacity for high-minded fervor for the emptiest and sappiest platitudes; their tendencies to make a fetish of procedure over substance and to look for technical fixes to political problems; their ability to screen out the mounting carnage in the cities they inhabit as they seek pleasant venues for ingesting good coffee and scones; their propensity for aestheticizing other people's oppression and calling that activism; their reflex to wring their hands and look constipated in the face of conflict; and, most of all, their spinelessness and undependability in crises.[39]

Reed was an early critic of Obama, whom he saw as embodying all of these tendencies. As early as 1996, he described Obama as practicing a policy of "form over substance," calling him a "smooth Harvard lawyer with impeccable do-good credentials and vacuous-to-repressive neoliberal politics." In 2008, he warned, "Obama's empty claims to being a candidate of progressive change and to embodying a 'movement' that exists only as a brand will dissolve into disillusionment," and his presidency would "continue the politics he's practiced his entire career."[40] Reed saw the devotion Obama inspired as a "faddish, utterly uninformed exuberance," and said that Obama's "miraculous ability to inspire and engage the young replaced specific content in his patter of Hope and Change."

Matt Taibbi described Obama similarly, saying that he was

> an ingeniously crafted human cipher . . . a sort of ideological Universalist . . . who spends a great deal of rhetorical energy show- ing that he recognizes the validity of all points of view, and con- versely emphasizes that when he does take hard positions on issues, he often does so reluctantly . . . You can't run against him on issues because you can't even find him on the ideological spectrum.[41]

If you read the memoirs of Obama administration staffers, you'll see that Reed and Taibbi were exactly right. David Litt and Dan Pfeif- fer, who both wrote speeches for Obama, describe themselves as huge *West Wing* fans who watched the series on an endless loop in college. They were drawn to Obama not because they were strong political par- tisans who wanted to accomplish a particular kind of social transfor- mation, but because of Obama's personal magnetism. Litt describes Obama in downright messianic terms, and makes the campaign sound very much like a cult of personality.

> We had no doubt that everyone would soon see the light . . . Our critics would later mock the depths of our devotion. Obamabots, they'd call us. And really, weren't they right? Becoming obsessed with Barack Obama wasn't a choice I made . . . My switch had been flipped . . . Obama wasn't just fighting for change. He was change. He was the messenger and message all at once. It's one thing to fol- low a prophet who speaks glowingly of a promised land. It's another thing entirely to join him once he parts the sea . . . Given the circum- stances, it seemed selfish not to spread the good news.[42]

There was always a certain emptiness to Obama's politics. Pfeiffer says that while conventional wisdom in politics is that you should talk about "issues and policy positions," for Obama, "the campaign was the message." Litt admits that while he fell into a "patriotic ecstasy" when listening to Obama speak, when the speeches ended, he couldn't remember a single word of them. It was Obama the person, not Obama the representative of a set of concrete ideas, that people liked.

The actual politics of the Obama administration were often repugnant to left values. He came in with lofty promises of "hope" and "change," then immediately began stuffing his cabinet with Goldman Sachs alumni. He deported staggering numbers of immigrants, let Wall Street criminals off the hook, failed to take on the fossil fuel industry, sold over $100 billion in arms to Saudi Arabia, killed American citizens with drones, killed lots more non–American citizens with drones (including Yemenis going to a wedding), promised "the most transparent administration ever" and then was "worse than Nixon" in his paranoia about leakers, and showered Israel with both public support and military aid even as it systematically violated the human rights of Palestinians.[43]

Scott Brown, the Republican who won Ted Kennedy's Senate seat in 2010, destroying the Democratic supermajority, pointed out that Democrats hadn't done much when they *had* had a supermajority:

> They had two years to do whatever they wanted and they did hardly anything. They didn't do minimum wage. They didn't do climate change. They didn't do immigration. They didn't do health care. They just assumed they would always have this supermajority.[44]

The things they did do were often distinctly unprogressive. Look, for example, at Obama's education policy. Obama hired "reformer" Arne Duncan to be his secretary of education. Their signature initiative was called "Race to the Top," which forced struggling school districts to compete against one another for federal funding.[45] In order to get federal money, the school districts had to comply with a series of federal rules, like making it easier to start charter schools. The policy was born out of the "education reform" movement, which united liberals and conservatives around the position that "school choice" and "teacher accountability" were what was needed to fix the school system. But, as Diane Ravitch has shown in her books on the education system like *Reign of Error* and *The Death and Life of the Great American School System*, this movement was founded on fundamentally erroneous, conservative premises. Instead of trying to pay teachers competitive wages in order to attract the best talent, the policy encouraged the establishment of privatized schools, which are independent of school districts and could therefore fire "bad" teachers more easily. Instead of asking teachers what resources they needed for their schools to function well, the policy relied heavily on "performance" tests and punished schools whose students did poorly. This kind of approach to policy is not egalitarian or democratic. It makes teachers' lives worse—the fruits of Obama's education policy can be seen in the recent wave of teachers' strikes—and shuns principles of equity in favor of market competition and efficiency. Nowhere can we more starkly see the difference between how a liberal approaches a social problem and how a leftist would approach it.

* * *

WHAT ARE THE most pernicious qualities of liberalism? What exactly are we leftists trying to rid politics of? A few essential things:

- **Reluctance to Challenge the Powerful:** If you are giving paid speeches to Goldman Sachs rather than trying to build a world without Goldman Sachs in it, you are on the wrong side. Democratic officials have shown perpetual fealty to Wall Street, pharmaceutical companies, and oppressive governments like those of Saudi Arabia and Israel. Grow some vertebrae!

- **Lack of Movement Building:** Upon his election, Obama dismantled the formidable grassroots organizing apparatus that he had built, Organizing for America.[46] This meant that there was no social movement to support him in office, which is part of why he wasn't able to muster much political power. But liberals don't really think about how to organize (Ochs sang about the liberal who will "send you all the money you ask for" but won't actually leave the house and join in), which is part of why they have missed how important the labor movement is to counterbalance conservative power.

- **Belief in Bipartisanship:** Sometimes you have to make compromises with the other side and reach negotiated settlements. But although politicians like Cory Booker put out books with titles like *Unity: Thoughts on Finding Common Ground and Advancing the Common Good*, bipartisanship, in and of itself, is not inherently a good thing. The Iraq War was bipartisan. So were welfare reform, mass incarceration, and the Patriot Act. Bill Clinton achieved political consensus with Republicans repeatedly—by adopting Republican positions. Ultimately, a person of principle needs to be more concerned with building power than with reaching agreement.

- **Politics of Attributes:** Liberalism thinks more about who a candidate *is* than what that candidate is actually going to do with power. For example, when South Bend, Indiana, mayor Pete Buttigieg was asked why he would be the best Democratic candidate in 2020, he replied:

  > You have a handful of candidates from the middle of the country, but very few of them are young. You have a handful of young candidates, but very few of them are executives. We have a handful of executives but none of them are veterans, and so it's a question of: What alignment of attributes do you want to have?[47]

  The "alignment of attributes" is a perfect phrase. It shows a politics that is symbolic rather than substantive, that doesn't think about policies but about characters. (Sure enough, articles about Buttigieg are about things like what socks he wears and what books he reads, rather than his record as a mayor.[48])

- **Whitewashing of History:** America has a shameful history. The land we live on was stolen from its original inhabitants, who were systematically wiped out. But "liberal history" wants to tell an uplifting narrative about America, as a country that has had its problems and flaws, but is constantly getting better. So, for example, Harvard historian Jill Lepore's *These Truths* treats America's story as a story of democratic ideas, but almost entirely leaves out the history of labor struggles and Native people and gives only a small fraction of its space to black history. Or look at the musical *Hamilton*, which turns the Framers into people of color and sets slavery aside, so that people can love America while still feeling "woke" and avoiding having to grapple with uncomfortable truths.[49]

- **Use of Right-Wing Premises:** Sometimes liberals say things like "we're the *real* patriots" or "we're the ones who *really* embody the Founding Fathers' principles." A leftist wouldn't say these things. They would say, "Patriotism is overrated and many of the Founding Fathers beat and raped slaves, so a principle isn't good just because the Founding Fathers happened to believe in it." Liberals often adopt the right's premises even when they are making ostensibly left arguments. For example, when the Republicans passed their massive corporate tax giveaway, the Democratic response was, in part, that the Republicans were actually raising taxes on middle-class people and disguising it as a tax cut. Democrats, they said, were the *real* party of middle-class tax cuts. In doing so, they affirmed the idea that tax cuts are a wonderful thing that everyone should be working toward. If a Republican says, "I want to cut your taxes and they want to raise them," and you respond, "No, they want to raise your taxes and I want to cut them," you are implicitly adopting the same principle, namely that politics should be a competition to see who can cut taxes the most.[50]

* * *

THE LIBERALISM OF Hollywood, Harvard, and the Hamptons is not capable of advancing egalitarian values. Luke Savage says that it puts "etiquette over equality, manners before morals, procedure ahead of program, [and] conciliation over conflict." It calls for civility and decorum before calling for justice. It laments inequality but takes no steps that would actually reduce it, such as making it easier to unionize. (Inequality is a very popular topic at the Davos World Economic Forum, where billionaires wring their hands about poverty over canapés rather than just give poor people all their money.)

The great socialist writer Alexander Cockburn, when he worked at *The Nation*, used to ask all of his interns the same question: "Is your hate pure?" If they said no or looked confused, Cockburn would shake his head in disappointment. At one point, a young Ed Miliband, a future British Labour leader, worked at the magazine. Cockburn posed his usual question, and Miliband "replied with shock that he did not, in fact, hate anyone." "It tells you all you need to know," Cockburn said.[51]

What did Cockburn mean? Why did he want his interns to have hate in their hearts? Well, because the world is full of terrible injustice! If that injustice doesn't absolutely enrage you, then your moral compass is busted. You don't have to hate *people*, necessarily (though when I look at George W. Bush dancing on the *Ellen* show, and I think about the faces of Iraqi orphans, I seethe uncontrollably). But you do have to hate the things that happen to people: the way some grow up with unbelievable privilege while millions of children are homeless (in the United States alone), the eviction of families in the middle of winter, the way American leaders can casually destroy the lives of foreigners without a second thought, the killing of children and journalists by our allies. Contemporary liberalism often gives voice to outrage, but it talks more of the need to get past "partisanship" and achieve "unity" than the scandal of low teacher salaries or the private health insurance system.

*   *   *

IT WAS NOT always this way. There was, once upon a time, a more respectable liberalism that cared about the needs of working people.

Franklin Roosevelt was not a socialist. Far from it. He was an American aristocrat, with no interest in fundamentally upending the country's system of government. Roosevelt's labor secretary, Frances Perkins, said that the president "took the status quo in our economic system as much for granted as his family . . . [H]e was content with it."[52] A nation furious at Wall Street had given Roosevelt a mandate to take radical steps to alleviate the suffering caused by the Great Depression, but the president declined opportunities to nationalize the banking sector. His intent was to "save capitalism from the capitalists" and ensure that widespread rage against big business didn't spark a populist uprising. Economic radicals like Huey Long were openly advocating for the massive redistribution of wealth from rich to poor. Roosevelt knew that unless the American people were given a measure of financial security, the torches and pitchforks would soon be visible outside his window.

Yet even though Roosevelt's instincts were fundamentally conservative, he voiced sentiments that are startling in their radicalism when compared with contemporary political rhetoric. Speaking at Madison Square Garden in 1936, Roosevelt condemned those who put profit over people:

> We had to struggle with the old enemies of peace—business and financial monopoly, speculation, reckless banking, class antagonism, sectionalism, war profiteering. They had begun to consider the Government of the United States as a mere appendage to their own affairs. We know now that Government by organized money is just as dangerous as Government by organized mob. Never before in all our history have these forces been so united against one candidate as they stand today. They are unanimous in their hate for me—and I welcome their hatred. I should like to have it said of my first Administration that in it the forces of selfishness and of lust for power met their match. I should like to have it said of my second Administration that in it these forces met their master.[53]

It was a remarkable sentiment from a U.S. president, though other presidents had previously issued their own criticisms of the propertied classes. Thomas Jefferson concluded, "Whenever there is in any country, uncultivated lands and unemployed poor, it is clear that the laws of property have been so far extended as to violate natural right," because "the earth is given as a common stock for man to labour and live on."[54] Abraham Lincoln went even further, writing, "Capitalists generally act harmoniously and in concert to fleece the people," and because "labor is the superior of capital," it was a "most worthy object of good government" to secure "to each laborer the whole product of his labor."[55] Lincoln pointed out, as Karl Marx did, that when the world was divided between owners and laborers, owners could reap the fruits of workers' labor without having to do any labor themselves.

Roosevelt's New Deal may not have seized the means of production. It didn't introduce a universal healthcare program (as the United Kingdom would do in 1945) or guarantee housing and a basic income, and it didn't bring major industries under popular control. It also had racially exclusionary aspects, to the point where nobody should hold up FDR as a champion of the oppressed.[56] But in its bold approach to the economic crisis, it represented a gutsy and ambitious liberalism, one unafraid to incur the "hate" of some powerful forces. For most of the rest of the twentieth century, American progressives would look to the New Deal as the model for robust government response to social problems, while American radicals would view it as a good start that didn't go nearly far enough.

In a sane political universe, Rooseveltian progressive liberals would be the right wing, and revolutionary socialists the left wing. Yet, as Thomas Frank points out in *Listen, Liberal: Or, What Ever Happened to the Party of the People?*, from the 1970s to the present day, liberals abandoned Roosevelt's vision altogether.[57] The vision of the Democratic Party as the representatives of "working people" was dropped; the Democrats became the party of Wall Street. In 2012, Barack Obama received more donations from Wall Street than Mitt Romney did. People who in a previous generation would have been obvious Republicans, like JPMorgan Chase CEO Jamie Dimon, are now Democrats. As Frank writes, when rich professionals come to dominate the Democratic Party, it isn't going to be very concerned with the maldistribution of rewards:

> Professional-class liberals aren't really alarmed by oversized rewards for society's winners; on the contrary, this seems natural to them— because they are society's winners. The liberalism of professionals just does not extend to matters of inequality; this is the area where soft hearts abruptly turn hard.[58]

Left politics means supporting the losers against the winners, and the liberalism of the wealthy is never going to challenge the status quo. The left not only have soft hearts, but we have fire in our bellies.

Response to Criticisms

Why Opponents of Socialism Are All Wrong

> "Socialism is the philosophy of failure, the creed of ignorance, and the gospel of envy."
>
> —Winston Churchill, Perth, Scotland (1948)

> "The inherent virtue of Socialism is the equal sharing of miseries."
>
> —Winston Churchill, House of Commons (1945)

THERE ARE APPROXIMATELY 900,000 COMMON criticisms of socialism, give or take a few. And because I've assumed you're extremely skeptical of socialism, I have to spend at least a bit of time going through at least some of them. By this point I hope that, at the very least, I have successfully shown the YouTubers who think "socialism is cancer" that socialism is not, in fact, cancer. However, there are some slightly more sophisticated critiques that merit a response. Let me show why the standard criticisms of socialism can be dismissed.

1. SOCIALISTS DISLIKE FREEDOM; THEY ONLY CARE ABOUT EQUALITY

> "A major source of objection to a free economy is precisely that it gives people what they want instead of what a particular group thinks they ought to want. Underlying most arguments against the free market is a lack of belief in freedom itself."
>
> —Milton Friedman, *Capitalism and Freedom*, 1962

I hope you've seen why this is false. Democratic socialists believe deeply in freedom. Our largest criticism of society today is that, in many ways, capitalism actually restricts people's freedom. We believe that the choices capitalism gives people—obey your employer or starve to death—are not really choices at all, and that without meaningful choice, there can be no freedom. Economist Rob Larson, in *Capitalism vs. Freedom*, shows that free-market economies actually restrict individual freedom in a number of ways.[1] By concentrating economic power in the hands of a small class of elites, they reduce the amount of control that ordinary people have over the world. By restricting working people's leisure time and not giving them access to necessary services (like affordable healthcare and paid parental leave), laissez-faire policies undermine people's capacity to pursue their own happiness.

We are made less free when corporations have disproportionate power over our elections and government policy. We are made less free when we are manipulated by unrestrained capitalism. Edward Bernays, the pioneer of the modern-day public relations industry, noted, "We are governed, our minds molded, our tastes formed, our ideas suggested, largely by men we have never heard of."[2] He was referring to advertising, and the pernicious ways in which people's weaknesses are preyed on through marketing. We are encouraged to fulfill our desires through consumption and billions of dollars are spent shaping those desires.

It's absolutely not the case, then, that socialists only care about equality and do not care about freedom. Freedom is one of our central concerns, and one of the main reasons we're socialists in the first place is that we want people to be free from having to spend their lives putting money in the pockets of their bosses and landlords.

There are some, however, who say socialists are wrong to care about equality at all. Harry Frankfurt, in *On Inequality*, says that it's actually *irrational* to think that inequality is some kind of problem. Don Watkins and Yaron Brook, in *Equal Is Unfair*, actually go further; they say that the very concept of equality is actually unjust, because it involves treading on people's liberties in order to pursue some kind of arbitrary standard of sameness. We have already seen why economic equality is important: for the same reason inequality in the number of votes each person has would lead to some people dominating and ruling over others, economic inequality turns some people into lords and others into peasants. Equality doesn't mean ensuring everybody is the same, it means making sure some people don't get godlike power to determine the fates of others.

2. VENEZUELA, VENEZUELA, VENEZUELA

> "Inflation in Venezuela is reminiscent of Weimar Germany. Roughly 85 percent of Venezuelan companies have stopped production to one extent or another, in the most oil-rich country in the world . . . The disconnect between socialism's record and its invincible appeal also stems from leftists' denial of what it really entails."
>
> —Jonah Goldberg, *Los Angeles Times*

Every time a socialist opens her mouth, the first thing you'll hear in reply is "Venezuela." Venezuela has been suffering a debilitating economic crisis, with runaway inflation, shortages of essential goods, and widespread unemployment. It's a tragic humanitarian disaster. For many, it also discredits socialism because much of the crisis has been brought about through poor government economic policies introduced by a supposedly leftist administration.

It's worth noting that unless we simply define all bad economic decisions as socialist, there isn't anything resembling socialism in Venezuela. Here, for example, is leftist Venezuelan union leader José Bodas Lugo, who says that none of the left principles he is fighting for are practiced by the present authoritarian government:

Maduro is not from the Left, his is a bourgeois government that imposes austerity on the workers, that binds workers in a state of semi-slavery in agreements that benefit the multinationals . . . It is a government that criminalizes protest, which criminalizes the right to strike . . . They have criminalized workers who fight for an autonomous union . . . We activists are fighting for our rights, for union autonomy, for our right to bargain collectively, for decent wages, for better working conditions . . . The government of Chavez and Maduro, the government of "Socialism of the 21st Century" is nothing

more than a scam. This government is not socialist, it is not a workers' government. It is a bourgeois government. It is a government
that applies a bourgeois, anti-worker and anti-popular [package of
austerity measures], which includes miserable wages . . . This government is not left-wing . . . this government is right-wing.[3]

Even the chief Venezuela correspondent of the *Wall Street Journal* (which is not exactly the *Daily Worker*) has said that the leftism of
Nicolás Maduro's government is mostly a flimsy cover for what is ultimately a corrupt kleptocracy.

What struck me on arriving was how little the Socialist leaders cared
about even the appearance of equality . . . As the recession took hold
in Venezuela, the so-called Socialist government made no attempt to
shield health care and education, the two supposed pillars of its program. This wasn't socialism. It was kleptocracy—the rule of thieves.
Even Mr. Maduro has given up on the Socialist pretense, chucking
leftist slogans in favor of straightforward clientelism: Vote for me
and you'll get a food handout.[4]

Of course, one might reply that such kleptocracies are the inevitable result of leftist ideas. There's a problem with that logic, though:
in recent years, nearby Bolivia has been running on leftist ideas and
hasn't had the same problems. *Washington Post* columnist Francisco
Toro has noted that under a socialist government, Bolivia "has experienced a spectacular run of economic growth and poverty reduction
with no hint of the chaos that has plagued Venezuela," meaning that
"the supposedly obvious link between socialism and economic ruin
doesn't check out."[5]

Venezuela's crisis has not occurred because its government was too
dedicated to ensuring workplace democracy and a decent standard of
living; nobody thinks it has made meaningful attempts to give people
these things.[6] Critics suggest that all economic mismanagement is
automatically socialism. But American democratic socialists have no
interest in pursuing the policies that damaged Venezuela's fortunes.
The "Venezuela" criticism is mindless and cheap, and too often it is

used to avoid having to engage with the policies that socialists are advocating here.[7]

3. SOCIALISM IS WHEN THE GOVERNMENT CONTROLS THE ECONOMY, AND THAT'S ALWAYS A DISASTER

> "The trouble with Socialism is that eventually you run out of other people's money."
>
> —Margaret Thatcher, speech to the
> Conservative Party Conference, 1975

> "The capitalist ideal is that government plays very little role in the economy—and the socialist ideal is that government plays the leading role in the economy . . . I say that capitalism is awesome, and socialism is terrible."
>
> —Bryan Caplan, debate at LibertyCon

First, socialism *isn't* about the government controlling the economy. If that was all there was to it, then it would be strange to have so many anarchists self-identifying as socialists. *Socialism*, as we have seen, is a term that describes a bundle of different political philosophies, some of which emphasize greater state control of the economy, and some of which actually want less of it, but all of which seek to empower the working class and deplore the concentration of capital in the hands of rich people.[8] If we are going to deal fairly with socialists, we can't just talk about "the government," because many of them loathe the government.

It should also be said, however, that many of the arguments about socialists advocating for government control of the economy are poor. One of the key defenses of American capitalism asks others to look at how the Soviet Union fared, then look at our own extremely prosperous country. Case closed. The structure of this argument has remained the same for about a century. Here's how Ludwig von Mises argued in 1947:

> The only certain fact about Russian affairs under the Soviet regime with regard to which all people agree is: that the standard of living of the Russian masses is much lower than that of the masses in the country which is universally considered as the paragon of capitalism, the United States of America. If we were to regard the Soviet

regime as an experiment, we would have to say that the experiment has clearly demonstrated the superiority of capitalism and the inferiority of socialism.[9]

In that paragraph, we can see that people who make this type of argument are not always intellectually honest. Look how Mises reasoned: the Soviet standard of living is much lower than the U.S. standard. Therefore, the experiment has demonstrated the inferiority of socialism. But hang on a minute: that's not the case at all. For that to be true, the United States and the Soviet Union would have had to be similarly situated when the "experiment" began. But in 1917, when the Russian Revolution occurred, the United States was *post*industrial, whereas Russia was largely *pre*industrial. It was a nation of peasants, "backward, agrarian, and semi-feudal," not to mention having suffered eight years of war (World War I and the Civil War).[10] The average standard of living was far lower than that in the United States during the Tsar's time as well. In order to make a comparison between the Soviet and the American systems, you wouldn't look at *raw* standard of living measurements, you'd look at growth. When you use the proper measurement, Soviet economic performance doesn't look nearly so dismal. As a UCLA/RAND Corporation study noted in 1988, "Since the Bolshevik Revolution of 1917, the Soviet Union has transformed itself from an underdeveloped economy into a modern industrial state with a GNP second only to that of the United States."[11] (That does not, of course, justify all of the atrocities!)

In fact, we know that greater state intervention in the economy isn't inherently bad. Plenty of countries that exert far greater control over the economy than the United States have become economic powerhouses, such as China, Germany, and Sweden. Norway's economy is robust, despite the state owning a colossal portion of the country's wealth. Denmark collects 46 percent of its GDP in taxes, versus 26 percent in the United States, and Denmark does fine.[12] (They haven't yet "run out of other people's money.") That's not to say that the United States should follow any of these countries' models. But those who talk about the "disaster" that results from government interference in the economy are usually selectively picking cases where socialist governments have done disastrous things and ignoring the numerous instances where they have operated benignly or beneficially.

There is a highly dishonest cherry-picking that goes on in evaluating what "government" does. For example, many people will cite the failures of U.S. public schools, which do not do as good a job as schools in other countries, as an example of how "government" shouldn't manage a task best left to the private sector—Kevin Williamson makes public schools a centerpiece of his anti-socialist argument in *The Politically Incorrect Guide to Socialism*. But think how absurd that is: the other countries we're "losing" to aren't running their schools for profit. If U.S. public schools are an example of socialism's failure, why aren't Chinese and Finnish schools examples of its success? It's the same kind of silly argument that sees Amtrak as an indictment of government, while conveniently ignoring the superior performance of the public Chinese and French high-speed rail systems.

It's also the case that the line between "planned economies" and "free markets" can be quite blurry. It often goes unnoticed that large companies are frequently run internally like centrally planned economies, and large parts of our lives are "planned" by unseen, unelected private-sector bureaucrats. In *People's Republic of Walmart*, Leigh Phillips and Michal Rozworski point out that large companies like Walmart already operate like "socialist economies"—just not in the way they treat their workers—insofar as decisions are made by central planners and there is no internal market within the company. Phillips and Rozworski observe that inside corporate firms, free-market transactions don't exist, and when companies try to introduce them, the results can be disastrous.[13]

The libertarian CEO of Sears, for instance, decided that the company should operate on free-market principles *internally* as well as externally.[14] This meant that the store's various departments would all operate as their own self-interested entities, competing against each other (hardware vs. shoes vs. appliances, etc.). Previously, different units of Sears cooperated with one another—if one department wanted something from another, it would simply request it. Under the new system, it would have to buy it and negotiate a contract. The effect was catastrophic: the departments tried to take advantage of each other and ended up hurting the collective interest of Sears. The appliance department would try to screw over the hardware department and vice versa. Executives from different parts of Sears hid information from each other and spied. The collective good of the enterprise was ill served by internal market competition. Phillips and Rozworski point out that, in some ways, society is like one big Sears: we are all hurting each other and duplicating work instead of recognizing our common interests. Markets, they say, can undermine the collective well-being, which is why companies never operate internally on free-market principles.

Paul Krugman summarizes why the Sears debacle has discomforting implications for those who oppose central planning:

> We may live in a market sea, but that sea is dotted with many islands that we call firms, some of them quite large, within which decisions are made not via markets but via hierarchy—even, you might say, via central planning. Clearly, there are some things you don't want to leave up to the market—the market itself is telling us that, by creating those islands of planning and hierarchy . . . For a free-market true believer the recognition that some things are best not left up to markets should be a disturbing notion. If the limitations of markets in providing certain kinds of shared services are important enough to justify the creation of command-and-control entities with hundreds of thousands or even millions of workers, might there not even be some goods and services (*cough* health care *cough*) best provided by non-market means even at the level of the economy as a whole?[15]

4. SOCIALISTS ELEVATE THE COLLECTIVE AND FORGET THE INDIVIDUAL

> "The disrespect socialist-inclined policy exhibits toward the equal moral agency of individual human beings rests . . . on a crucial factual mistake, namely, seeing people as essentially members of classes or groups, instead of as individuals . . . The great mistake that socialism makes lies not in its assumption that there are groups . . . Socialism's mistake is instead in its attempt to treat people as mere members of groups."
> —James Otteson, *The End of Socialism*

I have to say, I am always a little confused when I hear criticisms like Otteson's. Ben Shapiro says something similar in his "intersectionality" video: that there is a left-wing "hoax" that says "we aren't individuals . . . but are merely members of groups."[16] Perhaps some on the left do forget that all of us are unique, individual people. But I think the left is very pro-individual, since we all subscribe to the Mr. Rogers notion that each person is valuable in and of themselves, and that we are all special (yes, like *snowflakes*).

I've always agreed with Oscar Wilde that "socialism itself will be of value simply because it will lead to Individualism."[17] Wilde was a socialist *because* he wanted to liberate individuals to pursue their own ends, which they are better equipped to do when their basic material needs are taken care of. In "The Soul of Man Under Socialism," Wilde noted that in a society with significant inequality, it was a life of "individual agency" for some and "subsistence toil" for others.

> At present, in consequence of the existence of private property, a great many people are enabled to develop a certain very limited amount of Individualism. They are either under no necessity to work for their living, or are enabled to choose the sphere of activity that is really congenial to them, and gives them pleasure . . . Upon the other hand, there are a great many people who, having no private property of their own, and being always on the brink of sheer starvation, are compelled to do the work of beasts of burden, to do work that is quite uncongenial to them, and to which they are forced by the peremptory, unreasonable, degrading Tyranny of want . . . From their collective force Humanity gains much in material prosperity. [The man who is poor] is merely the infinitesimal atom of a force that, so far from regarding him, crushes him: indeed, prefers him crushed, as in that case he is far more obedient.[18]

Socialists, at least those of us in the libertarian tradition, are critical of economic hierarchy precisely because we care about each individual person. We don't just look at aggregated collective statistics showing that there is "economic growth" or that people as a whole are "better off" than they were a few decades ago. We are interested in looking at the real lives of each person in society to see whether overall prosperity is coming at the expense of particular members. You know who *isn't* interested in people's individuality? The board of Walmart, for whom all employees are fungible units who exist to serve the collective. In a corporation, the "individual" is simply a labor unit to serve the ends of central planners.[19] For socialists, that's a monstrous degradation of individual worth.

It is necessary to *talk* about groups, of course. "Rich people" as a group have particular capacities that people without wealth lack. Black people face problems that white people do not; immigrants have troubles that nonimmigrants don't. This doesn't mean that people are "mere" members of groups. Nobody knows that better than the members of those groups: they don't think of one another as nothing more than a demographic trait, but as multidimensional human beings. It's unclear to me why one can't believe that group characteristics have important implications in society *and* that people are more than the sum of their identity traits.

Otteson has another criticism in this group-versus-individual vein, which is that socialistic policies allow groups to override the agency of individuals.

> The moral objection . . . is that its mandate to override people's de-centralized decisions and choices—even if ostensibly out of respect for those individuals' true, authentic, or proper wishes—cannot take place without authorizing some group of people a scope of agency that is denied to others. Because the paternalistic coercers have no actual knowledge of what individuals want, desire, or value, in prac-tice their policies cannot but reflect their own wants, desires, and values.[20]

Socialists are thought to be "paternalistic coercers" because they assume they know what individuals want. But our whole position is that people should get to participate in decisions that affect their own lives! Libertarian socialists in particular are *highly* suspicious of force-ful coercion, believing it should be used only as a very last resort, and that, generally, decisions should be made through collective delibera-tion rather than administrative fiat. There is always going to be a small element of "paternalistic coercion" when you live in a community—decisions will be made at your workplace that you hate, and you're going to have to live with them. Getting along with others means abid-ing by some rules you wouldn't have chosen yourself. But the less in-equality of wealth and power there is, the more economic and social outcomes will reflect the will of the many rather than the will of the few who are able to impose their preferences.

5. PEOPLE ARE INHERENTLY GREEDY AND/OR LAZY

> "Is there some society you know that doesn't run on greed? You
> think Russia doesn't run on greed?"
> —Milton Friedman, interview with Phil Donahue, 1979

I think people who say things like "humans are naturally selfish" are saying more about themselves than they are about humanity. Most people are a mixture: we're a bit generous and a bit selfish. We'll always help out a friend, up to a point, and usually help out a stranger, also up to a point. Experimental evidence shows that people are not sim-ply "rational maximizers" who want to grab as much for themselves as possible. If you give people money and ask them to decide how much they will share with a stranger, most of them will share at least some of it.[21] We have social and antisocial impulses, but on the whole, we are a cooperative species whose success has come from our ability to work together rather than fight each other to the death.[22]

Some people think socialists have a naive view of human nature, that we think people are naturally good, and that once our horrible economic system is replaced, our inner perfection will be set free. This is not what we think. In fact, it's because we recognize that everyone is a mixture of greed and goodness that we want to make sure greed doesn't triumph. We want to encourage people's best and most community-spirited impulses, and discourage their nastiest and most callous ones. One reason we're suspicious of "competition" is that competitions tend to be won by the most ruthless people, thereby encouraging cut-throat rather than cooperative behavior. If you play a game in which selfishness increases your chances of winning, and notice that every-one seems to be behaving extremely selfishly, this is not proof that people are naturally inclined toward selfishness. If you offered $10,000 to anyone willing to perform a jig in the nude, and then noticed a lot of people performing jigs in the nude, you would not have discovered a natural human tendency toward jigging *au naturel.*

Well-designed institutions don't necessarily make people good, but they can incentivize constructive social behavior. Take the theory of the "Tragedy of the Commons." In a famous 1968 article, Garrett Hardin envisaged a situation in which village herdsmen used an unowned pas-ture for grazing.[23] If everybody uses only the amount of land necessary to keep the land sustainable, there is no problem. But, Hardin said, "as a rational being, each herdsman seeks to maximize his gain," and "each man is locked into a system that compels him to increase his herd with-out limit." This means that each herdsman's cows will gobble up more and more of the pasture, ultimately leading to the destruction of the commons that could have served everyone fairly well.

In fact, as it turns out, that this is not what happens to commonly owned land. Elinor Ostrom's fascinating Nobel Prize–winning work *Governing the Commons* goes beyond theory and empirically outlines the ways in which people actually manage public commons to ensure that they aren't destroyed. People develop social rules and governance structures to make sure that the commons are well managed. Ostrom notes that despite empirical evidence, "unfortunately, many analysts—in academia, special-interest groups, governments, and the press—still presume that common-pool problems are all dilemmas in which the participants themselves cannot avoid producing suboptimal results, and in some cases disastrous results."[24]

Just as greed is falsely presumed, so is laziness. A common, casual assumption is that if you give a basic income to people, they will become indolent and do nothing. In reality, people enjoy doing work *when that work is satisfying.* They don't hate being productive, they hate their *jobs!* Improve working conditions and make work a pleasure rather than a burden, and there's no reason why people won't engage in it. Very few people *want* to do nothing. They want to find meaning and feel accomplished and useful. Rosy views of human nature may be naive, but so are views that presume the natural state of humankind is slothful and selfish.

6. SOCIALISTS ALWAYS DENY THAT SOCIALIST GOVERNMENTS ARE "TRUE SOCIALISM"

When socialists point out, correctly, that there is nothing socialistic about oppressing people, we are often met with the same reply: we live in theory-land, and because our theory is perfect we do not have to take responsibility for its failure in the real world. Usually, the critic will say something like, "Every time a socialist government produces disastrous consequences, socialists say, 'It wasn't really socialism. Real socialism would be flawless!'"

This is a misunderstanding of the point. In fact, when I look at countries like, for example, North Korea, the reason I don't consider them socialist is that ultimately, it's not about whether you use the word, it's about whether you do what the word is supposed to describe. What I care about is maximizing ordinary people's control over their lives. North Korea is not socialistic because it doesn't have any kind of democracy, and the whole point of my politics is to increase democratic control and reduce the degree to which people are tyrannized over by authorities, both public and private. It is not because these countries failed that I don't consider them good demonstrations of my principles; it's because they never cared about those principles to begin with.

This sounds like a sneaky dodge, I know. But it isn't. It's really quite simple: people don't need the illusory freedom of free-market choice (aka, the freedom to die when your medical bill exceeds your paycheck), nor the farcical freedom of an authoritarian police state; they need the ability to meaningfully choose between a lot of different routes to happiness. If this isn't what's happening, then you're not creating a socialist state, you're building an abominable perversion of socialism's ideals.

7. NICE IPHONE, HYPOCRITE

> "Ocasio-Cortez can rant about capitalism from her iPhone while wearing her Sephora lipstick, but she should realize that she's a beneficiary of the capitalism she so despises. It's easy to rip on capitalism's shortcomings while living amidst its benefits."
> —Ben Shapiro, *The Daily Wire*

This is the least persuasive of the criticisms, though it's also one of the most common. It doesn't actually tell us anything about how workplaces ought to operate, what healthcare ought to look like, or whether nuclear arms should be eliminated. It's an attack on people rather than on their ideas. If you want to distract attention away from the question of whether the Black Lives Matter policy agenda is sound and justifiable, or whether child agricultural labor is an outrage, you can just go, "Oh yeah, well look at your fancy lipstick."

Even if we assume that wearing nice lipstick means your social justice beliefs are invalid, we haven't actually come up with an intellectual response to someone who *wasn't* wearing lipstick or receiving the benefits of capitalism. Since, however, we all live in the economy, using the goods and services provided by "capitalism" (actually, mostly by wage workers), there *isn't* anybody who doesn't receive the benefits. This argument would make capitalism immune to criticism, which seems awfully convenient.

I can never understand why using an iPhone means you cannot object to the conditions under which iPhones are produced and sold and advocate for changing them. Under any other system, this objection would be absurd. If a resident of the Soviet Union had gotten a free education in state schools and a job in the state bureaucracy, would they be a hypocrite if they criticized the way these institutions were run or the structure of the Soviet economy? There is a wonderful comic by the left-wing cartoonist Matt Bors, in which a feudal peasant says, "We should improve society somewhat," only to be told, "Yet you participate in society. Curious!"[25]

We can imagine countless other scenarios in which such a criticism is made, and each time it sounds ludicrous. A father rules like a tyrant over his family, and they are terrified of him. Whenever one of them criticizes him, he replies, "How can you stand there in the clothes I bought you and tell me there's something 'fundamentally wrong with the way this family operates'? Without me, you'd have nothing." This is a bad defense even if it's factually true that the family would have nothing without this man. Being better than some other horrible alternative is not license to abuse people. Similarly, the fact that living under Stalin is worse than having to do the Walmart cheer does not justify making people do the Walmart cheer.[26]

Yet this criticism can be formulated in a slightly more sophisticated way than Ben Shapiro types tend to articulate it: those who criticize capitalism while using iPhones are failing to actually understand how wondrous the achievements of capitalism are. They are taking them for granted, which is objectionable not because it makes them hypocrites, but because they are oblivious to the bounties our economic system is yielding. But even in this much stronger version, the criticism doesn't work. I am just as impressed with supermarkets and iPhones and the six different kinds of "poop emoji pool floats" you can get on Amazon as any member of the American Enterprise Institute.[27] Yet I still believe that workplaces should be democratic, hedge fund managers produce nothing of social worth, and wealth is immoral. We are supposed to believe that every aspect of contemporary production must be accepted or rejected as a package, that there's no way to have innovation without exploitation. I see no reason to think we can't keep the good and ditch the bad.

Finally, it's worth discussing the basic question: Are you a hypocrite if you profess socialist values but do not live as an ascetic? I do not think you are—or rather, if you were, then by this standard it would be almost impossible *not* to be a hypocrite.[28] But it's a difficult moral question. Socialism shouldn't require people to give up ordinary comforts because a central point of the idea is that there are plenty of comforts to go around, and there's no reason *anyone* should be deprived of them. Joy and pleasure and indulgence are crucial parts of life; everyone deserves good lipstick and nice clothes. From a purely utilitarian perspective, one should personally redistribute one's goods and never have any more than is strictly necessary for subsistence (if even subsistence can be justified). But socialism can't be purely utilitarian; that gets you dreary worker housing and a diet of gruel, a world in which nobody would want to live.

And yet I also realize that colossal wealth is indefensible, and that I have more than I truly need. To what extent should the value of egalitarianism entail self-sacrifice? What do we owe one another? I think it's fine for Bernie Sanders to own a cute little vacation cottage by a lake, because a hardworking old man should get to have a little cottage he can visit! Yet I think it's a huge waste for Elon Musk to fire a sports car into space,[29] or for Jeff Bezos to build a $42-million, 10,000-year clock in the desert. Am I being inconsistent? I don't think I am, because I do think we can draw lines between reasonable and unreasonable luxury, and that it's possible to have a world in which everyone can have lakeside vacations, but not possible to have a world in which everyone gets to build gigantic, pointless clocks. "Live as you think everyone should reasonably be able to live if we distribute resources equitably" is the principle I try to follow, but admittedly I haven't done the calculations to determine whether I'm exceeding my share.

Once again, though, we're drifting away from the actual issues. The real question is whether the principles of socialism—that human beings should care about one another and share their resources in a way that ensures nobody is deprived—make sense. I say they do, others say they don't. But most of the arguments they make are cruel, silly, and/or beside the point. They distract us from the serious questions: What kind of world should we live in? What is the difference between that kind of world and the world we live in now? How do we get from one to the other?

8. FINAL ARGUMENT: SOCIALISTS ARE BORING

Perhaps the most offensive charge of all against the socialist left is that we're humorless. It is said that we cannot take a joke and are no fun at a party. The alt-right used to claim that the "transgressive" humor of its Holocaust jokes and frog cartoons was a reaction to a left that had become prissy and moralizing. You hear it from all the "anti-PC" comedians—you can't say *anything* these days without being denounced.

If the left has no sense of humor, that would indeed not speak well of us. The world is an extremely funny place. Animals are funny. The presidency is funny. The existence of Elon Musk is funny. Fortunately, you can quite easily combine humor and left politics. See, for example, *The Onion*, which runs left-leaning satirical headlines from the absurd ("Pope Francis Reverses Position on Capitalism After Seeing Wide Variety of American Oreos") to the extremely dark ("ICE Agent Decides He Wants Kids After Seeing Incredible Love and Devotion of Parents Begging Him Not to Take Their Child"). Frankly, the most entertaining people I know are scathing socialists who enjoy noting the absurdities of a country where you can buy a $100 gold-coated donut but there is a national debate about whether we can "afford" a basic social democratic welfare state.[30]

But it's true that when you start every day thinking about the horrors of human and animal suffering, you risk becoming a bit of a *downer*. And if you realize that your free time is zero sum, that every second you spend baking lemon squares or goofing off at modern art museums is time you aren't spending working toward the defeat of global capitalism . . . well, you can even accidentally develop a principled belief that fun is bad. Nobody wants to spend time around someone who believes it's literally immoral to enjoy yourself or hectors people on their poor use of time.

Socialism needs to be fun, or what's the point? The left isn't about reducing people to undifferentiated, monk-like drones. That's what happens in Amazon warehouses, not in colorful, leftist utopias. We need a "luxury leftism" that doesn't bring everyone down to the same poor level, but raises them all up equally to the same heights.

The socialist project is not just to create better living standards, but to create collective joy. It is a response to the loneliness, alienation, and deep sadness that occurs when everything is commodified and people are left on their own, without communal ties or collective support, to satisfy themselves through the purchase of consumer goods. Part of why the Democratic Socialists of America has grown so popular is that DSA meetings are places to be with others and come together to work on an exciting project. This is what made the Occupy encampments such special places; they filled, temporarily, people's deep need to be part of a community rather than a marketplace.

If you want a vision of the bleak, bland capitalist future, go to Hudson Yards in New York City, the new, billion-dollar complex of gleaming skyscrapers.[31] It's a lifeless shopping mall for luxury goods, intensely policed and surveilled, where every aspect of life is curated by a corporation. Justin Davidson of *New York* magazine writes of visiting this boring "billionaires' fantasy city":

> Everything is too clean, too flat, too art-directed. This para-Manhattan, raised on a platform and tethered to the real thing by one subway line, has no history, no holdover greasy spoons, no pockets of blight or resident eccentrics—no memories at all.[32]

And this is what you get if you're *lucky*. This is the city for the winners. The losers will be in homeless encampments outside the city gates.

The left's city of the future looks very different. It is a *Star Trek* world, where we can travel through space together and meet aliens. It is public libraries and free colleges, where all can come and learn without worrying about money. It is Mardi Gras in New Orleans, where everyone expresses their individuality through art and costume without any regard for profit or commerce.[33] It is camping trips and cookouts, book clubs and street cafés. It is the theory that life is meant to be enjoyed, and that nobody should lack the basic ingredients for a decent existence. It is, above all, the conviction that we're here to help each other through this thing, whatever it is.

> "In our narrow, confined existence, we tend to forget the essence of life . . . All of us, whatever our occupation or class, are equally guilty: the employer is lost in the running of his business; the workers, sunk in the abyss of their misery, raise their heads only to cry in protest; we, the politicians, are lost in daily battles and corridor intrigues. All of us forget that before everything else, we are men, ephemeral beings lost in the immense universe, so full of terrors. We are inclined to neglect the search for the real meaning of life, to ignore the real goals—serenity of the spirit and sublimity of the heart . . . To reach them—that is the revolution."
> —Jean Jaurès, speech on Tolstoy, 1911

*   *   *

"We need to come together and call out democratic socialism for what it is: a scam being perpetrated on the American people by a few who prey upon the blitheful ignorance of many in the hope it will net them political power. It must be vociferously denounced with an equally fierce defense of our shared American values."
—Giancarlo Sopo, *The Federalist*

The word *socialism* still gives a lot of people the jitters. This is understandable, given what they have been told about socialism and socialists. But I hope I've managed to show you, *at the very least*, that democratic socialists are neither stupid nor malicious. They operate on the basis of humane principles, and they are not proposing insane, economically illiterate ideas. The socialist instinct is a legitimate and rational one, and it constitutes the only set of ideas which gives plausible explanations for the problems of our times and also provides prescriptions.

To be a socialist is to depart significantly from political orthodoxy. It requires a certain amount of faith, because at its core it involves thinking that a better world is possible. But there is nothing about being a utopian that prohibits one from being a pragmatist, and the sensible socialist pursues realistic, short-term improvements in the service of an ambitious, long-term dream.

If you're not a socialist before you're 30, you have no heart. If you're not a conservative after 30, you have no brain.

As I write this, I have just turned 30, and am therefore officially brainless. With each passing year, I have only become more convinced that the critics are wrong and Sanders and Ocasio-Cortez are right. Perhaps this is my foolish, bleeding heart, and in a year my brain will finally wake up and realize what a naive nincompoop it has been. But for now, this slogan still looks like something cruel people made up to rationalize their heartlessness.

Conclusion

Reflections on Hope, Justice, and Solidarity

"Boundless compassion for all living beings is the surest and most certain guarantee of pure moral conduct, and needs no casuistry. Whoever is filled with it will assuredly injure no one, do harm to no one, encroach on no man's rights; he will rather have regard for every one, forgive every one, help every one as far as he can, and all his actions will bear the stamp of justice and loving-kindness . . . In former times the English plays used to finish with a petition for the King. The old Indian dramas close with these words: 'May all living beings be delivered from pain.' Tastes differ; but in my opinion there is no more beautiful prayer than this."

—Arthur Schopenhauer, *The Basis of Morality*

"The final conclusion of the absurdist protest is, in fact, the rejection of suicide and persistence in that hopeless encounter between human questioning and the silence of the universe."

—Albert Camus, *The Rebel*

IN THE BEGINNING THERE WAS . . .

Well, I don't know what there was. But then there was a tremendous explosion. Then, for a few hundred million years, there was nothing much of interest. After that, stars and galaxies began to form, and they were fascinating and beautiful, but nobody was there to notice. Billions and billions of years went by, until a molecular cloud happened to collapse, inadvertently giving us the sun, moons, asteroids, etcetera. Our humble planet Earth formed by accident, and for billions more years it was wet and gassy, with little to recommend it save some bacteria here and there.

Plants emerged, then all of a sudden there were animals—weird ones—and they lived and died and evolved steadily into dinosaurs, who met an unfortunate fate. Very recently, we showed up, looking something of a mess. Our ancestors struggled to stay alive—they fashioned tools, built little dwellings, and made do. And then they died, and the next batch did the same, learning to farm and build. (They also were often killed or enslaved, or did the killing and enslaving.) Slowly something quite impressive emerged.

They built civilizations, discovered math, gave birth to Socrates, and then murdered Socrates for asking too many questions. They fumbled along and tried to figure things out, and they mostly failed. But they learned how to fill their bellies and minds, and they discovered their incredible potential, building printing presses, cotton gins, hundred-story buildings, and gigantic ships that sometimes sank. Together, based on what those before them had learned, they invented steam trains and then pickup trucks, jet airplanes, television game shows, internet pornography, and six different kinds of poop emoji pool floats.

And over this time, people fell in love, and were torn apart; worked their asses off; watched their children grow up to screw up or do well; went on adventures; stepped on Legos; built too many cars and clogged the roads but refused to carpool so they got stuck in traffic, and it served them right; did monstrously cruel things; tamed a lot of diseases; ate a lot of tacos; petted a lot of animals; treated the planet in highly irresponsible and ungrateful ways; and just generally acted out a stunningly violent, heartwarming, infuriating, inspiring collective drama on an inconceivable scale.

And what we socialists refuse to believe is that all of this was just the buildup to Donald Trump being given the power to end all human life, neoliberal capitalism devouring the Earth, Elon Musk buying all of outer space, and everyone eventually ending up working as a drone in an Amazon warehouse until the planet boils or the sun explodes.

That cannot possibly be the end of history, we say. Surely not. No. That isn't how this story goes. That would be a tale told by an idiot, signifying fuck-all. I would want my money back. Zero stars. Liked the plot, but that ending was garbage.

Yet this is the direction a lot of people believe we're heading in, and they're not wrong. I mean some of these things have already happened: The United States gave the world's most selfish and ignorant man control of its 4,018 nuclear weapons. He's joked about making himself president for life.[1] Monopolistic corporations are steadily wrapping their tentacles around every part of the economy. There should be hardly any doubt that the United States is one major terrorist event away from a frightening concentration of power in the hands of a single, unstable person, if you're not already frightened by the whole nuclear weapons thing.

This makes a lot of people I know feel hopeless and uncertain. They see people with no qualifications except wealth being put in charge, and they see Jeff Bezos building his giant clock in the desert while his workers pee in bottles because they can't take bathroom breaks.[2] They think that their fate is in the hands of grotesque individuals who could not care less about anyone but themselves, and many ask themselves the question that Navy veteran Seth King asked himself when he found himself in the "revolving door of bodies" known as an Amazon fulfillment warehouse: "If this is the best life is going to get why am I even still here?"[3] In the United States alone, every year 47,000 people take their own lives because they cannot find a satisfactory answer to that question.

From one perspective, it's strange that that should be the case, because we've come so far and done so much as a species. As Orwell put it, the Earth is a boat sailing through space, fully stocked with enough supplies for everyone. And yet, history is a record of brutality on an unthinkable scale, with violent competition among groups trying to secure as many of those supplies for themselves as possible. Chattel slavery was only ended recently, and the century that brought us Motown records and the Golden Gate Bridge was, for hundreds of millions of people, also a machine of death creating piles of corpses. For a few decades, it's been comparatively peaceful, but only because the world's great powers keep civilization-ending missiles pointed at each other, and one false move could destroy everything. Oh, and let's not even talk about climate catastrophe. (Living in New Orleans, I cannot bear to contemplate it.)

How can anyone have hope when Trump is the president? How can anyone have dreams about a *Star Trek* future, in which we all go on adventures through space together in a spirit of equality and shared purpose? The resurgence of nationalism spells absolute doom; nationalism is one of the silliest and most destructive ideas imaginable.[4] Silly because nobody, looking at human beings in the context of the universe, can think national distinctions are worth worrying about. (Even Ronald Reagan admitted that existing global conflicts would seem trivial if aliens showed up.[5]) "Most destructive" because nationalism operates like a purpose-built empathy inhibitor, making other humans seem less and less like ourselves and thus making it easy to distrust, detest, or destroy them. Nationalism makes it possible to put on a uniform, strut around, and denounce the enemies who will destroy our culture and way of life, without realizing how ridiculous you look to the universe.

Perhaps you're an optimist, like Steven Pinker, who thinks everything is getting better and people just don't know it. Well, you know who doesn't think that? Bezos, who has admitted that one reason he wants to invest in space travel is because it will be necessary to flee the Earth.[6] Many of the richest people in the world are scared to death of the near future. They think everything is going to collapse and are worried that when that happens, the people who work for them will turn on them, realizing that without an economy, capitalists have no function at all.[7] Our speculative fiction has turned dystopian, and even the *Star Trek* franchise seems to have given up on the possibility of a just and livable tomorrow.

And yet, with so much human good will, creativity, and potential, it is ridiculous to conclude that there is no way to avoid a dystopia. Not that I'm an optimist. An optimist thinks things will go well; I have absolutely no idea how things will go and don't care to try to predict the future. And I dislike the word *hope*, which feels cheap and empty. But I'm with Albert Camus: the right reaction to an absurd society is to revolt against it, even if it feels fruitless. That's not hope, exactly. More like obstinacy, an unwillingness to reconcile yourself to the obvious.

Otherwise, what would this great cosmic journey have been for? Is it all leading up to self-immolation and the triumph of greed? History cannot be over; nobody should be willing to let it end like that.

The democratic socialist creed is the belief not only that things ought to be better, but that they *must* be better, and we will do what we can to make them so. There are internal debates on what that better world would look like, but socialists have in common a fierce outrage at injustice and a belief that everyone should share alike in the Earth's prosperity.

This philosophy is not necessarily optimistic, in that it doesn't predict its own success. But it involves an absolute determination not to let exploitation and injustice continue. When I think of the socialist attitude, I think of Sisyphus in Camus' *The Myth of Sisyphus*, doomed to roll a boulder up a mountain for all eternity, but hell-bent on putting his all into the task, and even doing it joyfully. Regardless of whether we stand a chance at succeeding, we are committed to doing our damnedest to revolt against intolerable conditions.

To my friends who feel hopeless, I would point out the extraordinary progress that has already been made, and the wonderful historical leftists whose torch we carry. In every generation, there have been those with sharpened moral vision who refused to satisfy themselves with the status quo excuses. Hindsight has looked favorably on these people, whether they were abolitionists, suffragists, or civil rights crusaders. Those who fought against slavery, child labor, and unsafe workplaces helped build the safer, freer world we are fortunate to inhabit today. They often faced far greater obstacles than we do now—just read about the history of labor violence, the deadly force employed against striking workers, or the beating and killing of anti-segregation activists in the South.[8]

There are people with us today who are just as brave. Looking up at the Confederate flag in front of the state capitol building in 2015, South Carolina activist Bree Newsome did not wait for change to show up on its own. Strapping on a harness, she ascended the flagpole illegally and tore the flag down with her own two hands. Soon after, the state officially got rid of it. Newsome's view of political change is instructive. Reflecting on her activism and that of others, she has said that while the past doesn't necessarily give cause for being optimistic, it does show that the impossible can sometimes be achieved.

> I'm more of a realist than an optimist. I have hope when I look at the past of this country: There was a time when the idea of an America without chattel slavery seemed impossible. The only reason that we're not in that condition now is because of the belief and the work of abolitionists and people who were alive then. With that kind of assessment, I'm able to have hope. It's possible that things can get better if we do what is necessary to ensure that, but it's not just something that happens with the natural progression of time. Without taking action and being proactive, things will actually get worse than they are now.[9]

We could all stand to follow Newsome's example.

* * *

PARADOXICALLY, EVEN THOUGH conservatives appear to have more political power than at any other time in recent memory, it is also a moment ripe with opportunity for progressives. Even though the Republican Party holds substantial power at the federal and state levels, internal division—combined with the unpopularity of the Republican agenda— has left the party unable to pass major legislation, and its long-anticipated Obamacare repeal collapsed and failed. Trump, while he has formidable powers over the military and the regulatory state, has floundered in his attempts to organize an effective White House, and the infighting of his chaotic and leak-prone administration has reached comical heights.

The American public is, by and large, sympathetic to core progressive goals. A significant majority of people think the distribution of wealth in the country is unfair, with too much going to those at the top. Sixty percent say that it's the government's responsibility to provide healthcare for people, while only 37 percent say it isn't, and there is growing support for a single-payer system.[10] People generally oppose Republican attempts to cut social welfare benefits, are skeptical of U.S. military action abroad, and believe corporations have too much influence. Large majorities support tuition-free college and raising the minimum wage. The most popular politician in America, by a significant amount, is Bernie Sanders,[11] the only political figure in the country to have a majority favorable rating.

To illustrate what I mean when I say that socialists are addressing problems that other political ideologies are incapable of dealing with, I just want to relate two anecdotes from my own observations in the past two days. First, at a coffee shop I sometimes go to, all of the staff recently walked out in the middle of a shift and refused to return to work. Why? Because the owners of the shop fired the store's beloved manager, who had worked there for years and had been promised that someday she would receive a share of the business. The staff were disgusted by the way they and their manager had been treated—alleging that the owners had been verbally and emotionally abusive to them. But here's the thing: they don't actually have any real recourse. The United States' economy is based on at-will employment, and owners can do as they please. If you don't have strong employment protections, if you don't have a union, your boss can do whatever they like and you're stuck. The American right is fine with this: They have nothing to say to people who are mistreated at their jobs, except, "If you don't like it, quit," which leaves anyone who actually needs their job completely stuck. Socialists, on the other hand, want workplace democracy. They want workers to have a say in what goes on at their companies and not be subject to the capricious whims of owners.

Here is the second anecdote: A friend of mine has been caught in all of the prevailing economic and political trends at once. She is pregnant and has just been laid off from her job. She was laid off because the school district she worked for is facing budget cuts because, well, they have to increase spending on school security because everyone is afraid of mass shootings. Now, my friend is stuck: she has to try to get another job and health insurance before having her baby, but knows it's going to be very hard to get a job while she's pregnant. She also knows that if she gets a job, she'll be lucky if she gets even a single month of maternity leave to spend with her newborn child.

Democratic socialists actually have answers for my friend. They're going to make sure schools are fully funded and don't cut important staff positions. They're going to make sure that new moms get to spend time with their babies. They're going to make sure that nobody has to worry about not being able to pay to go to the hospital just because they lost their job. The right's response to her dilemma is downright pitiful: They tell us how wonderful free-market capitalism is, and how we should all be grateful for its bounties. Or they say that paid leave is the first step on the road to the gulag. But they can't actually solve the problems facing my friend or the local baristas.

* * *

IN AUGUST 2018, 30-year-old Antoine Dangerfield was working as a welder at a UPS hub in Indianapolis, when one day he observed something small but remarkable.[12] A group of Hispanic coworkers, tired of being ordered around by a racist supervisor, decided to put down their tools and go home. About 100 fed-up workers all decided, with no outside coordination, to band together in solidarity against their employer. Dangerfield, in awe at their guts, recorded the moment on video, showing the workers slowly filing out. Dangerfield narrated in amazement:

> They are not bullshitting! They thought they was gonna play with these amigos, and they said, "Aw yeah, we rise together, homie." And they leaving! And they not bullshitting! Ain't no grinding, cutting, welding—this motherfucker dead-ass quiet. The Mexicans shut this motherfucker down.[13]

The video swiftly went viral, even though all it depicted was some men leaving a warehouse, along with a few shots of the empty workplace. But as labor journalist Micah Uetricht subsequently put it, it offered "a raw, unfiltered view of the human drama of workers fighting their bosses on the shop floor."[14] The video shows hardworking people who have decided not to take it anymore and asserted their dignity against the corporation that tells them what to do.

Dangerfield was fired for making and posting the video, naturally. But in an interview with *Jacobin*, he voiced pride, suggesting that the actions of the Hispanic UPS laborers could plant the seeds of revolt and show people what can be done.

> It was life-changing to me to see that happen. Because it was like, dang, they really came together. And that's why I'm not mad about the video, about getting fired. Because it's five million people who saw that. And it might change their view on things. Empowering people. So me losing a job is nothing compared to the big picture. If we can get it in our heads that we are the people, and if we make our numbers count, we can change anything.[15]

This was one moment, and a very small one. But Dangerfield is right. The political establishment is vulnerable. And if we make our numbers count, we can change anything. So here, in deepest sincerity, is a personal plea: come and join the left. We're more fun, we've got better plans, we'll make people's lives better, and we're not scary. There's no reason to find us dangerous or terrifying. Just stop worrying. Socialism will win, and it'll all be okay.

A Left Media Diet

I am wary of telling people what to think. I mean, in a way I've spent this entire book telling you what to think, but I am suspicious of pure propaganda that discourages independent thought. My position is that arguments should be examined carefully, that you should scrutinize every word, and that if someone cites a study you should go and look at the study to see if they're representing it accurately. I've targeted this book at "skeptics" because I think we should all be skeptics. Nobody should accept socialism just because it's cool these days (although it is). You should accept it because the socialist worldview is morally and rationally compelling.

Sometimes people ask me for a "reading list" of left ideas. And I'm hesitant to prescribe one, because it feels too much like giving them a list of the "correct things to think." Beware those who hand you a book, or a stack of books, and tell you they contain the Answers. I think you should read as many things by people whose political beliefs you disagree with as things by people whom you agree with. So I regularly read the conservative *National Review*, the op-ed page of the *Wall Street Journal*, and books by people like Ben Shapiro and Ann Coulter.

This is not because I enjoy them, and I'm not saying you yourself have to endure this kind of punishment. But examining how the other side thinks has helped me sharpen my arguments and understand what my political values actually are. I have learned as much about leftism from reading *Breitbart* as from reading Peter Kropotkin, because analyzing *Breitbart* has helped me realize precisely what I detest so much about right-wing politics and put my objections into words. The *Wall Street Journal* is worth reading because it's a borderline Marxist newspaper, in that it accepts the existence of a class struggle, but thinks the capitalists ought to win it.[1] The *New York Times* thinks ideas and culture rule the world, while the *Wall Street Journal* realizes that money rules the world. (You'll often find better coverage of labor issues in the *Wall Street Journal* than in the *New York Times*, for instance, because the bosses want to be kept apprised of what's going on with the angry masses.)

I do not, however, want to give you a list of horrible right-wing authors to read. So I'll just give you a general encouragement to seek out and understand the enemy. Not in order to compromise, but to be able to effectively respond. (Be careful. Some are better sophists than you might think, and you need to resist letting their terrible opinions eat your brain and convert you.[2]) Even if you are a committed socialist, you will be smarter if you read widely and have a better command of the right's talking points than they do.

That said, today there is an extraordinarily rich landscape of left media. From books and periodicals to podcasts and videos, sharp leftists are producing all kinds of engaging content, with a new level of professionalism and enthusiasm. It's *exciting*; all over the internet, you will find thoughtful commentary by socialists and progressives, people who are bringing devastating weaponry to the "battle of ideas." There is so much now that any catalog I could provide would be hopelessly incomplete, but if you're curious about left politics after reading this book, I'd like to give you a few possibilities for new material to read and listen to.

For left reporting and commentary, in addition to my own little magazine and *Jacobin*, it's worth regularly listening to *Democracy Now!* and reading *The Intercept, The Baffler, Dissent, CounterPunch, ZNet,* and *The Nation*. The *New Left Review, Catalyst,* and *Monthly Review* offer more scholarly work. For coverage of labor issues, *Labor Notes* and *In These Times* are strong. For economic analysis see *Naked Capitalism* and *Dollars and Sense,* plus the commentary of Richard Wolff and Michael Roberts. For the Middle East and U.S. foreign policy, see *Electronic Intifada, TomDispatch, Foreign Policy In Focus,* and *Mondoweiss.* For coverage of UK politics, check out *Novara Media* and *Tribune.* For Africa, see *Africa Is a Country.* For environmental and climate news, see *Grist, The Trouble,* and *Mongabay.* Libcom.org and Marxists.org host a lot of archival primary sources from left thinkers. The research papers being put out by the People's Policy Project offer practical examples of what left governance might look like.

There are many individual left writers and academics whose work is worth following. Some of my own favorites are: Carl Beijer, Yasmin Nair, Sarah Jaffe, Liza Featherstone, Elizabeth Bruenig, Kim Kelly, Allie Conti, Marshall Steinbaum, Seth Ackerman, Meagan Day, Asad Haider, Amber A'Lee Frost, Freddie deBoer, Matt Taibbi, Alex Press, Cedric Johnson, Maximilian Alvarez, Vijay Prashad, Ryan Cooper, Mehdi Hasan, Vivek Chibber, Ben Burgis, Molly Crabapple, Adam Gaffney, Sarah Jones, Kyle Kulinski, Eve Ewing, Libby Watson, Eric Levitz, Jeff Stein, Mike Konczal, Rebecca Nagle, Michael Parenti, Dean Baker, Ben Studebaker, Michelle Alexander, Jamelle Bouie, Branko Marcetic, Osita Nwanevu, and Abi Wilkinson.

The number of quality leftist podcasts and radio shows is impressive. It's also frustrating, because it means there is no way to listen to everything. But you're almost certain to find something that suits you! *Chapo Trap House* has built a substantial following for its acerbic and witty left commentary, but they're just the start. *Season of the Bitch* offers a socialist feminist perspective. *Citations Needed* does penetrating media criticism. The podcasts *What a Hell of a Way to Die, Eyes Left, Lions Led by Donkeys,* and *Radio War Nerd* offer foreign policy analysis, with many of the hosts being military veterans themselves. Excellent interviews with leftist intellectuals and activists can be heard on *Behind the News, The Dig, The Katie Halper Show,* and *Dead Pundits Society. Working People* offers raw and powerful interviews with ordinary workers. *The Intercept*'s podcasts *Intercepted* and *Deconstructed* are of consistently high quality. *Srsly Wrong* offers a hilarious utopian anarchist perspective. Other important left podcasts include: *Delete Your Account, Struggle Session, Michael & Us, Left Anchor, The Bruenigs, Street Fight Radio, Millennials Are Killing Capitalism, Revolutionary Left Radio, Pod Damn America, Trillbilly Workers Party, District Sentinel Radio, This Is Hell!,* and *The Zero Hour.*

For a long time, YouTube was dominated by the right. This is beginning to change, thanks to a wave of brilliant new creators offering well-produced and insightful video commentary. Natalie "ContraPoints" Wynn is the most famous, but there are lots more excellent lefty YouTube channels. These include:

- PhilosophyTube
- Hbomberguy
- Shaun
- Peter Coffin
- Innuendo Studios
- MeansTV
- The Michael Brooks Show
- The David Pakman Show
- The Majority Report

Here, and on other channels, you can find comprehensive and persuasive responses to right-wing talking points, and useful explanations of left political philosophy.[3]

There are a number of excellent leftist book publishers whose catalogs are worth investigating, the foremost being Verso, OR Books, Zero Books, Haymarket Books, and AK Press. In the endnotes to *Why You Should Be a Socialist*, you'll find many book recommendations on particular topics. But here are a few more for good measure. The book I give people most often is Noam Chomsky's *Understanding Power,* the most accessible introduction to his work and (in my opinion) to left ideas generally. For a basic introduction to economics from a left perspective, I would use Yanis Varoufakis' *Foundations of Economics,*

Ha-Joon Chang's *Economics: The User's Guide*, and Samuel Bowles et al.'s *Understanding Capitalism*. Rob Larson's *Capitalism vs. Freedom* does an excellent job explaining why leftists don't share the libertarian idea of freedom, and Murray Bookchin's works *The Ecology of Freedom* and *Remaking Society* expound an illuminating "social ecology" perspective on how we should think about politics.

For a good primer on the politics of climate change and its implications for capitalism, use Naomi Klein's *This Changes Everything*. Klein's *Shock Doctrine* shows the terrifying ways in which unpopular economic policies are foisted on an unwilling populace. For an explanation of how Wall Street works, look at Doug Henwood's unbeatable *Wall Street: How It Works and for Whom*. For an accessible introduction to Marxism, try Terry Eagleton's *Why Marx Was Right*. For a left perspective on why Marx was wrong, try Alan Carter's *Marx: A Radical Critique*. For more on labor strategy, try Alexandra Bradbury et al.'s *Secrets of a Successful Organizer* and Jane McAlevey's *No Shortcuts*. For a through explanation of anarchism and how it works, see Iain McKay's *Anarchist FAQ*, Colin Ward's *Anarchy in Action*, and Peter Gelderloos' *Anarchy Works*. For an understanding of the role of the state in developing economies, see Ha-Joon Chang's *Bad Samaritans*. Julia Serano's *Whipping Girl* explains transgender politics very well—Serano is also a PhD biologist, destroying the idea that transgender people are simply mistaken about biology. Mark Blyth's *Austerity* lucidly explains why neoliberal economic policy is such a disaster for ordinary people. Keeanga-Yamahtta Taylor's *From #BlackLivesMatter to Black Liberation* offers a solid introduction to the racial justice dimension of left politics, while Sherry J. Wolf's *Sexuality and Socialism: History, Politics, and Theory of LGBT Liberation* applies a socialist lens to gender and sexuality. The memoirs of Jessica Mitford, Vera Brittain, and Victor Serge will inspire you to want to live a life of defiant adherence to principle.

The essays of Alexander Cockburn, Barbara Ehrenreich, and Gore Vidal show how left ideas can be expressed with style and verve, free of dogma. Adolph Reed Jr.'s *Class Notes* shows, by examining particular political events of the 1990s, the difference between authentic politics and "cargo cult" politics. Studs Terkel's oral history books, particularly

Working and *Hard Times*, offer engrossing first-person accounts of ordinary people's struggle and toil. People know that Howard Zinn's *People's History of the United States* offers a left take on American history, but the accompanying volume, *Voices of a People's History*, edited by Anthony Arnove, offers a great deal more primary source material so you can hear history's protagonists in their own voices. Old, largely forgotten socialist books like Robert Blatchford's *Merrie England* or John Strachey's *Theory and Practice of Socialism*, still offer useful insight, while books like *News from Nowhere* and *The Conquest of Bread* give delightful visions of possible alternate societies.[4]

Finally, if I had to take ten left classics with me to a desert island, here are the ones I would bring:

Ursula K. Le Guin—*The Dispossessed*
Martin Luther King Jr.—*A Testament of Hope*
George Orwell—*Homage to Catalonia*
Simone de Beauvoir—*The Second Sex*
James Baldwin—*Collected Essays*
Angela Davis—*An Autobiography*
Peter Kropotkin—*Memoirs of a Revolutionist*
Emma Goldman—*Living My Life*
Ignazio Silone—*Bread and Wine*
Marge Piercy—*Woman on the Edge of Time*

We all cobble together our politics from eclectic sources. Someone could become a leftist from reading the Bible or watching reality television.[5] But there are so many thoughtful, empathetic, principled people on our side who are committed to explaining our ideas clearly and carefully. You won't hear them on the news. For all the right's talk about how conservative ideas are persecuted and silenced, it's the smart lefties who are mostly absent from the discourse.[6] I have only been able to cite a small fraction of them here. But I hope you'll be curious enough to investigate the writings and speeches of our comrades, and that you'll realize how deep and intelligent much of the contemporary left is.

ACKNOWLEDGMENTS

Without the staff and subscribers of *Current Affairs*, there would be no magazine and therefore no book. A socialist knows better than anyone else that all accomplishment is a collective effort. I am so grateful to you all for building an extraordinary project that has beyond anything I could have dreamed. This magazine has been in every way a team effort and I am fortunate to have found the most incredible team of colleagues and friends imaginable. Our readers send us such encouraging notes, and are generous enough to give us their hard-earned money, and I am so proud of our kind, supportive subscriber community. This includes donors, magazine readers, Patreon supporters, and the members of Facebook's "Current Affairs Aviary."

I would also like to thank the writers of *Current Affairs* whose talent and effort have given our magazine its reputation for high-quality prose, including contributors like Rob Larson, Malaika Jabali, Maximilian Alvarez, Sam Miller McDonald, Elle Hardy, Jaya Sundaresh, Luke Savage, Garrison Lovely, Amber A'Lee Frost, Benjamin Studebaker, and Emily Bartlett Hines. Then there are the artists who have graced our pages with brilliant illustrations and made the magazine sparkle. We have had so many dazzling pieces that have taken thousands of hours of work, but I'd especially like to thank regular contributors Christopher M. Duffy, Chelsea Saunders, Christopher Matthews, Tiffany Pai, Ellen Burch, Mike Freiheit, Matt Lubchansky, Ben "Skutch" McGehee, Nick Sirotich, Susannah Lohr, Tyler Rubenfeld, Jesse Rubenfeld, Mort Todd, Lizzy Price, Naomi Ushiyama, Hokyoung Kim, Katherine Lam, and Ben Clarkson. Libby Horacek and Cassie Moy at Position Development have done a great job keeping the *Current Affairs* website online. Jon White has produced beautiful design work for us. Pete Davis and Aisling McCrea have built a phenomenal *Current Affairs* podcasting operation to accompany our print edition. Lyta Gold has been essential to keeping the magazine production occurring smoothly, and to maintaining optimal levels of amusingness. Eli Massey has been an incredibly hardworking and loyal copy-editor and business manager who has made the last six months in the office a joy. Addison Kane has done diligent transcription work. Cate Root has worked administrative wonders in addition to making the best scones in the South. Vanessa A. Bee has given us a dynamic and hilarious social media presence. Nick Slater has been writing the most delightful newsletter any magazine could hope to have. Yasmin Nair had faith in us from the beginning and has never wavered.

In this book, I have relied on hundreds of works of journalism and scholarship from other authors. I have credited these in endnotes, and recommend that all readers check out the original sources, but the endnotes are insufficient to show just how indebted I am to the writers who produced the material I relied on. I would like to single out some whose work was especially useful, and whose original material I was heavily dependent on: Micah Uetricht, Rachel Sherman, Chrystia Freeland, Jeremy Lent, Jason Hickel, and Malcolm Harris.

I have been lucky enough to have four of my intellectual heroes treat me with great personal warmth and generosity. Thanks to Noam Chomsky, Adolph Reed Jr., Norman G. Finkelstein, and Glenn Greenwald. Their writings have made me a smarter and more empathetic person and their support has been incredibly meaningful.

My friends have, kept me sane during insane times. Oren Nimni and Sparky Abraham have been stalwart comrades as always. Brianna

Rennix is the most decent person I know, and a treasured collaborator and co-conspirator. Paul Waters-Smith is the man who made me a leftist, and I will love him always. Other friends who have been there for me include Amber Phelps, Sarah Hailey, Jessica Elliott, Lauren Lueder, and Amanda Miller. Then there are my great mostly-online friends like CJ Owens, Katie Halper, Doug Henwood, Albert Kim, Drew Hilliard, Erik Crouch, Chao Huang, Josh White, Johann Hari, Jeff Sorensen, Ted Thomas, Dana Jo Abraham Monk, Gabriel Kokoszka, Alik Myroniv, Angela López-c, and Justine Medina. I would also like to thank Theresa Sinnetta and promise her that I will never, ever forget the memory of Robert Pruett.

My agent, Mark Gottlieb, was impressively efficient and helpful. Adam Bellow took a chance on me that I'll always be grateful to him for. Kevin Reilly and Alan Bradshaw at St. Martin's have been very patient with me as I have blown deadline after deadline. Amana Fontanella-Khan at *The Guardian* has been the best editor a political columnist could hope for.

Family are everything. My dear sweet grandmother Audrey Matthews has seen less of me than she deserved because I have been consumed with *Current Affairs*, and has never loved me any less even though she disagrees with nearly every word I write. Lastly and most importantly, Peter and Rosemary Robinson are the best and most supportive parents one could ever hope for. I love you both so much.

NOTES

INTRODUCTION

1. Jeremy Berke, "Clinton Staffers Toyed with Using 'Because It's Her Turn' as a Campaign Rallying Cry," *Business Insider,* April 22, 2017, https://www.businessinsider.my/hillary-clinton-slogan-why-run-because-her-turn-2017-4/.
2. Nick Gass, "Clinton Ekes Out Win in Iowa Against Sanders," *Politico,* February 1, 2016, https://www.politico.com/story/2016/02/iowa-caucus-2016-donald-trump-bernie-sanders-218547.
3. Sydney Ember, "Bernie Sanders: Lion of the Left, but Not the Only One Roaring," *New York Times*, November 23, 2018, https://www.nytimes.com/2018/11/23/us/politics/bernie-sanders-president-2020.html.
4. Brandon Weber, "Eugene Debs Got 1 Million Votes for President—As Convict Number 9653," *The Progressive*, November 2, 2016, https://progressive.org/dispatches/eugene-debs-got-1-million-votes-president-as-convict-number-9653-Weber-161102/.
5. Paul Buhle and Mari Jo Buhle, "The Face of American Socialism Before Bernie Sanders? Eugene Debs," *The Guardian*, March 23, 2019, https://www.theguardian.com/commentisfree/2019/mar/23/american-socialism-bernie-sanders-eugene-debs.
6. Libby Nelson, "Bernie Sanders Has an 11-Point Advantage Over Hillary Clinton Among Voters Under 35," *Vox,* January 11, 2016, https://www.vox.com/2016/1/11/10750326/clinton-sanders-poll.

7. Charlotte Alter, "'Change Is Closer Than We Think.' Inside Alexandria Ocasio-Cortez's Unlikely Rise," *TIME*, March 21, 2019, https://time.com/longform/alexandria-ocasio-cortez-profile/.

8. "Gillibrand Endorses Crowley," *NY State of Politics,* June 11, 2018, https://www.nystateofpolitics.com/2018/06/gillibrand-endorses-crowley/.

9. Kristin Hugo, "Alexandria Ocasio-Cortez 'Can't Afford Washington Apartment' Before Job in Congress Starts," *The Independent,* November 9, 2018, https://www.independent.co.uk/news/world/americas/us-politics/alexandria-ocasio-cortez-senate-washington-dc-congress-apartment-money-election-a8626361.html.

10. Alexandria Ocasio-Cortez (@AOC), "A quick note to you all . . . ," Twitter, January 5, 2019, 9:37 p.m., https://twitter.com/AOC/status/1081786765403480064.

11. Sydney Ember and Alexander Burns, "Bernie Sanders Is Winning Converts. But Primary Victories Remain Elusive," *New York Times*, June 24, 2018, https://www.nytimes.com/2018/06/24/us/politics/bernie-sanders-midterm-elections.html.

12. Bill Scher, "Down Goes Socialism," *Politico*, August 8, 2018, https://www.politico.com/magazine/story/2018/08/08/democratic-socialism-sanders-ocasio-cortez-2018-primary-results-219161.

13. "Andrew Gillum Backs 'Medicare for All,'" *PolitiFact Florida*, September 24, 2018, https://www.nbcmiami.com/on-air/as-seen-on/Politifact-Florida-Andrew-Gillum-Backs-Medicare-for-All_Miami-494188341.html.

14. Phillip Longman, "How Big Medicine Can Ruin Medicare for All," *Washington Monthly,* November/December 2017, https://washingtonmonthly.com/magazine/novemberdecember-2017/how-big-medicine-can-ruin-medicare-for-all/.

15. Ibid.

16. Dana Milbank, "The Democrats Have Become Socialists," *Washington Post*, September 13, 2017, https://www.washingtonpost.com/opinions/socialized-health-care-in-the-us-suddenly-that-sounds-a-lot-less-crazy/2017/09/13/20b88d88-98cb-11e7-82e4-f1076f6d6152_story.html?utm_term=.a92bd80ac391. It is often not clear, however, what different candidates mean by "Medicare for All" and leftists have been critical of those who have used the term to refer to much less ambitious healthcare plans than full single payer. See Abdul El-Sayed, "Don't Let Medicare For All Be Rebranded," *Current Affairs*, February 22, 2019, https://www.currentaffairs.org/2019/02/dont-let-medicare-for-all-be-rebranded.

17. Farah Stockman, "'Yes, I'm Running as a Socialist.' Why Candidates Are Embracing the Label in 2018," *New York Times*, April 20, 2018, https://www.nytimes.com/2018/04/20/us/dsa-socialism-candidates-midterms.html.

18. Ibid.

19. Ryan Smith, "Democratic Socialists Now Control One-Tenth of the Chicago City Council," *Chicago Sun-Times*, April 3, 2019, https://chicago.suntimes.com/2019/4/3/18412913/democratic-socialists-now-control-one-tenth-of-the-chicago-city-council.

20. Benjamin H. Bradlow, "Somerville's Turn to 'Sewer Socialism,'" *Commonwealth*, November 18, 2017, https://commonwealthmagazine.org/opinion/somervilles -turn-sewer-socialism/.

21. Ben Austen, "In Philadelphia, a Progressive D.A. Tests the Power—and Learns the Limits—of His Office," *New York Times*, October 30, 2018, https://www .nytimes.com/2018/10/30/magazine/larry-krasner-philadelphia-district -attorney-progressive.html.

22. Stockman, "'Yes, I'm Running as a Socialist.' Why Candidates Are Embracing the Label in 2018."

23. Ibid.

24. For what it's worth, I hate that song.

25. Steve Chapman, "Why Young Americans Are Drawn to Socialism," *Reason*, May 21, 2018, https://reason.com/2018/05/21/why-young-americans-are-drawn -to-sociali/.

26. See Jesse Eisinger, *The Chickenshit Club: Why the Justice Department Fails to Prosecute Executives* (New York: Simon & Schuster, 2017). Pulitzer Prize–winning investigative journalist Eisinger has said that if the Obama administration had been committed to actually enforcing the law, "the history of the country would be different . . . We would think of the financial crisis differently, think of the Obama administration differently; there would be a sense that the government was legitimate. There would be a sense of accountability after the crisis, the reforms would be tougher . . . I don't think we would have Donald Trump as president." Quoted in Alexander C. Kaufman, "How Obama's Failure to Prosecute Wall Street Set the Stage for Trump's Win," *Huffington Post*, July 11, 2017, https://www.huffpost.com/entry/chickenshit-club_n _5963fcc6e4b005b0fdc7bacb.

27. David Graeber, *The Democracy Project* (New York: Spiegel & Grau, 2013).

28. See Dan Kopf, "Union Membership in the US Keeps on Falling, Like Almost Everywhere Else," *Quartz*, February 5, 2019, https://qz.com/1542019/union -membership-in-the-us-keeps-on-falling-like-almost-everywhere-else/.

29. For a detailed look at Obama's record of failure, see Adolph Reed Jr., "Nothing Left: The Long, Slow Surrender of American Liberals," *Harpers*, March 2014, https://harpers.org/archive/2014/03/nothing-left-2/.

30. Ramesh Ponnuru, "A Debate Renewed: Conservatives Are Questioning Their Allegiance to Capitalism and the Founding," *National Review*, November 27, 2017, https://www.nationalreview.com/magazine/2017/11/27/conservatives-against -capitalism-some-moving-away/. For a thorough examination of a sad conservative attempt to rebut socialist ideas, see Nathan J. Robinson, "The Best They've Got," *Current Affairs*, June 10, 2019, https://www.currentaffairs.org/2019/06/the -best-theyve-got.

31. Bill Kristol (@BillKristol), "The GOP tax bill's bringing . . . ," Twitter, November 21, 2017, 12:46 p.m., https://twitter.com/BillKristol/status/933074207637991424.

32. Dinesh D'Souza, *The Big Lie: Exposing the Nazi Roots of the American Left* (Washington, D.C.: Regnery Publishing, 2017).

33. Jocelyn Kiley, "Most Continue to Say Ensuring Health Care Coverage Is Government's Responsibility," *Pew Research Center*, October. 3, 2018, https://www.pewresearch.org/fact-tank/2018/10/03/most-continue-to-say-ensuring-health-care-coverage-is-governments-responsibility/.

34. Frank Newport, "Majority Say Wealthy Americans, Corporations Taxed Too Little," *Gallup*, April 18, 2017, https://news.gallup.com/poll/208685/majority-say-wealthy-americans-corporations-taxed-little.aspx.

35. 2016 Democratic Party Platform, Democratic Platform Committee, July 8–9, 2016, Orlando, FL, https://democrats.org/wp-content/uploads/2018/10/2016_DNC_Platform.pdf.

36. *For the Many, Not the Few*, Labour Party, 2017, https://labour.org.uk/wp-content/uploads/2017/10/labour-manifesto-2017.pdf; Adam Bienkov, "New Poll Finds Huge Public Support for Jeremy Corbyn's Manifesto Promises," *Business Insider*, May 12, 2017, https://www.businessinsider.com/poll-huge-public-support-for-jeremy-corbyns-manifesto-promises-2017-5.

37. Jim Pickard and Helen Warrell, "Conservative Manifesto Pledges Consigned to the Bin," *Financial Times*, June 12, 2017, https://www.ft.com/content/6dd1942a-4f88-11e7-bfb8-997009366969.

38. Quoted in Stockman, "'Yes, I'm Running as a Socialist.' Why Candidates Are Embracing the Label in 2018."

39. "Select a Subscription Level," *Current Affairs*, http://currentaffairs.org/subscribe.

40. This is, by the way, why you always need to set your sights high rather than low. I totally disagree with Hillary Clinton's position that it's pragmatic to aim for moderation. You aim for radical change and settle temporarily for moderation. If you aim for moderation, you will end up settling for nothing.

41. Richard Posner, *A Failure of Capitalism* (Cambridge, MA: Harvard University Press, 2009).

42. For a typical example, see Joseph Epstein, "Socialists Don't Know History," *Wall Street Journal*, May 29, 2019, https://www.wsj.com/articles/socialists-dont-know-history-11559171072.

43. Posner, *A Failure Of Capitalism*.

44. Maeve Reston, "Hillary Clinton Splits Younger, Older Democratic Women," *CNN*, June 10, 2016, https://www.cnn.com/2016/06/10/politics/hillary-clinton-women-generational-divide/index.html.

45. See Nathan J. Robinson, "How Horrific Things Come to Seem Normal," *Current Affairs*, July 4, 2018, https://www.currentaffairs.org/2018/07/how-horrific-things-come-to-seem-normal, in which I examine the way the *New York Times* reported on the rise of Adolf Hitler.

46. Ontologists may disagree with me on this, but the ontologists can hash it out among themselves.

47. Abdul El-Sayed was not a socialist, but he was a left progressive in the Sanders mold who ran an inspiring campaign. I wrote about his ideas for *Current Affairs* and covered him on the campaign trail for *New York* magazine. See Nathan J. Robinson, "Could Abdul El-Sayed Be The Real Deal?," *Current Affairs*, Febru-

ary 5, 2018, https://www.currentaffairs.org/2018/02/could-abdul-el-sayed-be-the
-real-deal; Nathan J. Robinson, "Abdul El-Sayed's Campaign Is A Test For Leftism in the Midwest," *New York*, August 5, 2018, http://nymag.com/intelligencer
/2018/08/leftist-abdul-el-sayeds-race-for-michigan-governor.html.

48. Jennifer Schuessler, "A Young Publisher Takes Marx into the Mainstream," *New York Times*, January 20, 2013, https://www.nytimes.com/2013/01/21/books
/bhaskar-sunkara-editor-of-jacobin-magazine.html.

49. They were not all political. See, e.g., Nathan J. Robinson, *The Man Who Accidentally Wore His Cravat to a Gymnasium* (Demilune Press, 2014).

50. Kyle Chayka, "The Rise of the Hard Left," *The Ringer*, March 23, 2017, https://www.theringer.com/2017/3/23/16044958/new-left-media-current-affairs-chapo
-trap-house-crooked-media-9cb016070532.

CHAPTER 1: REVULSION, CURIOSITY, MORAL INSTINCT

1. "Sterling Silver Protractor," Tiffany & Co., https://www.tiffany.com/accessories
/desk/everyday-objects-sterling-silver-protractor-60558523/.

2. Oliver Milman, "Americans Waste 150,000 Tons of Food Each Day," *The Guardian*, April 18, 2018, https://www.theguardian.com/environment/2018
/apr/18/americans-waste-food-fruit-vegetables-study; "Burberry Burns Bags, Clothes and Perfume Worth Millions," BBC News, July 19, 2018, https://www
.bbc.com/news/business-44885983. After the practice became a public scandal, the company announced that it would stop; Sarah Cliff, "I Read 1,182 Emergency Room Bills This Year. Here's What I Learned," *Vox*, December 18, 2018, https://www.vox.com/health-care/2018/12/18/18134825/emergency-room
-bills-health-care-costs-america; Marisa Kendall, "Rent a Bunk Bed for $1,200 a Month?," *Mercury News*, June 7, 2019, https://www.mercurynews.com/2019
/06/07/rent-a-bunk-bed-for-1200-a-month-idea-sparks-pushback-from-sf
-officials/.

3. Candace Taylor, "AOL Co-Founder's D.C.-Area Home Asks $62.95 Million," *Wall Street Journal*, May 24, 2018, https://www.wsj.com/articles/aol-co
-founders-d-c-area-home-asks-62-95-million-1527171415.

4. Katy McLaughlin, "Scott McNealy Asks Nearly $100 Million for Silicon Valley Estate," *Wall Street Journal*, June 21, 2018, https://www.wsj.com/articles/scott
-mcnealy-asks-nearly-100-million-for-silicon-valley-estate-1529592912.

5. Michael Hiltzik, "Crowdfunding for Medical Expenses Is Rising," *Los Angeles Times*, April 28, 2017, https://www.latimes.com/business/hiltzik/la-fi-hiltzik
-crowdfunding-medical-20170428-story.html.

6. Bopha Phorn, "Woman Slips Between Subway and Platform, Draws Huge Crowd of Good Samaritans," *ABC News*, July 3, 2018.

7. "Poverty," The World Bank, updated April 3, 2019, https://www.worldbank.org
/en/topic/poverty/overview. It is commonly argued that capitalism has "lifted billions out of poverty." In fact, the statistics here are grossly manipulated, both in regard to how many people have been made meaningfully less poor and how

responsible "capitalism" is for the progress. See Roge Karma, "5 Myths About Global Poverty," *Current Affairs*, July 26, 2019, https://www.currentaffairs.org/2019/07/5-myths-about-global-poverty. The best existing left scholar on global inequality and poverty statistics is anthropologist Jason Hickel, whose blog destroys many of the myths about how much progress has been made: https://www.jasonhickel.org/blog.

8. "Immunization Coverage," World Health Organization, July 16, 2018, https://www.who.int/news-room/fact-sheets/detail/immunization-coverage; "Up to 40 Percent of Annual Deaths from Each of Five Leading US Causes Are Preventable," Centers for Disease Control and Prevention, May 1, 2014, https://www.cdc.gov/media/releases/2014/p0501-preventable-deaths.html.

9. Quoted in Lucy Dalloway, "Principles for Living We Could Do Without," *Financial Times*, May 23, 2010, https://www.ft.com/content/be8ce2ce-650d-11df-b648-00144feab49a. For an in-depth review of Dalio's business management principles, see Nathan J. Robinson, "How to Make Everyone in Your Vicinity Secretly Fear and Despise You," *Current Affairs*, June 10, 2018, https://www.currentaffairs.org/2018/06/how-to-make-everyone-in-your-vicinity-secretly-fear-and-despise-you.

10. Robert Nozick, *Anarchy, State, and Utopia* (New York: Basic Books, 1974).

11. Ben Shapiro, "The Complete Transcript: Ben Takes Berkeley," *The Daily Wire*, September 15, 2017, https://www.dailywire.com/news/21144/complete-transcript-ben-takes-berkeley-daily-wire.

12. Henry George, *Progress and Poverty* (New York: Robert Schalkenbach Foundation, 1879, reprinted 1937), 274.

13. Ken Langone, *I Love Capitalism! An American Story* (New York: Portfolio, 2018).

14. Max Weber, *From Max Weber: Essays in Sociology*, ed. H. H. Gerth and C. Wright Mills (New York: Oxford University Press, 1946), 271.

15. Jack London, *The Iron Heel*. Available from Project Gutenberg: https://www.gutenberg.org/ebooks/author/120.

16. This is especially noticeable in Harvard Square, where every day good liberals from the university try hard to ignore a sizable homeless population.

17. Brianna Rennix and Oren Nimni, "Slavery Is Everywhere," *Current Affairs*, May/June 2016, https://www.currentaffairs.org/2016/07/slavery-is-everywhere.

18. Rachel Sherman, *Uneasy Street: The Anxieties of Affluence* (Princeton, NJ: Princeton University Press, 2017).

19. Edith Wharton, *The House of Mirth* (1905).

20. Brendan Maloy, "Prospective Clippers Owner Larry Ellison Has a Basketball Court on His Yacht," *Sports Illustrated*, May 1, 2014.

21. David Vine, "Where in the World Is the U.S. Military?," *Politico Magazine*, July/August 2015, https://www.politico.com/magazine/story/2015/06/us-military-bases-around-the-world-119321.

22. "Suicide Statistics," American Foundation for Suicide Prevention, 2017, https://afsp.org/about-suicide/suicide-statistics/.

23. For more on Pruett's life and writing, see Nathan J. Robinson, "The Autobio-

graphy of Robert Pruett," *Current Affairs*, October 9, 2017, https://www
.currentaffairs.org/2017/10/the-autobiography-of-robert-pruett.

24. Paul Bloom, in the book *Against Empathy*, argues exactly the opposite. Bloom
says that empathy makes us less rational and more emotional, thereby causing
us to make poor moral decisions. I think Bloom is wrong, because unless you
make an effort to understand what the pain of others is *like*, you won't know
how serious it is when you make those decisions. For my full argument see Nathan J. Robinson, "Empathy: Probably A Good Thing," *Current Affairs*, July/
August 2017.

25. Nathan J. Robinson, "What We Did," *Current Affairs*, July 8, 2018, https://www
.currentaffairs.org/2018/07/what-we-did.

26. T. Eisensee and D. Strömberg, "News Droughts, News Floods, and US Disaster
Relief," *Quarterly Journal of Economics* 122, no. 2 (2007): 693–728.

27. Thomas Paine, *The Rights of Man*. Available from Project Gutenberg: http://
www.gutenberg.org/ebooks/3742.

28. Peter Brannen, "Earth Is Not in the Midst of a Sixth Mass Extinction," *The Atlantic*, June 13, 2017, https://www.theatlantic.com/science/archive/2017/06/the
-ends-of-the-world/529545/.

29. Jeremiah Moss, *Vanishing New York: How A Great City Lost Its Soul* (New York:
Dey Street Books, 2017).

30. Nathan J. Robinson, "Everything You Love Will Be Eaten Alive," *Current Affairs*, February 9, 2018, https://www.currentaffairs.org/2018/02/everything-you
-love-will-be-eaten-alive.

31. George Orwell, "Politics and the English Language," *Horizon*, April 1946,
http://www.orwell.ru/library/essays/politics/english/e_polit.

32. Ian Cobain, "Obama's Secret Kill List—the Disposition Matrix," *The Guardian*,
July 14, 2013, https://www.theguardian.com/world/2013/jul/14/obama-secret
-kill-list-disposition-matrix.

33. George Carlin, *Parental Advisory: Explicit Lyrics*, Atlantic Records, 1990.

34. Yara Bayoumy, "Obama Administration Arms Sales Offers to Saudi Top $115
Billion," Reuters, September 7, 2016, https://www.reuters.com/article/us-usa
-saudi-security/obama-administration-arms-sales-offers-to-saudi-top-115
-billion-report-idUSKCN11D2JQ; Nathan J. Robinson, "I Refuse to Be Distracted from the Deaths of Palestinian Children," *Current Affairs*, March 8,
2019, https://www.currentaffairs.org/2019/03/i-refuse-to-be-distracted-from
-the-deaths-of-palestinian-children.

CHAPTER 2: NEOLIBERAL NIGHTMARES

1. Barack Obama, "Now Is the Greatest Time to Be Alive," *Wired*, October. 12, 2016,
https://www.wired.com/2016/10/president-obama-guest-edits-wired-essay/.

2. Scott Winship (@swinshi), "What's really clarifying . . . ," Twitter, August 15,
2018, 7:32 a.m., https://twitter.com/swinshi/status/1029737546731974656.

3. Steven Pinker, *Enlightenment Now: The Case for Reason, Science, Humanism,
and Progress* (New York: Viking, 2018).

4. William J. Ripple et al., "World Scientists' Warning to Humanity: A Second Notice," *BioScience* 67, no. 12 (December 2017): 1026–1028.

5. Jeremy Lent, "Steven Pinker's Ideas Are Fatally Flawed. These Eight Graphs Show Why," *OpenDemocracy*, May 21, 2018, https://patternsofmeaning.com /2018/05/17/steven-pinkers-ideas-about-progress-are-fatally-flawed-these -eight-graphs-show-why/.

6. This is contested. See Peter Brannan, "Earth Is Not in the Midst of a Sixth Mass Extinction," *The Atlantic*, June 21, 2017, https://www.theatlantic.com/science /archive/2017/06/the-ends-of-the-world/529545/.

7. Sydney Pereira, "NASA: Hole in Earth's Ozone Layer Finally Closing Up Because Humans Did Something About it," *Newsweek*, January 5, 2018, https:// www.newsweek.com/nasa-hole-earths-ozone-layer-finally-closing-humans -did-something-771922.

8. Albert Einstein, *Essays in Humanism* (New York: Philosophical Library, 2011).

9. "Nuclear Weapons: Who Has What At a Glance," Arms Control Association, https://www.armscontrol.org/factsheets/Nuclearweaponswhohaswhat (accessed May 31, 2019).

10. Quoted in James Carden, "Former Defense Secretary William Perry Sounds the Alarm over the Present Nuclear Danger," *The Nation*, November 30, 2017, https://www.thenation.com/article/former-defense-secretary-william-perry -sounds-the-alarm-over-the-present-nuclear-danger/.

11. Alex Wallerstein, "The Hawaii Alert Was an Accident. The Dread It Inspired Wasn't," *Washington Post*, January 6, 2018, https://www.washingtonpost.com /news/posteverything/wp/2018/01/16/the-hawaii-alert-was-an-accident-the -dread-it-inspired-wasnt/?noredirect=on&utm_term=.4102afe63815.

12. See Steven Pinker, *The Better Angels of Our Nature: Why Violence Has Declined* (New York: Penguin, 2011).

13. Quoted in Chrystia Freeland, *Plutocrats: The Rise of the New Global Super-Rich and the Fall of Everyone Else* (New York: Penguin, 2012).

14. "Plutonomy: Buying Luxury, Explaining Global Imbalances," Citigroup, October 16, 2005, http://www.lust-for-life.org/Lust-For-Life/CitigroupImbalances _October2009/CitigroupImbalances_October2009.pdf.

15. Oliver P. Hauser and Michael I. Norton, "(Mis)perceptions of Inequality," *Current Opinion in Psychology* 18 (2017): 21–25.

16. Noah Kirsch, "The 3 Richest Americans Hold More Wealth Than Bottom 50% of the Country, Study Finds," *Forbes*, November 9, 2017, https://www.forbes .com/sites/noahkirsch/2017/11/09/the-3-richest-americans-hold-more-wealth -than-bottom-50-of-country-study-finds/.

17. Some dispute Oxfam's representation of wealth. See Dylan Matthews, "Are 26 Billionaires Worth More than Half the Planet? The Debate, Explained," *Vox*, January 22, 2019, https://www.vox.com/future-perfect/2019/1/22/18192774/oxfam -inequality-report-2019-davos-wealth. But even if you slice the data differently than Oxfam does, you cannot escape the basic fact: billions of people have virtually nothing, and yet a few people have billions.

18. As shown by Matt Bruenig of the People's Policy Project, people at the top

have amassed a truly colossal amount of wealth over the last decades. Matt Bruenig, "We Really Need to Eat the Rich," *Jacobin*, June 16, 2019, https://www.jacobinmag.com/2019/06/wealth-inequality-united-states-statistics-one-percent.

19. David Adler, "Who Cares About Inequality," *Current Affairs*, November/December 2017, https://www.currentaffairs.org/2018/01/who-cares-about-inequality.

20. Freeland, *Plutocrats*.

21. Ibid.

22. Freeland, *Plutocrats*, 82. This is Freeland's summary of Deaton's work, not a direct quote from Deaton.

23. Chris Taylor, "How Money Changes Us, and Not for the Good," Reuters, February 16, 2016, https://www.reuters.com/article/us-money-behavior-piff/how-money-changes-us-and-not-for-the-good-idUSKCN0VP1QQ.

24. Benjamin Preston, "The Rich Drive Differently, a Study Suggests," *New York Times*, August 12, 2013, https://wheels.blogs.nytimes.com/2013/08/12/the-rich-drive-differently-a-study-suggests/.

25. Lauren Tousignant, "Amazon Gave Away Too Many Free Bananas and Messed Up Seattle," *New York Post*, May 23, 2017. https://nypost.com/2017/05/23/amazon-gave-away-too-many-free-bananas-and-messed-up-seattle/ The free banana program, which has given away 1.7 million bananas, has apparently annoyed those who sell bananas for a living, and also encouraged people who think they're funny to repeat the *Arrested Development* line "There's always money in the banana stand" ad nauseam.

26. In the time since I wrote this, Bezos has finally made a charitable pledge, promising to build a large number of preschools where "the child will be the customer," whatever that means. Even if these schools turn out to be good, and not just a privatization scheme, we should just have free universal pre-K instead of just hoping Jeff Bezos wakes up one day thinking about preschool instead of bananas. Harry Cheadle, "'The Child Will Be the Customer' at Jeff Bezos' Totally Normal Preschool," *VICE*, Sept. 13, 2018, https://www.vice.com/en_us/article/wjy8am/jeff-bezos-preschool-child-will-be-the-customer-vgtrn.

27. Catherine Clifford, "Jeff Bezos Says This Is How He Plans to Spend the Bulk of His Fortune," *CNBC*, April 30, 2018, https://www.cnbc.com/2018/04/30/jeff-bezos-says-this-is-how-he-plans-to-spend-the-bulk-of-his-fortune.html.

28. Isobel Asher Hamilton and Áine Cain, "Amazon Warehouse Employees Speak Out About the 'Brutal' Reality of Working During the Holidays, When 60-Hour Weeks are Mandatory and Ambulance Calls Are Common," *Business Insider*, February 19, 2019, https://www.businessinsider.com/amazon-employees-describe-peak-2019-2.

29. See Nathan J. Robinson, "Jeff Bezos: How the World's Richest Man Can Change His Stingy Reputation," *The Guardian*, July 28, 2017, https://www.theguardian.com/technology/2017/jul/28/jeff-bezos-amazon-rich-charity-warren-buffett.

30. Daphne Howland, "Why Amazon's 'Big Brother' Warehouse Theft Surveillance Is a Big Mistake," *Retail Dive*, March 23, 2016, https://www.retaildive

.com/news/why-amazons-big-brother-warehouse-theft-surveillance-is-a-big
-mistake/415764/.

31. Hamilton Nolan, "Inside an Amazon Warehouse, the Relentless Need to 'Make Rate,'" *Gawker*, June 6, 2016, https://gawker.com/inside-an-amazon-warehouse -the-relentless-need-to-mak-1780800336.

32. David Streitfeld, "Inside Amazon's Very Hot Warehouse," *New York Times*, September 19, 2011, https://bits.blogs.nytimes.com/2011/09/19/inside-amazons -very-hot-warehouse/.

33. Bloodworth's Amazon warehouse was in Britain, but if anything this probably means conditions were *better* than they would have been in the United States, where labor protections are minimal. James Bloodworth, *Hired: Six Months Undercover in Low-Wage Britain* (London: Atlantic Books, 2018).

34. Jodi Kantor and David Streitfeld, "Inside Amazon: Wrestling Big Ideas in a Bruising Workplace," *New York Times*, August 16, 2015, https://www.nytimes .com/2015/08/16/technology/inside-amazon-wrestling-big-ideas-in-a-bruising -workplace.html.

35. Catey Hill, "41% of Workers Took No Vacation Last Year," *MarketWatch*, Jan. 19, 2016, https://www.marketwatch.com/story/41-of-workers-took-no-vacation-last -year-2016-01-19. Note that many of these workers may be nominally entitled to time off but subject to informal sanctions from employers for actually taking it. As Joe Pinsker noted in *The Atlantic*, they are "deterred by the possible repercussions of taking time off," and even when they take it they often keep working during their vacations. Joe Pinsker, "41% of American Workers Let Paid Vacation Days Go to Waste," *The Atlantic*, Aug. 22, 2014. https://www.theatlantic .com/business/archive/2014/08/41-percent-of-american-workers-let-their-paid -vacation-go-to-waste/378950/.

36. Elise Gould and Jessica Schieder, "Work Sick or Lose Pay? The High Cost of Being Sick When You Don't Get Paid Sick Days," Economic Policy Institute, June 28, 2017, https://www.epi.org/publication/work-sick-or-lose-pay-the-high -cost-of-being-sick-when-you-dont-get-paid-sick-days/. Gould and Schieder note that the situation is far worse for low-wage workers in the food service and accommodation industries, 69% of whom lack paid sick days.

37. Monique Morrisey, "Private-Sector Pension Ccoverage Fell by Half over Two Decades," Economic Policy Institute, Jan. 11, 2013, https://www.epi.org/blog /private-sector-pension-coverage-decline/.

38. Gretchen Livingston, "Is U.S. fertility at an All-Time Low? Two of Three Measures Point to Yes," Pew Research Center, May 22, 2019, https://www.pewresearch .org/fact-tank/2019/05/22/u-s-fertility-rate-explained/.

39. Tom Allison, "Financial Health of Young America: Measuring Generational Declines Between Baby Boomers & Millennials," Young Invincibles, April 2018, https://younginvincibles.org/wp-content/uploads/2018/04/Financial-Health-of -Young-America-update.pdf.

40. Malcolm Harris, *Kids These Days: Human Capital and the Making of Millennials* (New York: Little, Brown and Company, 2017).

41. *Jacobin*'s Luke Savage has compiled a collection of the most absurd "Millen-

nials Are Ruining X" headlines to be found in the press, including "How Gen Y Workers Are Ruining Your Workplace," "Millennials Are Killing Lunch," "Why Do Millennials Hate Groceries?," "Millennials Are Killing Chains Like Buffalo Wild Wings and Applebees," "Pepsi's New Kendall Jenner Ad Is Everything Wrong with Millennials," "Blame Millennials for the Vanishing Bar of Soap," and "Millennials Are Ruining America's Sex Life." See Luke Savage (@ Lukewsavage), "This 'Millennials Killed X' . . ." Twitter, June 3, 2017, https://twitter.com/lukewsavage/status/871083837228544000?lang=en.

42. Eve Peyser, "Joe Biden Trashes Millennials in His Quest to Become Even Less Likable," *Vice*, January 12, 2018, https://www.vice.com/en_us/article/mbpxx8/biden-trashes-millennials-in-his-quest-to-become-even-less-likable.

43. "Household Debt and Credit Report," Federal Reserve Bank of New York, 2019, https://www.newyorkfed.org/microeconomics/hhdc.html.

44. "A Look at the Shocking Student Loan Debt Statistics for 2019," Student Loan Hero, February 4, 2019, https://studentloanhero.com/student-loan-debt-statistics/.

45. Beth Akers and Matthew M. Chingos, *Game of Loans: The Rhetoric and Reality of Student Debt* (Princeton: Princeton University Press, 2017). For a critical review of the book, explaining why student debt is indeed a serious problem worth being "very, very angry" about, see K. M. Lautrec, "Does Student Debt Matter?," *Current Affairs*, March 24, 2017, https://www.currentaffairs.org/2017/03/does-student-debt-matter.

46. Shannon Insler, "The Mental Toll of Student Debt: What Our Survey Shows," *StudentLoanHero*, September 7, 2017, https://studentloanhero.com/featured/psychological-effects-of-debt-survey-results/.

47. Josh Mitchell, "Mike Meru Has $1 Million in Student Loans. How Did That Happen?," *Wall Street Journal*, May 25, 2018, https://www.wsj.com/articles/mike-meru-has-1-million-in-student-loans-how-did-that-happen-1527252975.

48. Ryann Liebenthal, "The Incredible, Rage-Inducing Inside Story of America's Student Debt Machine," *Mother Jones*, September/October 2018, https://www.motherjones.com/politics/2018/08/debt-student-loan-forgiveness-betsy-devos-education-department-fedloan/.

49. David Dayen, "Betsy DeVos Quietly Making It Easier for Dying For-Profit Schools to Rip Off a Few More Students on the Way Out," *The Intercept*, April 12, 2019, https://theintercept.com/2019/04/12/betsy-devos-for-profit-colleges/.

50. Sparky Abraham, "How Student Debt Is Worsening Race and Gender Injustice," *Current Affairs*, June 26, 2018, https://www.currentaffairs.org/2018/06/how-student-debt-is-worsening-gender-and-racial-injustice.

51. Maurie Backman, "It's Official: Most Americans Are Currently in Debt," *Motley Fool*, February 15, 2018, https://www.fool.com/retirement/2018/02/15/its-official-most-americans-are-currently-in-debt.aspx; Melanie Lockert, "The Average U.S. Household Debt Continues to Rise," Credit Karma, October 30, 2017, https://www.creditkarma.com/studies/i/average-debt-american-household-on-rise/.

52. Esther Gross, Victoria Efetevbia, Alexandria Wilkins, "Racism and Sexism Against Black Women May Contribute to High Rates of Black Infant Mortality,"

ChildTrends, April 18, 2019, https://www.childtrends.org/racism-sexism
-against-black-women-may-contribute-high-rates-black-infant-mortality.

53. Max Ehrenfreund, "There's a Disturbing Truth to John Legend's Oscar Statement About Prisons and Slavery," *Washington Post,* February 23, 2015, https://www
.washingtonpost.com/news/wonk/wp/2015/02/23/theres-a-disturbing-truth
-to-john-legends-oscar-statement-about-prisons-and-slavery/?noredirect
=on&utm_term=.c600c34a7ebe.

54. As incarceration rates have declined, the odds have gotten somewhat less extreme, and the statistic should not be used to describe the odds facing children born today. Glen Kessler, "The Stale Statistic that One in Three Black Males 'Born Today' Will End Up in Jail," *Washington Post,* June 16, 2015, https://www
.washingtonpost.com/news/fact-checker/wp/2015/06/16/the-stale-statistic-that
-one-in-three-black-males-has-a-chance-of-ending-up-in-jail/.

55. Joshua Holland, "The Average Black Family Would Need 228 Years to Build the Wealth of a White Family Today," *The Nation,* August 8, 2016, https://www
.thenation.com/article/the-average-black-family-would-need-228-years-to
-build-the-wealth-of-a-white-family-today/.

56. Akilah Johnson, "That Was No Typo: The Median Net Worth of Black Bostonians Really Is $8," *Boston Globe,* Dec. 11, 2017, https://www.bostonglobe.com
/metro/2017/12/11/that-was-typo-the-median-net-worth-black-bostonians
-really/ze5kxC1jJelx24M3pugFFN/story.html. People often talk about "reparations" for historical racial injustice as if it would be an impossible number to calculate, but a good place to start is with concrete numbers like this. We can start to make reparations by closing this gap.

57. Matt Bruenig, "Baby Bonds Only Modestly Reduce the Racial Wealth Gap," *Peoples Policy Project,* January 22, 2019, https://www.peoplespolicyproject
.org/2019/01/22/baby-bonds-only-modestly-reduce-the-racial-wealth-gap/;
Matt Bruenig, "Wealth Inequality Across Class and Race in 5 Graphs," *Peoples Policy Project,* March 5, 2019, https://www.peoplespolicyproject.org/2019/03/05
/wealth-inequality-across-class-and-race-in-5-graphs/.

58. Facundo Alvaredo, Bertrand Garbinti, Thomas Piketty, "On the share of inheritance in aggregate wealth Europe and the United States, 1900-2010," Oct. 29, 2015, available at http://piketty.pse.ens.fr/files/AlvaredoGarbintiPiketty2015.pdf

59. Bernie Sanders on Twitter, April 5, 2019, https://twitter.com/berniesanders
/status/1114198592800079872?lang=en.

60. "Melissa Chan, "Life Expectancy Gap Between Black and White Americans Narrower Than Ever," *TIME,* May 9, 2016.

61. You often hear that the gender pay gap doesn't exist. Pay attention to how this argument proceeds, because it's extremely dishonest. In fact, those making it do not argue that the gender pay gap doesn't exist. They argue that it exists, *but* that it's the result of women's choices, and can therefore be dismissed. The people making this argument assert that within the same occupations, women and men tend to earn the same amount. But the whole point here is that women's occupations are less valued! Proving that female-dominated jobs earn less only serves to confirm that women's labor is systematically devalued.

62. Laura Bates, *Everyday Sexism: The Project That Inspired a Worldwide Movement* (New York: Thomas Dunne Books, 2016).

63. Garth Fowler, et al. "Women Outnumber Men in Psychology Graduate Programs," American Psychological Association, Dec. 2018, https://www.apa.org/monitor/2018/12/datapoint.

64. Dan Vergano, "Half-Million Iraqis Died in the War, New Study Says," *National Geographic*, Oct. 16, 2013, https://news.nationalgeographic.com/news/2013/10/131015-iraq-war-deaths-survey-2013/.

65. Julian Borger, "Fleeing a Hell the US Helped Create: Why Central Americans Journey North," *The Guardian*, Dec. 19, 2018, https://www.theguardian.com/us-news/2018/dec/19/central-america-migrants-us-foreign-policy.

66. Max Fisher, "Americans Have Forgotten What We Did to North Korea," *Vox*, Aug. 3, 2015, https://www.vox.com/2015/8/3/9089913/north-korea-us-war-crime.

67. Saeed Kamali Dehghan and Richard Norton-Taylor, "CIA Admits Role in 1953 Iranian Coup," *The Guardian*, Aug. 19, 2013, https://www.theguardian.com/world/2013/aug/19/cia-admits-role-1953-iranian-coup.

68. Tara Tidwell Cullen, "ICE Released Its Most Comprehensive Immigration Detention Data Yet. It's Alarming," National Immigrant Justice Center, March 13, 2018, https://immigrantjustice.org/staff/blog/ice-released-its-most-comprehensive-immigration-detention-data-yet.

69. Stef W. Kight and Alayna Treene, "Trump Isn't Matching Obama Deportation Numbers," *Axios*, June 21, 2019, https://www.axios.com/immigration-ice-deportation-trump-obama-a72a0a44-540d-46bc-a671-cd65cf72f4b1.html.

70. For more on why we need to place nonhuman animals front and center in our moral thinking, see Nathan J. Robinson, "Meat and the H-Word," *Current Affairs*, Jan. 17, 2018, https://www.currentaffairs.org/2018/01/meat-and-the-h-word.

71. Quoted in Jason Bellini, "Why 'Deaths of Despair' May Be a Warning Sign for America," *Wall Street Journal*, February 27, 2018, https://www.wsj.com/articles/why-deaths-of-despair-may-be-a-warning-sign-for-america-moving-upstream-1519743601.

72. See Nathan J. Robinson, "Suicide and the American Dream," *Current Affairs*, October 22, 2016, https://www.currentaffairs.org/2016/10/suicide-and-the-american-dream.

73. "Overdose Death Rates," National Institute on Drug Abuse, January 2019, https://www.drugabuse.gov/related-topics/trends-statistics/overdose-death-rates.

74. Michael Karpman, Stephen Zuckerman, and Dulce Gonzalez, "The Well-Being and Basic Needs Survey," Urban Institute, August 28, 2018, https://www.urban.org/research/publication/well-being-and-basic-needs-survey.

75. Dwyer Gunn, "Low-Income Americans Face a Harrowing Choice: Food or Housing?," *Pacific Standard*, November 2, 2018, https://psmag.com/economics/the-rent-and-mortgage-payments-are-still-too-damn-high.

76. "Suicide Statistics," American Foundation for Suicide Prevention, https://afsp.org/about-suicide/suicide-statistics/ (accessed June 1, 2019). There were 47,173 suicides in the United States in 2017. The population of Burlington is 42,239.

77. Lawrence H. Summers, "The Great Liberator," *New York Times*, November 19, 2006, https://www.nytimes.com/2006/11/19/opinion/19summers.html.

78. See Milton Friedman, *Capitalism and Freedom* (University of Chicago Press, 1962), 29.

79. In fact, some liberals talk about government this way to this day. Elizabeth Warren has said she is a "capitalist to her bones" who simply believes markets need to be made to function in the interests of the public through effective regulation. Former labor secretary Robert Reich was critical of the neoliberal turn when he served in the Clinton administration, but still wrote a book called *Saving Capitalism*.

80. Stephen Metcalf, "Neoliberalism: The Idea That Swallowed the World," *The Guardian*, August 18, 2017, https://www.theguardian.com/news/2017/aug/18/neoliberalism-the-idea-that-changed-the-world.

81. Wendy Brown, *Undoing the Demos: Neoliberalism's Stealth Revolution* (New York: Zone Books, 2015).

82. Panos Mourdoukoutas, "Amazon Should Replace Local Libraries to Save Taxpayers Money," *Forbes,* July 21, 2018, http://www.ala.org/yalsa/sites/ala.org.yalsa/files/content/AmazonShouldReplaceLocalLibrariestoSaveTaxpayersMoney.pdf. After librarians began deluging *Forbes* with complaints, arguing that the article was idiotic, the magazine removed the piece and pretended it had never published it. You can still find discussion of the controversy at: Thu-Huong Ha, "Forbes Deleted a Deeply Misinformed Op-ed Arguing Amazon Should Replace Libraries," *Quartz*, July 23, 2018, https://qz.com/1334123/forbes-deleted-an-op-ed-arguing-that-amazon-should-replace-libraries/.

83. Bryan Caplan, *The Case Against Education: Why the Education System Is a Waste of Time and Money* (Princeton, NJ: Princeton University Press, 2018).

84. For a lengthy critique of Caplan's vision for education, see Sparky Abraham and Nathan J. Robinson, "What Is Education For?," *Current Affairs*, August 11, 2018, https://www.currentaffairs.org/2018/08/what-is-education-for.

85. Kevin Carey, "Classless," *Washington Monthly,* April/May/June 2018, https://washingtonmonthly.com/magazine/april-may-june-2018/classless/.

86. Leslie Scism, "As Wildfires Raged, Insurers Sent in Private Firefighters to Protect Homes of the Wealthy," *Wall Street Journal*, November 5, 2017, https://www.wsj.com/articles/as-wildfires-raged-insurers-sent-in-private-firefighters-to-protect-homes-of-the-wealthy-1509886801.

87. Kimi Yoshino, "Another Way the Rich Are Different: 'Concierge-Level' Fire Protection," *Los Angeles Times*, October 26, 2007, https://www.latimes.com/business/la-fi-richfire26oct26-story.html.

88. Amy Julia Harris and Shoshana Walter, "They Thought They Were Going to Rehab. They Ended Up in Chicken Plants," *Reveal News*, October 4, 2017, https://www.revealnews.org/article/they-thought-they-were-going-to-rehab-they-ended-up-in-chicken-plants/.

89. Emma Pettit, "U. of Akron Will Phase Out 80 Degree Programs and Open New Esports Facilities," *Chronicle of Higher Education*, Aug. 16, 2018, https://www.chronicle.com/article/U-of-Akron-Will-Phase-Out-80/244293.

90. Harris, *Kids These Days,* p. 7.

91. Michael Cohen, "How For-Profit Prisons have Become the Biggest Lobby No One Is Talking About," *Washington Post,* April 28, 2015, https://www.washingtonpost.com/posteverything/wp/2015/04/28/how-for-profit-prisons -have-become-the-biggest-lobby-no-one-is-talking-about/?utm_term= .564c8e6fd948.

92. For a longer discussion of how "growth" has become a dangerous dogma, see Rob Larson and Nathan J. Robinson, "Stubborn Detachment," *Current Affairs* (Jan./Feb. 2019).

93. Christina Cauterucci, "The U.S. and Israel Are Trying to Cure Breast Cancer with Tasteful Pink Fighter Jet," *Slate,* October 27, 2016, https://slate.com /human-interest/2016/10/the-u-s-and-israel-are-trying-to-cure-breast-cancer -with-tasteful-pink-fighter-jets.html.

CHAPTER 3: THE ARMY OF PSYCHOPATHIC ANDROIDS

1. Milton Friedman, "The Social Responsibility of Business Is to Increase Its Profits," *New York Times,* September 13, 1970, http://umich.edu/~thecore/doc /Friedman.pdf.

2. Andrew Jacobs and Matt Richtel, "How Big Business Got Brazil Hooked on Junk Food," *New York Times,* September 16, 2017, https://www.nytimes.com /interactive/2017/09/16/health/brazil-obesity-nestle.html.

3. Ibid.

4. Ibid.

5. Barry Meier, "Sackler Scion's Email Reveals Push for High-Dose OxyContin, New Lawsuit Disclosures Claim," *New York Times,* January 31, 2019, https:// www.nytimes.com/2019/01/31/health/opioids-purdue-pharma-sackler.html.

6. Ibid.

7. Ibid.

8. Every time you point this out, some libertarian will scoff that the company "won't" do that, and give an explanation for why it wouldn't be rational. For example, it wouldn't be rational for an airplane manufacturer to cut corners on safety in pursuit of higher profits, because when the planes crash so will the profits. It's curious that people maintain that these things "won't" happen, because so many of them *do* happen. Boeing got caught up in a short-term race with rival Airbus, trying to outmaneuver them in the market. In doing so, it compromised its planes, resulting in two horrific accidents. See Peter Cohan, "Did Airbus Rivalry Drive Dangerous Tradeoffs for Boeing's 737 MAX?," *Forbes,* March 28, 2019, https://www.forbes.com/sites/petercohan/2019/03/28/did-airbus -rivalry-drive-dangerous-tradeoffs-for-boeings-737-max/#4aea1c972e18.

9. Adam Smith, *The Wealth of Nations* (London: W. Strahan and T. Cadell, 1776), vol. 1, ch. 8.

10. Vanessa Fuhrmans, "Tax Cuts Provide Limited Boost to Workers' Wages," *Wall Street Journal,* October 2, 2018, https://www.wsj.com/articles/tax-cuts-provide -limited-boost-to-workers-wages-1538472600 The article reports that even with

giant tax breaks, companies are "doing everything they can to avoid seeing their permanent payroll go up," which is exactly what you'd expect. Thomas Gryta, "Profits Surge at Big U.S. Firms," *Wall Street Journal*, August 5, 2018, https://www.wsj.com/articles/profits-surge-at-big-u-s-firms-1533489995. One argument I have heard in defense of profit goes as follows: Profit margins in public companies tend to be quite low. The difference between a nonprofit and for-profit company, then, can be around 2 percent. Perhaps it's true that for-profit companies must do everything they can to squeeze that extra 2 percent out of its customers, employees, and other stakeholders. But it's not clear that it will act substantially differently from a nonprofit institution. However, percentages aren't what we should pay attention to here. Instead, we should think about how a difference in an organization's mandate affects its choices. Let's say, hypothetically, that Coca-Cola makes a penny on every can of Coke sold. It's a tiny profit margin. But because the margin is so tiny, Coke will always be looking to sell as many cans of Coke as possible, and will be extremely aggressive in entering new markets. If I am only making a tiny profit on each unit, but my goal is to maximize the total amount I reap in profit, then in order to come away with a substantial sum, I will have to be ruthless in trying to crush my competitors. However, if I have no interest whatsoever in making a profit, then I don't actually need to grow the company *at all* once it is breaking even, and I can pursue other goals beyond increasing the consumption of my product. I see this difference in my own life as a magazine editor: I am not interested in doing anything other than breaking even, and that means I make substantially different choices. We don't market the magazine, we just focus on putting out the best possible product and keeping the enterprise afloat. If we wanted to make money, our entire operational strategy would change. There would be a total difference in the way our business was conducted *even if* our per-unit profit was quite low. Profit maximization changes the entire way you think about what your job is!

11. Frederick Taylor, *The Principles of Scientific Management* (New York and London: Harper & Brothers, 1911). Actually, many cogs are treated better than employees, because cogs are owned and therefore more costly to replace, whereas employees are fungible.

12. The collective character of capitalism is one of its great ironies. One major distinction between the Soviet system and the American one was supposedly that the United States is a country that serves the interests of the individual, yet many millions of people here spend their whole lives serving collective institutions. At Walmart, for instance, employees frequently start their shift by participating in the so-called Walmart cheer, which celebrates the company. (They do it, of course, while wearing their company uniforms.) The Walmart cheer has no parallel even in Maoist China. See Samuel Miller-Mcdonald, "Capitalism Is Collectivist," *Current Affairs*, May 9, 2018, https://www.currentaffairs.org/2018/05/capitalism-is-collectivist.

13. The idea was first introduced in Nick Bostrom, "Ethical Issues in Advanced Artificial Intelligence," in George Eric Lasker et al, eds., *Cognitive, Emotive and Ethical Aspects of Decision Making in Humans and in Artificial Intelligence*

(Tecumseh, ON: International Institute for Advanced Studies in Systems Research and Cybernetics, 2003).

14. P. J. Proudhon, *What Is Property* (1840), available at https://theanarchistlibrary.org/library/pierre-joseph-proudhon-what-is-property-an-inquiry-into-the-principle-of-right-and-of-governmen.

15. John Locke has a famous theory of property rights, whereby those who "mix their labor" with the world develop a right to the fruits of that labor. The theory sounds good, but in practice it becomes extremely difficult to determine what I have "mixed" my labor with, and the implications are actually quite radical. For example, the workers who build a factory plainly "mix" their labor with the resources used to build it, yet contemporary legal regimes do not recognize them as having developed any property interest in the place they have built. If we apply Lockean property theory seriously, workers should be entitled to own at least a significant piece of their firms.

16. Matt Bruenig, "If We Care About Inequality, We Must Confront Capital," People's Policy Project, August 5, 2017, https://www.peoplespolicyproject.org/2017/08/05/if-we-care-about-inequality-we-must-confront-capital/.

17. Aaron C. Davis and Shawn Boburg, "At Sean Hannity Properties in Working-Class Areas, an Aggressive Approach to Rent Collection," *Washington Post*, May 10, 2018, https://www.washingtonpost.com/investigations/at-hannitys-properties-in-low-income-areas-an-aggressive-approach-to-rent-collection/2018/05/10/964be4a2-4eea-11e8-84a0-458a1aa9ac0a_story.html?utm_term=.f8df268f7a83. Hannity reportedly owns 870 properties and is an extremely aggressive rent collector. At one 112-unit property, 94 eviction actions were filed in a single year. Among the tenants Hannity sought to evict, according to the *Post*, were "a double amputee who had lived in an apartment with her daughter for five years but did not pay on time after being hospitalized" and "a single mother of three whose $980 rent check was rejected because she could not come up with a $1,050 cleaning fee for a bedbug infestation."

18. For a look at the soul-destroying emptiness of the Bilzerian lifestyle, see Julian Morgans, "I Tried Living Like Dan Bilzerian and Realized What His Problem Is," *Vice*, May 3, 2016. https://www.vice.com/en_us/article/3b4q5y/i-tried-living-like-dan-bilzerian-and-realised-what-his-problem-is.

19. Charles E. Hurst, *Social Inequality: Forms, Causes, and Consequences* (New York: Pearson Education, Inc., 2007), 31.

20. This is not the only way, of course, in which capitalism is inefficient and wasteful. Competition can be extravagantly wasteful because of all the resources that are spent trying to poach customers from elsewhere rather than improving the product. And, of course, pursuing profit leads to absolutely *absurd* inefficiencies like the incineration of Burberry handbags or the attempt to sell people a new iPhone model every couple of years. Capitalism involves trying to convince people to buy things that they neither want nor need because this is the only way for companies to continue growing. The production and marketing of unneeded items are colossal wastes of time and resources that could be put to a thousand better uses.

Cornell's Robert Frank has reported on another important way in which extreme wealth is wasteful. Many wealthy people purchase status symbols in order to feel proud of themselves, a phenomenon Thorstein Veblen called "conspicuous consumption." Frank points out that these goods are "positional," meaning that their status is not intrinsic but arises relative to other goods. So I don't want a 5,000-square-foot house because I want a 5,000-square-foot house, I want it because the Joneses have a 4,000-square-foot house. If the Joneses only had a 1,000-square-foot house, I would be content with a 1,200-square-foot house, because my aim is not to maximize my square footage but to beat the Joneses. Because of that, heavy taxes on luxury goods can slow down this competition without reducing anyone's ultimate happiness. If I and the Joneses are both taxed on our ridiculous houses, the extra wealth can be used to give children free preschool while I still get the satisfaction of knowing my house is slightly larger than theirs. Robert H. Frank, *Luxury Fever: Weighing the Cost of Excess* (Princeton, NJ: Princeton University Press, 2010).

21. David Gauthier, "No Need for Morality: The Case of the Competitive Market," *Philosophic Exchange Vol. 13 : No. 1, Article 2* (1982), available at https://digitalcommons.brockport.edu/cgi/viewcontent.cgi?article=1228&context =phil_ex; Francis Ysidro Edgeworth, *Mathematical Psychics: An Essay on the Application of Mathematics to the Moral Sciences* (London: C.K. Paul & Co., 1881), 16–17.

22. Samuel Bowles, *The Moral Economy* (New Haven, CT: Yale University Press, 2016).

23. For a representative "price gouging is actually good" take, see Benjamin Zycher, "In Defense of Price Gouging and Profiteering," *American Enterprise Institute*, August 7, 2014, http://www.aei.org/publication/in-defense-of-price-gouging-and -profiteering/. Usually, the arguments made here are something like "if prices of useful supplies go up after a disaster, it will incentivize profiteers to bring more useful supplies so they can make money." Note, however, that while this may be an argument for not *criminalizing* price gouging, it does not actually tell us that it's okay to charge $1,000 for a bottle of water if someone needs it to keep their baby alive. Free market economists will present the empirical argument that banning price gouging yields fewer supplies *as if* it's a moral argument that it's okay to extort money from desperate people. For lengthy rebuttals of the "price gouging is good" hot take, see Nathan J. Robinson, "Do Economists Actually Know What Money Is?," *Current Affairs*, October 27, 2016, https://www.currentaffairs .org/2016/10/do-economists-actually-know-what-money-is; and Nathan J. Robinson, "Incentives and Price Gouging," *Current Affairs*, October 28, 2016, https://www.currentaffairs.org/2016/10/incentives-and-price-gouging.

24. John Stuart Mill, "On the Definition of Political Economy," in *Essays on Economics and Society Part I* (1836).

25. Nick Hanauer, "The Pitchforks Are Coming . . . for Us Plutocrats," *Politico*, July/August 2014, https://www.politico.com/magazine/story/2014/06/the-pitchforks -are-coming-for-us-plutocrats-108014.

26. Ibid.

27. Bess Levin, "At Davos, Elites Simulate The Refugee 'Experience' By 'Pretend-

ing to Flee Advancing Armies,'" *Vanity Fair*, January 17, 2017, https://www
.vanityfair.com/news/2017/01/davos-elites-simulate-the-refugee-experience-by
-pretending-to-flee-advancing-armies.

28. Kristen Majewski, "Marie Antoinette Built a Fake Peasant Village; Real Peasants Not Pleased," *Modern Notion*, October 21, 2014, http://modernnotion.com
/marie-antoinette-built-entire-peasant-village-versailles-real-peasants-pleased/.

29. Steven Pinker, *Enlightenment Now: The Case for Reason, Science, Humanism,
and Progress* (New York: Viking, 2018).

30. Harry Frankfurt, *On Inequality* (Princeton, NJ: Princeton University Press,
2015).

31. The United States, however, is an undemocratic country. Some people's votes
are worth far more than others. In the U.S. Senate, for instance, every state gets
the same number of senators (2) regardless of its population size. That means
that in larger states, the value of individuals' votes is significantly diluted. As a
result, Californians' votes are worth a fraction of those of people in Wyoming.
Even more scandalously, people who live in Puerto Rico and Washington, D.C.,
do not get to vote in congressional elections, meaning that they have "taxation
without representation."

32. Warren Buffett, "Better Than Raising the Minimum Wage," *Wall Street Journal*,
May 21, 2015, https://www.wsj.com/articles/better-than-raising-the-minimum
-wage-1432249927.

33. Chris Bertram, Corey Robin, and Alex Gourevitch, "Let It Bleed: Libertarianism and the Workplace," *Crooked Timber*, July 1, 2012, http://crookedtimber
.org/2012/07/01/let-it-bleed-libertarianism-and-the-workplace/.

34. Elizabeth Anderson, *Private Government: How Employers Rule Our Lives*
(Princeton, NJ: Princeton University Press, 2017).

35. Robert Shiller, *Finance and the Good Society* (Princeton, NJ: Princeton University
Press, 2003), 218.

36. Chrystia Freeland, *Plutocrats: The Rise of the New Global Super-Rich and the Fall of
Everyone Else* (New York: Penguin, 2012).

37. Sadef Ali Kully, "What Happened When Seattle Tried to Tax Amazon," *City-
Limits*, December 3, 2018, https://citylimits.org/2018/12/03/what-happened-when
-seattle-tried-to-tax-amazon/.

38. Ana Swanson, "Meet the Four-Eyed, Eight-Tentacled Monopoly That Is Making Your Glasses So Expensive," *Forbes*, September 10, 2014, https://www
.forbes.com/sites/anaswanson/2014/09/10/meet-the-four-eyed-eight-tentacled
-monopoly-that-is-making-your-glasses-so-expensive/#a7df4a26b66b.

39. Jonathan Tepper, "Competition Is Dying, and Taking Capitalism with It," *Bloomberg*, November 25, 2018, https://www.bloomberg.com/opinion/articles/2018
-11-25/the-myth-of-capitalism-exposed. Some other reports put the percentage
closer to 70 percent, but do not dispute that two players dominate the industry.

40. Friedrich Hayek, *The Road to Serfdom* (Chicago: University of Chicago Press,
1944, 2007), 136.

41. Jefferson Cowie, *Capital Moves: RCA's Seventy-Year Quest for Cheap Labor*
(New York: The New Press, 2001).

42. Rob Larson, *Capitalism vs. Freedom* (Alresford, UK: Zero Books, 2018).

43. Friedrich Hayek, *Law Legislation and Liberty, Volume 2: The Mirage of Social Justice* (Chicago: University of Chicago Press, 1976).

44. Buffett, "Better Than Raising the Minimum Wage."

45. Freeland, *Plutocrats*.

46. Quoted in Jörg Guido Hülsmann, *Mises: The Last Knight of Liberalism* (Auburn, AL: Ludwig von Mises Institute, 2007), 996.

47. It's because *capitalists have the capital!*

48. Peter Thiel, "Competition Is for Losers," Stanford University lecture, https://www.youtube.com/watch?v=bVV26yRjwq0. Thiel points out that people like Albert Einstein who make the most important contributions to human knowledge hardly ever become millionaires or billionaires. Thiel advises business students to simply become monopolists rather than innovators.

49. Don Watkins and Yaron Brook, "The Two Fundamentally Flawed Assumptions at the Heart of the Inequality Crusade," *Medium*, April 14, 2016, https://medium.com/@dwatkins3/the-two-fundamentally-flawed-assumptions-at-the-heart-of-the-inequality-crusade-4ec53dacc061.

50. For a lucid explanation of how the state creates markets through law, see Robert B. Reich, *Saving Capitalism: For the Many, Not the Few* (New York: Vintage, 2016).

51. I say *large* and *powerful* because this government must be able to enforce all private property rights, which is no small task!

52. Address of Hon. Fred. Douglass, delivered before the National Convention of Colored Men, at Louisville, Kentucky, September 24, 1883.

53. Errico Malatesta, *At the Café: Conversations on Anarchism*, trans. Paul Nursey-Bray (Fifth Estate Books, 2006).

CHAPTER 4: SOLIDARITY FOREVER

1. Luke's essay is one of the best available explanations of just what *liberalism* is and what is wrong with it. Luke Savage, "Liberalism in Theory and Practice," *Jacobin*, December 17, 2018, https://jacobinmag.com/2018/12/liberalism-theory-practice-obama-trudeau.

2. Frank Newport, "Democrats More Positive About Socialism Than Capitalism," Gallup, August 13, 2018, https://news.gallup.com/poll/240725/democrats-positive-socialism-capitalism.aspx.

3. Eugene V. Debs, Statement to the Federal Court, Cleveland, Ohio, upon being convicted of violating the Sedition Act (September, 18, 1918).

4. Niraj Choksi, "94 Percent of U.S. Teachers Spend Their Own Money on School Supplies, Survey Finds," *New York Times,* May 16, 2018, https://www.nytimes.com/2018/05/16/us/teachers-school-supplies.html.

5. Erin Einhorn, "Crumbling Detroit School Buildings Will Cost $500 Million to Repair. It's Money the District Doesn't Have," *Chalkbeat,* June 22, 2018, https://www.chalkbeat.org/posts/detroit/2018/06/22/crumbling-detroit-school-buildings-will-cost-500-million-to-repair-its-money-the-district-doesnt-have/.

6. Jennifer Chambers, "Price Tag to Fix DPSCD Buildings: $500M," *Detroit News*, June 22, 2018, https://www.detroitnews.com/story/news/education/2018/06/22/price-tag-fix-dpscd-buildings-500-million/726186002/.

7. M. H. Morton, A. Dworsky, and G. M. Samuels, *Missed Opportunities: Youth Homelessness in America: National Estimates* (Chicago: Chaplin Hall, 2017), http://voicesofyouthcount.org/brief/national-estimates-of-youth-homelessness/.

8. Jack London, "How I Became a Socialist," War of the Classics, http://london.sonoma.edu/writings/WarOfTheClasses/socialist.html.

9. Jason Brennan, *Against Democracy* (Princeton, NJ: Princeton University Press, 2016). In a somewhat similar but less explicitly authoritarian vein see Bryan Caplan, *The Myth of the Rational Voter: Why Democracies Choose Bad Policies* (Princeton, NJ: Princeton University Press, 2011). The libertarians are pretty clear: they want enlightened capitalists to decide what's best for the irrational and emotional proletariat.

10. Joseph Heath, *Economics Without Illusions: Debunking the Myths of Modern Capitalism* (New York: Crown Publishing, 2009).

11. It's also very easy, when you meet extremely wealthy people and they turn out to be human, to conclude that they are not greedy and are just like everybody else. I think this is a mistake, because a lot of greed is not actually conscious. It's true that nearly everyone means well. But some people are blind to the consequences of their actions. The millionaires who think of themselves as poor because all of their friends are multimillionaires are not necessarily cruel or evil. They are just oblivious, in part because they have sealed themselves in a bubble. The fact that people do not *appear* selfish or do not think of themselves as selfish does not mean that they are not acting selfishly. For that, we should look at what they actually do.

12. Heath, *Economics Without Illusions*.

CHAPTER 5: A BETTER WORLD

1. Quoted in Lyta Gold, "The Dismal Frontier," *Current Affairs*, May 13, 2018, https://www.currentaffairs.org/2018/05/the-dismal-frontier.

2. Ibid.

3. Some aspects of this were more appealing than others. Personally I am against philosopher kings but in favor of exiling poets.

4. Edward Bellamy, *Looking Backward* (1888).

5. For a lovely essay on these remarkable books, see Lyta Gold, "World Without Men," July 2, 2019, https://www.currentaffairs.org/2019/07/world-without-men.

6. Ursula K. Le Guin, *The Dispossessed: An Ambiguous Utopia* (New York: HarperCollins, 2009).

7. A full-color diagram of the *Current Affairs* editorial utopia is available on pages 122–123 of Lyta Gold and Nathan J. Robinson, eds., *The Current Affairs Big Book of Amusements* (New Orleans: Current Affairs Press, 2019).

8. As I am someone who is afraid of flying, this person's utopia is my dystopia.

9. For an example of practical utopian thinking, see Meagan Day's discussion of the difference it would make if every worker was given a one-year sabbatical every

seven years. Meagan Day, "One Year Off, Every Seven Years," *Jacobin*, May 22, 2019, https://www.jacobinmag.com/2019/05/workers-sabbatical-demand-leisure.

10. George Orwell, *The Road to Wigan Pier* (New York: Harcourt Brace, 1958), 203.

11. Noah Smith, "Do Property Rights Increase Freedom?," Noahpinion, August 12, 2011, http://noahpinionblog.blogspot.com/2011/08/do-property-rights-increase-liberty.html.

12. Matt Gephardt and Michelle Poe, "How Much Does the USPS Profit When They Lose Your Mail and It's Sold at Auction?," *WJLA*, May 14, 2019, https://wjla.com/features/7-on-your-side/usps-profit-lost-mail-auction. The *WJLA* journalists point out that auctions of people's "lost" mail are handled by a private company called "GovDeals." The magic of public-private partnerships!

13. For irrefutable proof that "property is theft," see P. J. Proudhon, *What Is Property? An Inquiry into the Principle of Right and of Government* (Humboldt Publishing Company, 1890)

14. Hillary Clinton mocked Bernie Sanders for his promises by suggesting it was like offering everyone a "free pony." To be honest, free ponies—or at least pony rides—are an excellent idea. Every child should get a chance to ride a pony, irrespective of their parents' income. I don't see why free access to the city petting zoo is so inconceivable as to be inherently risible. See Hillary Clinton, *What Happened* (New York: Simon & Schuster, 2017).

15. A. W. Geiger, "Millennials Are the Most Likely Generation of Americans to Use Public Libraries," Pew Research Center, June 21, 2017, https://www.pewresearch.org/fact-tank/2017/06/21/millennials-are-the-most-likely-generation-of-americans-to-use-public-libraries/. For a rousing defense of libraries, and an exploration of their connection to socialism, see Nathan J. Robinson, "Why Public Libraries Are Amazing," *Current Affairs*, July 21, 2017, https://www.currentaffairs.org/2018/07/why-libraries-are-amazing.

16. Peter Wagner and Leah Sakala, "Mass Incarceration: The Whole Pie," Prison Policy Initiative, March 12, 2014, https://www.prisonpolicy.org/reports/pie.html.

17. U.S. Department of Justice Civil Rights division, U.S. Attorney's Office for the Northern, Middle, and Southern Districts of Alabama, *Investigations of Alabama's State Prisons for Men*, April 2, 2019, https://www.justice.gov/opa/press-release/file/1150276/download?utm_medium=email&utm_source=govdelivery.

18. John Gramlich, "The Gap Between the Number of Blacks and Whites in Prison Is Shrinking," *Pew Research Center*, April 30, 2019, https://www.pewresearch.org/fact-tank/2019/04/30/shrinking-gap-between-number-of-blacks-and-whites-in-prison/.

19. Angela Davis, *Are Prisons Obsolete?* (New York: Seven Stories Press, 2003).

CHAPTER 6: SOCIALISM, DEMOCRACY, SOCIAL DEMOCRACY

1. G. D. H. Cole, *A History of Socialist Thought* (London: Macmillan, 1957).

2. Matt Bruenig, "Norway Is Far More Socialist than Venezuela," People's Policy Project, January 27, 2019, https://www.peoplespolicyproject.org/2019/01/27/norway-is-far-more-socialist-than-venezuela/; Matt Bruenig, "The State Owns

76% of Norway's Non-Home Wealth," People's Policy Project, March 14, 2018, https://www.peoplespolicyproject.org/2018/03/14/the-state-owns-76-of -norways-non-home-wealth/.

3. For a comprehensive history of the establishment of the British welfare state, see Nicholas Timmins, *The Five Giants: A Biography of the Welfare State* (Harper-Collins, 2001).

4. See Aisha Gani, "Clause IV: A Brief History," *The Guardian*, August 9, 2015, https://www.theguardian.com/politics/2015/aug/09/clause-iv-of-labour-party -constitution-what-is-all-the-fuss-about-reinstating-it.

5. "Land Tenure System in Hong Kong," Legislative Council of Hong Kong, December 8, 2016, https://www.legco.gov.hk/research-publications/english/essentials-1617ise07 -land-tenure-system-in-hong-kong.htm.

6. Mariana Mazzucato, *The Entrepreneurial State: Debunking Public vs. Private Sector Myths* (Anthem, 2013). See also Rob Larson, "Cheating At Monopoly," *Current Affairs*, April 19, 2019. https://www.currentaffairs.org/2019/04 /cheating-at-monopoly For exploration of non-capitalist means of innovation, see Vanessa A. Bee, "Innovation Under Socialism," *Current Affairs*, October 24, 2018, https://www.currentaffairs.org/2018/10/innovation-under-socialism.

7. Quoted in E. H. Carr, *Michael Bakunin* (1937), 356.

8. Robert Blatchford, *Merrie England* (1893).

9. See, for example, Robert P. George's scathing review of Andrew Sullivan's *The Conservative Soul*, in George, *Conscience and Its Enemies: Confronting the Dogmas of Liberal Secularism* (Wilmington, DE: Intercollegiate Studies Institute, 2016).

10. Except Noam Chomsky himself, who rejects the label as meaningless.

11. For an exhaustive typology, see Leszek Kolakowski's 1,300-page *Main Currents of Marxism* (New York: Norton, 2008). Note that these are only the *main* currents.

12. Nathan J. Robinson, "The Sanders/Cruz Debate Was the Best Political TV in Ages," *Current Affairs*, February 8, 2017, https://www.currentaffairs.org/2017 /02/the-sanderscruz-debate-was-the-best-political-tv-in-ages.

13. From CNN: "The woman was clearly in a lot of pain, but she didn't want anyone to call an ambulance because she said she couldn't afford it. 'She made it a point to say "you don't understand, I have terrible insurance."'" David Williams, "Woman Feared She Couldn't Afford Ambulance After Her Leg Was Trapped by a Subway Train," CNN, July 3, 2018, https://www.cnn.com/2018/07 /03/health/subway-accident-insurance-fear-trnd/index.html.

14. Aris Folley, "Deforestation of the Amazon Rainforest Hits Nearly Three Football Fields per Minute: Report," *The Hill*, July 25, 2019, https://thehill.com /policy/energy-environment/454771-deforestation-of-the-amazon-rainforest -hits-nearly-three-football.

CHAPTER 7: ONE LONG STRUGGLE

1. See Albert Einstein, "Why Socialism?," *Monthly Review*, May 1949, https:// monthlyreview.org/2009/05/01/why-socialism/. Einstein based his socialism on his respect for the individual creative spirit: "This crippling of individu-

als I consider the worst evil of capitalism. Our whole educational system suffers from this evil. An exaggerated competitive attitude is inculcated into the student, who is trained to worship acquisitive success as a preparation for his future career. I am convinced there is only *one* way to eliminate these grave evils, namely through the establishment of a socialist economy, accompanied by an educational system which would be oriented toward social goals."

2. Thomas Paine, *Agrarian Justice*, in *The Life and Major Writings of Thomas Paine*, ed. Philip S. Foner (New York: Citadel, 1945). Elizabeth Anderson points out that many of Paine's positions would seemingly place him on the libertarian right today, but she also argues that this is in part because changes in capitalism itself have meant that it no longer means the same thing to argue for certain kinds of economic freedom. Elizabeth Anderson, "When the Market Was 'Left,'" The Tanner Lectures in Human Values, Princeton University, 2015. *Agrarian Justice* advocates limiting property accumulation, and the leftist anarchist Rudolf Rocker cites Paine as an influence in his important book *Pioneers of American Freedom* (Los Angeles: Rocker Publications Committee, 1945).

3. John Ball, Sermon at Blackheath, June 12, 1381, quoted in John Stow, Edmund Howes, *Annals, or a General Chronicle of England* (1631).

4. Quoted in Cory Doctorow, "When You think of Freedom, Remember the Charter of the Forest, Not the Magna Carta," *BoingBoing*, November 6, 2017, https://boingboing.net/2017/11/06/800-years-ago-today.html. The ABA has a number of fascinating resources on the Charter of the Forest, including printable posters explaining its importance: https://www.americanbar.org/groups/public_interest/law_library_congress/charter_of_the_forest/resources/.

5. "1642–1652: The Diggers and the Levellers," *LibCom*, September 12, 2006.

6. "The Chartist Movement," UK Parliament, https://www.parliament.uk/about/living-heritage/transformingsociety/electionsvoting/chartists/overview/chartistmovement/.

7. For a fascinating forgotten history of one utopian settlement, see Elle Hardy, "Seeking Utopia in Louisiana," *Current Affairs*, February 7, 2019, https://www.currentaffairs.org/2019/02/seeking-utopia-in-louisiana.

8. A lot of useful detail on the SPD's history can be found in chapter 3 of Bhaskar Sunkara's *The Socialist Manifesto* (New York: Basic Books, 2019).

9. Joseph Schumpeter, *Capitalism, Socialism, and Democracy* (London: George Allen and Unwin, 1944), p. 23.

10. Jim Sidanius and Felicia Pratto, *Social Dominance: An Intergroup Theory of Social Hierarchy and Oppression* (New York: Cambridge University Press, 2001), 21. I am grateful to Irami Osei-Frimpong for the source.

11. Karl Marx, "Wages of Labor," *Economic and Philosophic Manuscripts of 1844,* available at https://www.marxists.org/archive/marx/works/download/pdf/Economic-Philosophic-Manuscripts-1844.pdf.

12. Karl Marx, "Estranged Labour," *Economic and Philosophic Manuscripts of 1844*.

13. Karl Marx, *The Eighteenth Brumaire of Louis Bonaparte*, 1852, available at https://www.marxists.org/archive/marx/works/1852/18th-brumaire/ch01.htm.

14. Karl Marx, "A Contribution to the Critique of Hegel's Philosophy of Right,"

1844, available at https://www.marxists.org/archive/marx/works/1843/critique
-hpr/intro.htm.

15. Quoted in Peter Marshall, *Demanding the Impossible* (New York: HarperCollins, 1992), 241.

16. Ibid., 242.

17. Ibid., 259.

18. Murray Bookchin, *Post-Scarcity Anarchism* (Berkeley, CA: Ramparts Press, 1971), 173.

19. Emma Goldman, *My Disillusionment in Russia* (New York: Doubleday, Page & Company, 1923).

20. Ibid.

21. Ibid.

22. Bertrand Russell, *The Practice and Theory of Bolshevism* (1920), available at https://en.wikisource.org/wiki/The_Practice_and_Theory_of_Bolshevism.

23. Mikhail Bakunin, "Marxism, Freedom, and the State," https://www.marxists
.org/reference/archive/bakunin/works/mf-state/ch03.htm.

24. Elizabeth Bruenig, "How Augustine's Confessions and Left Politics Inspired My Conversion to Catholicism," *America*, August 7, 2017, https://www
.americamagazine.org/faith/2017/07/25/how-augustines-confessions-and-left
-politics-inspired-my-conversion-catholicism.

25. David Bentley Hart, "Are Christians Supposed to Be Communists?," *New York Times*, November 4, 2017, https://www.nytimes.com/2017/11/04/opinion
/sunday/christianity-communism.html.

26. Brian Terrell, "Dorothy Day's Anarchism Is the Antidote to Disappointing Political System," *National Catholic Reporter*, April 19, 2016, https://
www.ncronline.org/blogs/ncr-today/dorothy-days-anarchism-antidote
-disappointing-political-system. See also Day's memoir, Dorothy Day, *The Long Loneliness: The Autobiography of the Legendary Catholic Social Activist* (San Francisco: HarperOne, 2009).

27. Stephen Beale, "The Dorothy Day Few of Us Know," *Crisis*, March 19, 2013, https://www.crisismagazine.com/2013/the-dorothy-day-few-of-us-know.

28. Dorothy Day, "Poverty Is to Care and Not to Care," *The Catholic Worker*, April 1953, https://www.catholicworker.org/dorothyday/articles/647.html.

29. Jeremy Harmon, "Fifty Years Ago, a Catholic Anarchist Tried to Help Solve Homelessness in Salt Lake City. Here's What Happened," *Salt Lake Tribune*, September 24, 2017, https://www.sltrib.com/news/2017/09/24/fifty-years-ago-a
-catholic-anarchist-tried-to-help-solve-homelessness-in-salt-lake-city-heres
-what-happened/. See also Ammon Hennacy, *The Autobiography of a Catholic Anarchist* (New York: Catholic Worker Books, 1954).

30. Leo Tolstoy, *The Kingdom of God and Peace Essays* (London: Oxford University Press, 1960).

31. See Gustavo Gutiérrez, *A Theology of Liberation: History, Politics, and Salvation* (Ossining, NY: Orbis Books, 1988).

32. Quoted in Mark Rice-Oxley, "Pope Francis: The Humble Pontiff with Practical

Approach to Poverty," *The Guardian*, March 13, 2013, https://www.theguardian
.com/world/2013/mar/13/jorge-mario-bergoglio-pope-poverty.

33. Peter Dreier, "Radicals in City Hall: An American Tradition," *Dissent*, December
19, 2013, https://www.dissentmagazine.org/online_articles/radicals-in-city
-hall-an-american-tradition.

34. Jack Ross, "Socialist Party Elected Officials 1901–1960," Mapping American
Social Movements Project, University of Washington, http://depts.washington
.edu/moves/SP_map-elected.shtml.

35. Emily Birnbaum, "Dem Senator: Ocasio-Cortez's Platform Is Future of Party in
the 'Bronx,' Not Country," *The Hill*, July 1, 2018, https://thehill.com/homenews
/sunday-talk-shows/395064-dem-lawmaker-ocasio-cortez-represents-the
-bronx-not-the-future-of.

36. Peter Dreier, "Why Has Milwaukee Forgotten Victor Berger?," *Huffington Post*,
May 6, 2012, https://www.huffpost.com/entry/why-has-milwaukee-forgott_b
_1491463.

37. Peter Dreier, "Berger One of the Greatest Americans," *Milwaukee Journal Sentinel*, May 5, 2012, http://archive.jsonline.com/news/opinion/berger-one-of-the
-greatest-americans-kb57psj-150305515.html/.

38. Dreier, "Why Has Milwaukee Forgotten Victor Berger?"

39. Peter Dreier and Pierre Clavel, "What Kind of Mayor Was Bernie Sanders?," *The
Nation*, June 2, 2015, https://www.thenation.com/article/bernies-burlington
-city-sustainable-future/. For a dissenting opinion on Sanders' mayoralty from
a socialist perspective, see Murray Bookchin, "The Bernie Sanders Paradox:
When Socialism Grows Old," *Socialist Review* (November/December 1986),
https://theanarchistlibrary.org/library/bookchin-sanders.

40. Ethelwyn Mills, "Legislative Program of the Socialist Party," 1914, http://fau
.digital.flvc.org/islandora/object/fau%3A5198.

41. Ibid.

42. You can find a good history of the eight-hour-day movement in, of all places,
Teen Vogue. Kim Kelly, "How American Workers Won the Eight-Hour Workday," *Teen Vogue*, July 11, 2019, https://www.teenvogue.com/story/american
-workers-eight-hour-workday.

43. Helen Keller, "What Is the IWW?," speech at the New York City Civic Club,
1918, available at https://www.marxists.org/reference/archive/keller-helen
/works/1910s/18_01_x01.htm.

44. Helen Keller, "How I Became a Socialist," *New York Call*, 1912, https://www
.marxists.org/reference/archive/keller-helen/works/1910s/12_11_03.htm.

45. Ibid.

46. Gail Friedman, "March of the Mill Children," Encyclopedia of Greater Philadelphia, https://philadelphiaencyclopedia.org/archive/march-of-the-mill-children/.

47. Peter H. Clark, "Socialism: The Remedy for the Evils of Society," in Philip S.
Foner, *The Voice of Black America: Major Speeches by Negroes in the United
States, 1797–1971* (New York: Simon and Schuster, 1972), 455.

48. See Jeffrey B. Perry, *Hubert Harrison: The Voice of Harlem Radicalism, 1883-
1918* (New York: Columbia University Press, 2009).

49. For an important collection of Robeson's words, see *Paul Robeson Speaks: Writings, Speeches, Interviews, 1918–1974*, ed. Philip S. Foner (New York: Brunner/Mazel, 1978).

50. For an account of Ella Baker's remarkable life, see Barbara Ransby, *Ella Baker and the Black Freedom Movement: A Radical Democratic Vision* (Chapel Hill, NC: University of North Carolina Press, 2005).

51. For more on the life and assassination of Fred Hampton, see Jefrey Haas, *The Assassination of Fred Hampton: How the FBI and the Chicago Police Murdered a Black Panther* (Chicago: Lawrence Hill Books, 2011).

52. For an account of the strike see Harvey O'Connor, *Revolution in Seattle: A Memoir* (Chicago: Haymarket Books, 2009). Reading labor history is truly inspiring, because when you realize the obstacles faced by workers during the Pullman Strike of 1894 or the Bread and Roses Strike of 1912, you realize how comparatively easy our own struggle is. I strongly recommend Erik Loomis, *A History of America in Ten Strikes* (New York: New Press, 2018). The film *The Salt of the Earth* (1954) is also a gritty and moving portrayal of the realities of labor organizing.

53. Matilda Rabinowitz, *Immigrant Girl, Radical Woman: A Memoir from the Early Twentieth Century* (Ithaca, NY: ILR Press, 2017).

54. As of this writing, Manning is still imprisoned indefinitely for refusing to testify before a grand jury. Jacey Fortin, "Chelsea Manning Ordered Back to Jail for Refusal to Testify in WikiLeaks Inquiry," *New York Times*, May 16, 2019, https://www.nytimes.com/2019/05/16/us/chelsea-manning-jail.html. Manning is a great underappreciated hero of our time.

CHAPTER 8: MAKING OUR PLANS

1. Martin Luther King Jr., "Letter from Birmingham Jail," April 16, 1963, in "The Negro Is Your Brother," *The Atlantic,* August 1963, https://www.theatlantic.com/magazine/archive/2018/02/letter-from-birmingham-jail/552461/.

2. For more on the unexpected surge in support for the Labour Party under Corbyn, see Nathan J. Robinson, "This Is Why You Don't Listen When They Tell You That You'll Fail," in *Interesting Times: Observations & Arguments* (New Orleans, LA: Current Affairs Press, 2018).

3. The phrase is also used as the title of an excellent and readable history of anarchist thinking. Peter Marshall, *Demanding the Impossible: A History of Anarchism* (Oakland, CA: PM Press, 2010).

4. "What Is Democratic Socialism?," Democratic Socialists of America, https://www.dsausa.org/about-us/what-is-democratic-socialism/.

5. Elisabeth Rosenthal, *An American Sickness: How Healthcare Became Big Business and How You Can Take It Back* (New York: Penguin Books, 2017).

6. "US Health System Ranks Last Among Eleven Countries on Measures of Access, Equity, Quality, Efficiency, and Healthy Lives," Commonwealth Fund, June 16, 2014, https://www.commonwealthfund.org/press-release/2014/us-health-system-ranks-last-among-eleven-countries-measures-access-equity.

7. "The U.S. Healthcare Cost Crisis," Gallup, March 26, 2019, https://news.gallup
.com/poll/248129/westhealth-gallup-us-healthcare-cost-crisis-press-release
.aspx?g_source=link_newsv9&g_campaign=item_248090&g_medium=copy.

8. For the most persuasive explanation of why single-payer healthcare makes sense,
and responses to common counterarguments, see Timothy Faust, *Health Justice Now: Single Payer and What Comes Next* (Brooklyn, NY: Melville House,
2019). For cogent responses to questions about financing, see Dylan Scott, "A
Single-Payer Advocate Answers the Big Question: How Do We Pay for It?," *Vox*,
March 4, 2019, https://www.vox.com/policy-and-politics/2019/3/4/18249888
/medicare-for-all-cost-matt-bruenig-voxcare; Matt Bruenig, "Universal Health
Care Might Cost Less Than You Think," *New York Times*, April 29, 2019, https://
www.nytimes.com/2019/04/29/opinion/medicare-for-all-cost.html.

9. Abdul El-Sayed and Micah Johnson, "Caring For All," *Current Affairs*, October 15,
2018, https://www.currentaffairs.org/2018/10/caring-for-all. For explanations
of why we need full single-payer, and not simply a "public option," see Abdul
El-Sayed, "Don't Let Medicare for All Be Rebranded," *Current Affairs*, February 22, 2019, https://www.currentaffairs.org/2019/02/dont-let-medicare-for-all
-be-rebranded; Benjamin Studebaker and Nathan J. Robinson, "Why a 'Public
Option' Isn't Enough," *Current Affairs,* July 14, 2019, https://www.currentaffairs
.org/2019/07/why-a-public-option-isnt-enough.

10. E. C. Schneider, D. O. Sarnak, D. Squires, A. Shah, and M. M. Doty, *Mirror, Mirror: How the U.S. Health Care System Compares Internationally at a Time of Radical Change*, The Commonwealth Fund, July 2017, https://www.commonwealth
fund.org/sites/default/files/documents/___media_files_publications_fund
_report_2017_jul_pdf_schneider_mirror_mirror_exhibits.pdf.

11. Mollyann Brodie, Elizabeth V. Hamel, and Mira Norton, "Medicare as Reflected in Public Opinion," *Generations* (Summer 2015), https://www.asaging
.org/blog/medicare-reflected-public-opinion.

12. There is a lot of confused discussion around single-payer healthcare. Opponents mention that it would "cost trillions of dollars" or that it would introduce a large new payroll tax. It's irresponsible to talk about the costs without
talking about the savings, because only talking about the costs misleads people
into thinking they'll be spending *more* money under a Medicare for All system
rather than less. If I say, "Would you like to pay $1,000 in new taxes?," you
would likely say no. If, on the other hand, I say, "Would you prefer a $1,000 tax
or a $2,000 insurance premium with a $10,000 deductible?," your choice is a no-
brainer. If you're running a company and considering making an investment,
you don't just look at the cost, you also look at the return. Conservative opponents of Medicare for All emphasize the cost while denying the existence of
the return, thereby fooling people into thinking they are going to be financially
worse off rather than better off. For more on how to think clearly about this, see
Nathan J. Robinson, "Looking at the Bottom Line," *Current Affairs*, March 1,
2019, https://www.currentaffairs.org/2019/03/looking-at-the-bottom-line.

13. Quoted in John Cassidy, *How Markets Fail* (New York: Farrar, Straus, 2009),
159.

14. Matt Bruenig, "Family Fun Pack," People's Policy Project, https://www.peoples
policyproject.org/projects/family-fun-pack/.

15. Conservatives respond to the data on the success of social welfare programs by
cherry-picking downsides and ignoring upsides. For an explanation of how this
dishonesty works, see Nathan J. Robinson, "Never Trust the Cato Institute,"
Current Affairs, October 13, 2018, https://www.currentaffairs.org/2018/10
/never-trust-the-cato-institute.

16. Robert Pollin, James Heintz, Peter Arno, Jeannette Wicks-Lim, and Michael
Ash, *Economic Analysis of Medicare for All* (Amherst, MA: Political Economy Research Institute, November 30, 2018), https://www.peri.umass.edu
/publication/item/1127-economic-analysis-of-medicare-for-all.

17. H.Res.109: Recognizing the Duty of the Federal Government to Create a Green
New Deal, 116th Congress, 2019–2020, https://www.congress.gov/bill/116th
-congress/house-resolution/109/text.

18. Steve Cohen, "The Politics of a Green New Deal," Columbia University Earth
Institute, January 14, 2019, https://blogs.ei.columbia.edu/2019/01/14/politics
-green-new-deal/.

19. However, there *have* been serious attempts to think through exactly what ought
to be involved. If you would like to begin to understand the specifics, and why
a Green New Deal is feasible, I strongly recommend reading Robert Pollin,
"Degrowth vs. a Green New Deal," *New Left Review* (July/August 2018), https://
newleftreview.org/issues/II112/articles/robert-pollin-de-growth-vs-a-green
-new-deal.

20. In a Pew survey across 25 countries, 70 percent of people said that the United
States "does not take into account the interests of other countries," which is
true. Kristin Bialik, "How the World Views the U.S. and Its President in 9
Charts," Pew Research Center, October 9, 2018, https://www.pewresearch.org
/fact-tank/2018/10/09/how-the-world-views-the-u-s-and-its-president-in-9
-charts/.

21. You can watch the video of the debate here: https://www.youtube.com/watch?v
=7UiGCjgY2v4. You will see that capitalist arguments are in every way inferior
and easily refuted.

22. Free to Speak, "Ben Shapiro—EPIC—On Why You're Poor," YouTube, January 25, 2017, https://www.youtube.com/watch?v=cdEMw_lDUx0. This "three
things you need to do" framework is sometimes called the "success sequence"
and was first pushed by the liberal Brookings Institution.

23. Some conservatives literally do believe in bringing back child labor. See Bryan
Caplan, *The Case Against Education: Why the Education System Is a Waste of
Time and Money* (Princeton, NJ: Princeton University Press, 2018); and Jeffrey A. Tucker, "Let the Kids Work," Foundation for Economic Education, November 3, 2016, https://medium.com/fee-org/let-the-kids-work-jeffrey-a-tucker
-c8f7ba9d2cb3.

24. See Nathan J. Robinson, "Elizabeth Warren's Excellent Ideas," *Current Affairs*, April 16, 2019, https://www.currentaffairs.org/2019/04/elizabeth-warrens
-excellent-ideas.

25. For a detailed look at the contents of these mailers, see Nathan J. Robinson, "Anatomy of a Propaganda Campaign," *Current Affairs,* September 17, 2017, https://www.currentaffairs.org/2017/09/anatomy-of-a-propaganda-campaign.

26. If you would like proof that the Supreme Court is political, see Nathan J. Robinson, "How the Supreme Court Pretends to Be Reasonable," *Current Affairs,* June 29, 2018, https://www.currentaffairs.org/2018/06/how-the-supreme -court-pretends-to-be-reasonable; Nathan J. Robinson, "Why Everyone Should Oppose Brett Kavanaugh's Nomination," *Current Affairs,* August 6, 2018, https://www.currentaffairs.org/2018/08/why-everyone-should-oppose-brett -kavanaughs-confirmation. In these articles, I show how the justices delude themselves into believing they are deciding the law "neutrally" as "umpires" rather than according to obvious normative political values. For a more scholarly treatment of the same subject, see Duncan Kennedy, *A Critique of Adjudication* (Cambridge, MA: Harvard University Press, 1998).

27. For a more detailed explanation of why "court packing" is important and justified, see Vanessa A. Bee, "Court-Packing Is Necessary to Save Democracy," *Current Affairs,* October 10, 2018, https://www.currentaffairs.org/2018/10/court -packing-is-necessary.

28. See Sparky Abraham, "This Burrito Contains an Arbitration Clause," *Current Affairs,* August 16, 2018, https://www.currentaffairs.org/2018/08/this-burrito -includes-an-arbitration-clause.

29. *Connick v. Thompson,* 563 U.S. 51 (2011).

30. *Wal-Mart v. Dukes,* 564 U.S. 338 (2011).

31. If you need to be persuaded that unions matter, see Michael D. Yates, *Why Unions Matter* (New York: Monthly Review Press, 2009; second ed.). It is a highly readable introduction to labor issues. On broader economic issues, I recommend Michael D. Yates, *Naming the System: Inequality and Work in the Global Economy* (New York: Monthly Review Press, 2003).

32. David Macaray, "Friends Without Benefits: Obama's Betrayal of Labor," *Huffington Post,* August 9, 2011, https://www.huffpost.com/entry/obama-labor -unions-workers_b_922576.

33. See Rosemary Feurer and Chad Pearson, "Five Ways Bosses Fight Labor," *Jacobin,* May 1, 2018, https://jacobinmag.com/2018/05/employer-business-organizing -bosses-capitalists-public-relations.

34. For an explanation of why right-to-work laws are misleading and unfair, see Nathan J. Robinson, "How Expanding the Right to Contract Can Limit Rights," *Current Affairs,* May 23, 2018, https://www.currentaffairs.org/2018/05/why -expansions-of-the-right-to-contract-are-limitations-on-rights.

35. Nobody is more critical of top-down unionism than democratic socialists. It is not enough to have a union; that union must also actually represent the interests of its rank-and-file members. If it isn't internally democratic, then it's not doing its job. Many, many unions have betrayed the workers they represent.

36. Matthew Yglesias, "Top House Democrats Join Elizabeth Warren's Push to Fundamentally Change American Capitalism," *Vox,* December 14, 2018,

https://www.vox.com/2018/12/14/18136142/pocan-lujan-warren-accountable-capitalism-act.

37. Richard D. Wolff, *Democracy at Work: A Cure for Capitalism* (Chicago: Haymarket Books, 2012).

38. For criticism of employee ownership models, see Sam Gindin, "Chasing Utopia," *Jacobin*, March 10, 2016, https://www.jacobinmag.com/2016/03/workers-control-coops-wright-wolff-alperovitz/.

39. Andrew Yang, *The War on Normal People: The Truth About America's Disappearing Jobs and Why Universal Basic Income Is Our Future* (New York: Hachette, 2018), 168–169. The fact that Yang's UBI is intentionally only enough to "scrape by" has led some leftists to criticize it, and Benjamin Studebaker has suggested Yang's plan involves "eroding the welfare state and kicking the poor in the face." Benjamin Studebaker, "Andrew Yang's Basic Income Is Stealth Welfare Reform," benjaminstudebaker.com, March 20, 2019, https://benjaminstudebaker.com/2019/03/20/andrew-yangs-basic-income-is-stealth-welfare-reform/.

40. Jesse Eisinger and Paul Kiel, "The IRS Tried to Take on the Ultrawealthy. It Didn't Go Well," *ProPublica*, April 5, 2019, https://www.propublica.org/article/ultrawealthy-taxes-irs-internal-revenue-service-global-high-wealth-audits.

41. Movement for Black Lives Platform, https://policy.m4bl.org/platform/ (accessed June 2, 2019).

42. Evan Halper, "The Trump Administration Has Native American Tribes Feeling Under Siege," *Los Angeles Times*, May 15, 2018, https://www.latimes.com/politics/la-na-pol-trump-native-tribes-20180515-story.html.

43. See Brianna Rennix, "At the Border," *Current Affairs*, July 25, 2017, https://www.currentaffairs.org/2017/07/at-the-border; Brianna Rennix, "Can We Have Humane Immigration Policy?," *Current Affairs*, November 9, 2017, https://www.currentaffairs.org/2017/10/can-we-have-humane-immigration-policy; Brianna Rennix, "What Would Humane Immigration Policy Look Like?," *Current Affairs*, December 10, 2017, https://www.currentaffairs.org/2017/12/what-would-humane-immigration-policy-actually-look-like; Brianna Rennix, "Understanding the Administration's Monstrous Immigration Policies," *Current Affairs*, June 17, 2018, https://www.currentaffairs.org/2018/06/understanding-the-administrations-monstrous-immigration-policies; Brianna Rennix, "What's Actually Happening at the Border," *Current Affairs*, November 11, 2018, https://www.currentaffairs.org/2018/11/whats-actually-happening-at-the-border; Brianna Rennix, "Waiting for the Holy Infant of Atocha," *Current Affairs*, May 15, 2019, https://www.currentaffairs.org/2019/05/waiting-for-the-holy-infant-of-atocha.

44. See Caitlin Bellis, "Abolishing ICE Is Only the First Step," *Current Affairs*, July 20, 2018, https://www.currentaffairs.org/2018/07/abolishing-ice-is-only-the-first-step.

45. See Brianna Rennix and Nathan J. Robinson, "Death and the Drug War," *Current Affairs*, June 4, 2018, https://www.currentaffairs.org/2018/06/death-and-the-drug-war; Brianna Rennix and Nathan J. Robinson, "The U.S. Media's Failure to Report on Violence in Mexico Is Inexcusable," *Current Affairs*, Feb-

ruary 14, 2018, https://www.currentaffairs.org/2018/02/the-u-s-medias-failure -to-report-on-violence-in-mexico-is-inexcusable.

46. Matt Taibbi, "Why We Know So Little About the U.S.-Backed War in Yemen," *Rolling Stone*, July 27, 2018, https://www.rollingstone.com/politics/politics -news/yemen-war-united-states-704187/.

47. For a useful discussion of how leftists can adopt an "internationalist" view of trade and labor, see Benjamin Studebaker, "How The Left Should Think About Trade," *Current Affairs*, May 17, 2019, https://www.currentaffairs.org/2019/05 /how-the-left-should-think-about-trade.

48. Relatedly, it is important for the left to begin to devise new principles to guide U.S. foreign policy, principles based on supporting actual democratic governments and popular movements rather than simply furthering U.S. self-interest. For an introduction to the issues involved, see Azis Rana, "The Left's Missing Foreign Policy," *nplusone,* March 28, 2018, https://nplusonemag.com /online-only/online-only/the-lefts-missing-foreign-policy/. See also *Dissent* magazine's Winter 2017 issue "Toward a Left Foreign Policy." For a crucial essay on American military power, see Lyle Jeremy Rubin, "As a Former Marine, America's War-Making Haunts Me—It Should Haunt Our Politicians Too," *The Nation*, April 12, 2016, https://www.thenation.com/article /my-experience-of-americas-war-making-haunts-me-it-should-haunt-our -politicians-too/.

49. "Glenn Greenwald Talks About Animals," *Current Affairs,* March 30, 2019, https://www.currentaffairs.org/2019/03/glenn-greenwald-talks-about-animals.

50. See Nathan J. Robinson, "Can We End Animal Farming Forever?," *Current Affairs*, November 12, 2018, https://www.currentaffairs.org/2018/11/can-we-end -animal-farming-forever.

51. For some examples of what items on the animal rights agenda in the near future should include, see Nathan J. Robinson, "Animals and 2020," *Current Affairs*, April 11, 2019, https://www.currentaffairs.org/2019/04/animals-and-2020.

52. David French, "Identity Politics Are Ripping Us Apart," *National Review*, May 18, 2016, https://www.nationalreview.com/2016/05/identity-politics-race -ripping-us-apart/.

53. Ben Shapiro, "What Is Intersectionality?," PragerU, June 17, 2018, https://www .prageru.com/video/what-is-intersectionality/.

54. Dave Rubin, "Identity Politics Must Come to an End," YouTube, November 15, 2017, https://www.youtube.com/watch?v=JtDYS6w7ArY.

55. Adolph Reed Jr., "The Limits of Anti-Racism," *Left Business Observer* 121 (September 2009), http://www.leftbusinessobserver.com/Antiracism.html.

56. Kimberlé Williams Crenshaw, "Demarginalizing the Intersection of Race and Sex: A Black Feminist Critique of Antidiscrimination Doctrine, Feminist Theory and Antiracist Politics," *University of Chicago Legal Forum* 1989, no. 8: https://chicagounbound.uchicago.edu/cgi/viewcontent.cgi?article =1052&context=uclf.

57. Shapiro, "What Is Intersectionality?"

58. Quoted in Briahna Joy Gray, "Beware the Race Reductionist," *The Inter-*

cept, August 26, 2018, https://theintercept.com/2018/08/26/beware-the-race
-reductionist/.

CHAPTER 9: GETTING IT DONE

1. "Jane McAlevey on How to Organize for Power," *Current Affairs*, April 21, 2019,
   https://www.currentaffairs.org/2019/04/jane-mcalevey-on-how-to-organize
   -for-power. See also Jane McAlevey, *No Shortcuts: Organizing for Power in the
   New Gilded Age* (New York: Oxford University Press, 2016).
2. For the full text of the memo, see "The Lewis Powell Memo: A Corporate Blueprint to
   Dominate Democracy," *Greenpeace*, https://www.greenpeace.org/usa/democracy
   /the-lewis-powell-memo-a-corporate-blueprint-to-dominate-democracy/.
3. Mark Schmitt, "The Myth of the Powell Memo," *Washington Monthly*, September/
   October 2016.
4. See Nathan J. Robinson, "Why Won't the Right Debate Us?," *Current Affairs*,
   March 21, 2019, https://www.currentaffairs.org/2019/03/why-wont-the-right
   -debate-us; Rafael Garcia and Bailey Britton, "Turning Point USA Tried Influ-
   encing Elections at K-State. SGA Just Allocated Them $3,000 to Host Speak-
   ers on Campus," *The Collegian*, April 2, 2019, https://www.kstatecollegian
   .com/2019/04/02/turning-point-tried-influencing-elections-at-k-state-sga-just
   -allocated-them-3000-to-host-speakers-on-campus/.
5. See Evan Mandery, "Why There's No Liberal Federalist Society," *Politico*, January 23, 2019, https://www.politico.com/magazine/story/2019/01/23/why-theres
   -no-liberal-federalist-society-224033; Andrew Prokop, "How ALEC Helps
   Conservatives and Businesses Turn State Election Wins into New Laws," *Vox*,
   March 27, 2015, https://www.vox.com/2014/11/17/7186057/american-legislative
   -exchange-council.
6. For an example, see Nathan J. Robinson, "Never Trust the Cato Institute," *Current Affairs*, October 13, 2018, https://www.currentaffairs.org/2018/10/never
   -trust-the-cato-institute. I go through a random Cato study to show how it ma-
   nipulates the evidence to support free-market conclusions. For a representative
   piece of right-wing pseudo scholarship, look at C. A. DeAngelis, P. J. Wolf, L. D.
   Maloney, and J. F. May, *A Good Investment: The Updated Productivity of Public
   Charter Schools in Eight U.S. Cities* (Fayetteville: University of Arkansas, Department of Education Reform, 2019). The study, produced for the University
   of Arkansas' pro-charter Department of Education Reform, purports to show
   that private charter schools offer a better "return on investment" than public
   schools, using only two variables: per-pupil spending and test scores. Anyone
   who has taken a high school statistics class can see why this doesn't prove a
   thing: the schools with the lowest-performing students might *need* the highest
   per-pupil spending. The study is not scholarship, it is simply a thing for the *Wall
   Street Journal* to cite, and sure enough, they cited it. See Jason Riley, "Progressives Threaten to Destroy School Reform," *Wall Street Journal*, April 2, 2019,
   https://www.wsj.com/articles/progressives-threaten-to-destroy-school-reform
   -11554246593.

7. For an example of how nonsense is spread on Fox, I recommend this video in which I break down Tucker Carlson's misuse of immigrant crime statistics: *Current Affairs*, "Exposing Tucker Carlson's Immigration Ignorance," You-Tube, September 18, 2018, https://www.youtube.com/watch?v=7hRpWZe0lbw.

8. Alexander Coppock, Emily Ekins, and David Kirby, "The Long-lasting Effects of Newspaper Op-Eds on Public Opinion," *Quarterly Journal of Political Science* 13, no. 1 (2018): 59–87, http://dx.doi.org/10.1561/100.00016112.

9. Stefano Della Vigna and Ethan Kaplan, "The Fox News Effect: Media Bias and Voting," *The Quarterly Journal of Economics* 122, no. 3 (August 2007): 1187–1234, https://doi.org/10.1162/qjec.122.3.1187; Joshua David Clinton and Ted Enamorado, *The Fox News Factor: How the Spread of Fox News Affects Position Taking in Congress* (April 18, 2012), available at http://dx.doi.org/10.2139/ssrn.2050570. For a terrifying report on how Fox News has transformed individuals, see Luke O'Neil, "What I've Learned from Collecting Stories of People Whose Loved Ones Were Transformed by Fox News," *New York*, April 9, 2019, http://nymag.com/intelligencer/2019/04/i-gathered-stories-of-people-transformed-by-fox-news.html. O'Neil describes a common experience people had with relatives:

> They sat down in front of Fox News, found some kind of deep, addictive comfort in the anger and paranoia, and became a different person— someone difficult, if not impossible, to spend time with. The fallout led to failed marriages and estranged parental relationships. For at least one person, it marks the final memory he'll ever have of his father: "When I found my dad dead in his armchair, fucking Fox News was on the TV," this reader told me. "It's likely the last thing he saw. I hate what that channel and conservative talk radio did to my funny, compassionate dad. He spent the last years of his life increasingly angry, bigoted, and paranoid."

10. Prager University, prageru.com (accessed June 1, 2019).

11. John Herrman, "For the New Far Right, YouTube Has Become the New Talk Radio," *New York Times*, August 3, 2017, https://www.nytimes.com/2017/08/03/magazine/for-the-new-far-right-youtube-has-become-the-new-talk-radio.html.

12. Kelly Weill, "How YouTube Built a Radicalization Machine for the Far-Right," *The Daily Beast*, December 17, 2018, https://www.thedailybeast.com/how-youtube-pulled-these-men-down-a-vortex-of-far-right-hate.

13. Ryan Broderick, "YouTubers Will Enter Politics, and the Ones Who Do Are Probably Going to Win," *BuzzFeed*, October 21, 2018, https://www.buzzfeednews.com/article/ryanhatesthis/brazils-congressional-youtubers.

14. For more on Natalie Wynn's ContraPoints channel and why her work is valuable, see Nathan J. Robinson, "God Bless ContraPoints," *Current Affairs*, May 6, 2018, https://www.currentaffairs.org/2018/05/god-bless-contrapoints. There are other left-leaning YouTube channels, including PhilosophyTube and hbomberguy.

15. PragerU, however, spends a lot of money promoting its videos.
16. See Nathan J. Robinson, "Should Leftists Go on Fox?," March 2, 2019, https://www.currentaffairs.org/2019/03/should-leftists-go-on-fox.
17. Diamond Naga Siu, "Democratic Socialists of America Scored Wins in the Midterms. What's on Their Agenda?," NBC, December 8, 2018, https://www.nbcnews.com/politics/politics-news/democratic-socialists-america-scored-wins-midterms-what-s-their-agenda-n941911.
18. Duxbury is the one place in the country that actually has an elected dog catcher. See Amy Kolb Noyes, "Can't Get Elected Dogcatcher? Try Running in Duxbury, Vt," NPR, March 24, 2018, https://www.npr.org/2018/03/24/595755604/cant-get-elected-dogcatcher-try-running-in-duxbury-vt.
19. "In Conversation: Vaughan Stewart on Transforming from a Poster into a Politician," *Current Affairs Podcast*, December 26, 2018, https://www.patreon.com/posts/in-conversation-23563269.
20. Keri Blakinger, "Houston: Ground Zero for the Death Penalty," *Houston Chronicle*, November 27, 2017, https://www.chron.com/news/houston-texas/houston/article/Houston-Ground-zero-for-the-death-penalty-12385007.php.
21. Joan Mar, "Meet the Dream Defenders: 5 Key Members—What Have the DDs Achieved?," *Daily Kos*, September 20, 2013, https://www.dailykos.com/stories/2013/9/20/1239998/-Meet-the-Dream-Defenders-5-Key-Members-What-Have-the-DDs-Achieved.
22. "White House Bafflingly Claims Trump Actually Said 'Oringes,' Not 'Oranges,'" *The Week*, April 3, 2019, https://theweek.com/speedreads/833032/white-house-bafflingly-claims-trump-actually-said-oringes-not-oranges-.
23. See Adolph Reed Jr., "Splendors and Miseries of the Antiracist 'Left,'" *Nonsite*, November 6, 2016, https://nonsite.org/editorial/splendors-and-miseries-of-the-antiracist-left-2.

CHAPTER 10: MEAN, FALSE, AND HOPELESS

1. Rand removed this passage for subsequent editions and it does not appear in the version in print today. One can see why.
2. Michael Oakeshott, "On Being Conservative," in *Rationalism in Politics and Other Essays* (London: Methuen, 1962).
3. Corey Robin, *The Reactionary Mind: Conservatism from Edmund Burke to Sarah Palin* (Oxford: Oxford University Press, 2011), 5.
4. Ibid., 13.
5. Ibid., 4.
6. Kevin D. Williamson, "Chaos in the Family, Chaos in the State: The White Working Class's Dysfunction," *National Review*, March 17, 2016, https://www.nationalreview.com/2016/03/donald-trump-white-working-class-dysfunction-real-opportunity-needed-not-trump/.
7. Ann Coulter, ¡*Adios America! The Left's Plan to Turn Our Country into a Third World Hellhole* (Washington, D.C.: Regnery Publishing, 2015). For a devastating review of the book and a thorough explanation of why Coulter is both

wrong and monstrous, see Brianna Rennix, "The Cruelties of Coulter," *Current Affairs*, March 11, 2018, https://www.currentaffairs.org/2018/03/the-cruelties -of-coulter.

8. Ibid.

9. Nathan J. Robinson, "What We'll Tolerate and What We Won't," *Current Affairs*, February 21, 2017, https://www.currentaffairs.org/2017/02/what-well-tolerate -and-what-we-wont.

10. William F. Buckley Jr., "Why the South Must Prevail," *National Review*, August 24, 1957.

11. H. L. Mencken, "Bayard vs. Lionheart," *Baltimore Evening Sun*, July 26, 1920. This kind of antidemocratic rhetoric lives on in the works of *National Review*'s Kevin Williamson, who writes: "There are plenty of people out there who have nothing useful or interesting to say, whose exercise of the franchise is only a great infantile 'I WANT!' endlessly reiterated every four years or so. There is no special moral value in bundling together complex problems and policy ideas and asking 50 percent plus one of a sprawling and almost pristinely ignorant group of barely improved chimpanzees only a relatively few generations of evolution removed from habitual public masturbation and ritual poo-flinging what they think about those bundles and which of them they prefer." Kevin D. Williamson, *The Smallest Minority: Independent Thinking in the Age of Mob Politics* (Washington, D.C.: Regnery, 2019), 50–51.

12. Albert O. Hirschman, *The Rhetoric of Reaction: Perversity, Futility, Jeopardy* (Cambridge: Belknap Press, 1991).

13. The phrase was one of Thatcher's most powerful and irritating contributions to political discourse and has become lastingly associated with her. See Claire Berlinksi, *There Is No Alternative: Why Margaret Thatcher Matters* (New York: Basic Books, 2008).

14. John Muir, *Our National Parks* (Boston: Houghton Mifflin, 1901), 4.

15. Theodore Roosevelt, *Theodore Roosevelt on Bravery: Lessons from the Most Courageous Leader of the Twentieth Century* (New York: Skyhorse, 2015).

16. F. A. Hayek, "Why I Am Not a Conservative," in *The Constitution of Liberty* (London: Routledge & Kegan Paul, 1959), 397.

17. G. K. Chesterton, *The Thing* (1929).

CHAPTER 11: POLISHING TURDS

1. James Poniewozik, "A Rudderless Night, as News Networks Struggle with a Surprise Victory," *New York Times*, November 10, 2016, https://www.nytimes .com/2016/11/10/arts/television/a-rudderless-night-as-news-networks-struggle -with-a-surprise-victory.html?_r=0.

2. Chris Cillizza and Aaron Blake, "Donald Trump's Chances of Winning Are Approaching Zero, *Washington Post*, October 24, 2016, https://www .washingtonpost.com/news/the-fix/wp/2016/10/24/donald-trumps-chances-of -winning-are-approaching-zero/.

3. Jonathan Chait (@jonathanchait), "Trump won't win Michigan . . . ," Twitter, November 7, 2016, 7:22 a.m., https://twitter.com/jonathanchait/status/795647665463824384?lang=en.

4. Rachael Revesz, "Survey Finds Hillary Clinton Has 'More Than 99% Chance' of Winning Election over Donald Trump," *The Independent*, November 5, 2016, http://www.independent.co.uk/news/world/americas/sam-wang-princeton-election-consortium-poll-hillary-clinton-donald-trump-victory-a7399671.html.

5. On November 7, *Wired* magazine called Wang the "new election data king," and predicted that the election would be a triumph for Wang, validating the use of mathematical modeling for elections. Jeff Nesbit, "2016's Election Data Hero Isn't Nate Silver. It's Sam Wang," *Wired*, November 7, 2016, https://www.wired.com/2016/11/2016s-election-data-hero-isnt-nate-silver-sam-wang/.

6. Corey Robin, "Donald Trump: The Michael Dukakis of the Republican Party," coreyrobin.com, September 27, 2016, http://coreyrobin.com/2016/09/27/donald-trump-the-michael-dukakis-of-the-republican-party/; Corey Robin, "If I Were Worried That Clinton Might Lose, Here's What I Would—and Wouldn't—Do . . . ," coreyrobin.com, August 10, 2016, http://coreyrobin.com/2016/08/10/if-i-were-worried-that-clinton-might-lose-heres-what-i-would-and-wouldnt-do/. Political scientist Corey Robin of Brooklyn College, anticipating that "Clinton is going to win big-time" and calling Trump the "Michael Dukakis of the Republican Party," said that he didn't believe his Democratic friends who insisted Hillary Clinton might lose, because if they were truly afraid, they would be spending their time campaigning for her.

7. Kristen Hare, "Huffington Post Is Going to Cover Trump as Entertainment, Not Politics," *Poynter*, July 17, 2015, https://www.poynter.org/reporting-editing/2015/huffington-post-is-going-to-cover-trump-as-entertainment-not-politics/.

8. Lloyd Grove, "How Stephen Colbert Became Late Night's King of Trump Resistance," *The Daily Beast*, February 20, 2017, https://www.thedailybeast.com/how-stephen-colbert-became-late-nights-king-of-trump-resistance.

9. Todd Shepherd, "Hillary Clinton Concedes: 'I Had Not Drafted a Concession Speech,'" *Washington Examiner*, September 10, 2017, http://www.washingtonexaminer.com/hillary-clinton-concedes-i-had-not-drafted-a-concession-speech/article/2633949.

10. The confetti would later be incorporated into an inspirational snow globe. Nancy Coleman, "An Artist Creates a Giant Snowglobe with Hillary Clinton's Unused Election Night Confetti," CNN, July 14, 2017, http://www.cnn.com/2017/07/14/politics/hillary-clinton-confetti-art-trnd/index.html.

11. Daily Mirror (@DailyMirror), "Tomorrow's Daily Mirror front . . . ," Twitter, November 9, 2016, 1:42 p.m., https://twitter.com/dailymirror/status/796467942435262464?lang=en.

12. Annabeth Leow, "'OMG! It's Trump!': Newspapers Around the World React to Donald Trump's Victory," *Straits Times*, November 10, 2016, https://www

.straitstimes.com/world/united-states/omg-its-trump-newspapers-around-the
-world-react-to-donald-trumps-victory.

13. Paul Colgan, "'WTF': One of Australia's Biggest Newspapers Has Reacted to Trump's Shock Win," *Business Insider*, November 9, 2016, https://www .businessinsider.com/australias-daily-telegraph-reacts-to-trump-win-with -front-page-2016-11.

14. Brent Griffiths, "Plouffe: 'Never Been as Wrong on Anything in My Life,'" *Politico*, November 9, 2016, https://www.politico.com/story/2016/11/david-plouffe -wrong-2016-election-231045.

15. Nathan J. Robinson, "Unless the Democrats Run Sanders, a Trump Nomination Means a Trump Presidency," *Current Affairs*, February 23, 2016, https://static .currentaffairs.org/2016/02/unless-the-democrats-nominate-sanders-a-trump -nomination-means-a-trump-presidency. My record of predictions during 2016 was not perfect. Later, after the "pussy tape" came out, I believed Trump would lose. But in this February article, I concluded: "Donald Trump is one of the most formidable opponents in the history of American politics. He is sharp, shameless, and likable. If he is going to be the nominee, Democrats need to think very seriously about how to defeat him. If they don't, he will be the President of the United States, which will have disastrous repercussions for religious and racial minorities and likely for everyone else, too."

16. Michael Moore, "5 Reasons Why Trump Will Win," Michaelmoore.com, July 21, 2016, https://michaelmoore.com/trumpwillwin/.

17. "Party Images," Gallup, https://news.gallup.com/poll/24655/party-images.aspx. Public opinion of the Democratic Party was about 10 points lower than it was when Obama was elected in 2008. The Republican Party's image was actually worse, but Trump had successfully distanced himself from the party establishment.

18. "Hillary Clinton or Bernie Sanders: Who Can Trump Trump?," *Democracy Now!* March 10, 2016, https://www.democracynow.org/2016/3/10/hillary_clinton _or_bernie_sanders_who.

19. Bogus or not, it *did* turn out to be an electoral risk when FBI director James Comey made a bombshell announcement about the investigation mere days before the election.

20. See Joshua Benton, "The Game of Concentration: The Internet Is Pushing the American News Business to New York and the Coasts," *Nieman Lab*, March 25, 2016, https://www.niemanlab.org/2016/03/the-game-of-concentration-the -internet-is-pushing-the-american-news-business-to-new-york-and-the-coasts/.

21. After the 2016 election, Hillary Clinton remarked that she won parts of the country that were "moving forward," a remark that nicely demonstrates the view from the bubble. John Bowden, "Clinton: I Won Places Moving Forward, Trump Won Places Moving Backward," *The Hill*, March 13, 2018, https://thehill .com/homenews/campaign/378070-clinton-i-won-places-moving-forward -trump-won-places-moving-backward.

22. Barack Obama, "Now Is the Greatest Time to Be Alive," *Wired*, October 12, 2016, https://www.wired.com/2016/10/president-obama-guest-edits-wired

-essay/. It is still stunning to me that in the month before the election, Obama thought this was, first, a good message and, second, a good use of time.

23. I wrote about these at the time. Nathan J. Robinson, "Democrats Need to Stop Insisting That Everything Is Going Well," *Current Affairs*, July 23, 2016, https://www.currentaffairs.org/2016/07/democrats-need-to-stop-insisting-that -everything-is-going-well.

24. Ryan Cooper and Matt Bruenig, *Foreclosed: Destruction of Black Wealth During the Obama Presidency*, People's Policy Project, https://www.peoplespolicyproject .org/wp-content/uploads/2017/12/Foreclosed.pdf.

25. For a look at the political disillusionment of working class black Milwaukeeans, and how this has affected the Democratic Party's political fortunes, see Malaika Jabali, "The Color of Economic Anxiety," *Current Affairs*, October 3, 2018, https://www.currentaffairs.org/2018/10/the-color-of-economic-anxiety.

26. See Lori Wallach and Murshed Zaheed, "TPP: How Obama Traded Away His Legacy," *Huffington Post*, December 29, 2017, https://www.huffpost.com/entry /tpp-how-obama-traded-away_b_13872926. Wallach and Zaheed look at the way Bill Clinton's North American Free Trade Agreement and Barack Obama's Trans-Pacific Partnership (TPP) were political disasters, concluding, "Support for the TPP signaled to those whose lives have been turned upside down by the trade policies of the past 25 years that the Democratic Party did not care about them. That message was conveyed repeatedly to the administration and Clinton campaign by union officials who heard it from their angry members."

27. For a detailed report on Hillary Clinton's involvement in the Libya debacle, see Jo Becker and Scott Shane, "Hillary Clinton, 'Smart Power,' and a Dictator's Fall," *New York Times*, February 27, 2016, https://www.nytimes.com/2016/02 /28/us/politics/hillary-clinton-libya.html.

28. Michael Anton, aka "Publius Decius Mus," "The Flight 93 Election," The Claremont Institute, September 5, 2016, https://www.claremont.org/crb/basicpage /the-flight-93-election/.

29. See Matthew Yglesias, "The Democratic Party's Down-Ballot Collapse, Explained," *Vox*, January 10, 2017, https://www.vox.com/policy-and-politics/2017 /1/10/14211994/obama-democrats-downballot/.

30. Jonathan Allen and Amie Parnes, *Shattered: Inside Hillary Clinton's Doomed Campaign* (New York: Crown, 2017). For a longer review of the book and the mistakes of the Clinton campaign, see Nathan J. Robinson, "The Clinton Comedy of Errors," *Current Affairs*, April 26, 2017, https://www.currentaffairs.org /2017/04/the-clinton-comedy-of-errors.

31. Jeremy Berke, "Clinton Staffers Toyed with Using 'Because It's Her Turn' as a Campaign Rallying Cry," *Business Insider*, April 22, 2017, https://www .businessinsider.com/hillary-clinton-slogan-why-run-because-her-turn-2017-4.

32. Luke Savage, "How Liberals Fell in Love with *The West Wing*," *Current Affairs*, June 7, 2017, https://www.currentaffairs.org/2017/04/how-liberals-fell-in-love -with-the-west-wing.

33. Ben Rhodes, *The World As It Is: A Memoir of the Obama White House* (New York: Random House, 2019), 257. For a review of the amusingly naive mem-

oirs written by former Obama White House staff, see Nathan J. Robinson, "The Obama Boys," *Current Affairs*, March 10, 2019, https://www.currentaffairs.org /2019/03/the-obama-boys.

34. Quoted in Brian Abrams, *Obama: An Oral History* (New York: Little A, 2018), 52.

35. Erin Kelly, "Michelle Obama: George W. Bush Is 'My Partner in Crime' and 'I Love Him to Death,'" *USA Today*, October 11, 2018, https://www.usatoday.com /story/news/politics/onpolitics/2018/10/11/michelle-obama-george-w-bush-my -partner-crime/1603296002/.

36. For a long discussion of Joe Biden's history with racists see Nathan J. Robinson, "Everybody's Chum," *Current Affairs*, March 20, 2019, https://www .currentaffairs.org/2019/03/everybodys-chum.

37. Caitlynn Peetz, "Racial Equity Concerns Surface at Public Forum on School Redistricting," *Bethesda Magazine*, April 5, 2019, https://bethesdamagazine.com /bethesda-beat/schools/racial-equity-concerns-surface-at-boundary-meeting/.

38. Quoted in Dianna Douglas, "Are Private Schools Immoral?," *The Atlantic*, December 14, 2017, https://www.theatlantic.com/education/archive/2017/12 /progressives-are-undermining-public-schools/548084/?utm_source=atlfb.

39. Adolph Reed Jr., "Liberals I Do Despise," *Village Voice*, November 12, 1996, available at https://www.commondreams.org/views/2009/12/09/liberals-i-do-despise.

40. Adolph Reed Jr., "Obama No," *The Progressive*, April 28, 2008, https:// progressive.org/magazine/obama/.

41. Matt Taibbi, "Obama Is the Best BS Artist Since Bill Clinton," *Rolling Stone*, February 14, 2007, available at https://www.alternet.org/2007/02/obama_is_the _best_bs_artist_since_bill_clinton/.

42. David Litt, *Thanks, Obama: My Hopey Changey White House Years* (New York: Ecco, 2017), 22.

43. Jessica Campisi, "Trump Deporting Immigrants at Slower Pace than Obama," *The Hill*, June 21, 2019, https://thehill.com/homenews/administration/449665 -trump-deporting-immigrants-at-slower-pace-than-obama-report; Glenn Greenwald, "The Untouchables: How the Obama Administration Protected Wall Street from Prosecutions," *The Guardian*, January 23, 2013, https://www.theguardian .com/commentisfree/2013/jan/23/untouchables-wall-street-prosecutions-obama; Sonali Prasad et al., "Obama's Dirty Secret: The Fossil Fuel Projects the US Littered Around the World," *The Guardian*, December 1, 2016, https://www.theguardian .com/environment/2016/dec/01/obama-fossil-fuels-us-export-import-bank -energy-projects. Obama now brags about how good his presidency was for the industry: Valerie Richardson, "Obama Takes Credit for U.S. Oil-and-Gas Boom: 'That Was Me, People'" AP, November 28, 2018, https://www.apnews.com/5dfb c1aa17701ae219239caad0bfefb2; Yara Bayoumy, "Obama Administration Arms Sale Offers to Saudi Arabia Top $115 Billion," Reuters, September 7, 2016, https:// www.reuters.com/article/us-usa-saudi-security/obama-administration-arms -sales-offers-to-saudi-top-115-billion-report-idUSKCN11D2JQ; Conor Friedersdorf, "How Team Obama Justifies The Killing of a 16-Year-Old American," *The Atlantic*, October 24, 2012, https://www.theatlantic.com/politics/archive/2012/10

/how-team-obama-justifies-the-killing-of-a-16-year-old-american/264028/; Micah Zenko, "Do Not Believe the U.S. Government's Official Numbers on Drone Strike Civilian Casualties," *Foreign Policy*, July 5, 2016, https://foreignpolicy.com /2016/07/05/do-not-believe-the-u-s-governments-official-numbers-on-drone -strike-civilian-casualties/; Kira Goldenberg, "Obama's Broken Promises on Transparency," *Columbia Journalism Review*, October 10, 2013, https://archives .cjr.org/behind_the_news/cjp_report_on_us_press_freedom.php (the "worse than Nixon" quote is from the chief attorney who represented the *New York Times* during the Pentagon Papers case); Colin Kahl, "Obama Has Been Great For Israel," *Foreign Policy*, August 16, 2012, https://foreignpolicy.com/2012/08 /16/obama-has-been-great-for-israel/; Geoffrey Aronson, "How Barack Obama Failed to Stop Israeli Settlements," *Al Jazeera*, October 31, 2016, https://www .aljazeera.com/indepth/opinion/2016/10/barack-obama-failed-stop-israeli -settlements-161030075936848.html.

44. Quoted in Abrams, *Obama: An Oral History*, 162.

45. For a more detailed critique of Obama's education policy, see Nathan J. Robinson, "The Kind of Policy We Must Never Make Again," *Current Affairs*, February 6, 2019, https://www.currentaffairs.org/2019/02/the-kind-of-policy-we-must -never-make-again.

46. Micah L. Sifry, "Obama's Lost Army," *New Republic*, February 9, 2017, https:// newrepublic.com/article/140245/obamas-lost-army-inside-fall-grassroots -machine.

47. Quoted in Gabrial Debenedetti, "A Long Talk with Pete Buttigieg: The 2020 Hopeful on College Contemporary Mark Zuckerberg, How Sewers Are Like National Security, and Ulysses," *New York*, February 14, 2019, http://nymag .com/intelligencer/2019/02/a-long-talk-with-democratic-2020-candidate-pete -buttigieg.html.

48. See, for example, Katy Waldman, "The Coming-of-Age Tale That Inspired Mayor Pete to Learn Norwegian," *New Yorker*, May 2, 2019, https://www .newyorker.com/books/page-turner/the-coming-of-age-tale-that-inspired -mayor-pete-to-learn-norwegian; Elizabeth Murray, "Potential Presidential Candidate Pete Buttigieg Can't Live Without These Vermont-Made Socks," *Burlington Free Press*, April 4, 2019, https://www.burlingtonfreepress.com/story /news/local/2019/04/04/2020-election-pete-buttigieg-potential-presidential -candidate-vermont-made-socks/3362269002/. For a detailed critique of Pete Buttigieg's policies and record, as well as the media hype surrounding him, see Nathan J. Robinson, "All About Pete," *Current Affairs*, March 29, 2019, https:// www.currentaffairs.org/2019/03/all-about-pete.

49. Nathan J. Robinson, "The Limits of Liberal History," *Current Affairs*, October 28, 2018, https://www.currentaffairs.org/2018/10/the-limits-of-liberal-history; Alex Nichols, "You Should Be Terrified That People Who Like *Hamilton* Run Our Country," *Current Affairs*, July 29, 2016, https://www.currentaffairs.org /2016/07/you-should-be-terrified-that-people-who-like-hamilton-run-our -country.

50. For a deeper explanation of how this happens with many more examples see

Nathan J. Robinson, "Don't Use the Right's Assumptions to Make the Left's Arguments," *Current Affairs*, March 1, 2018, https://www.currentaffairs.org /2018/03/dont-use-the-rights-assumptions-to-make-the-lefts-arguments.

51. Connor Kilpatrick, "Alexander Cockburn: The Last Polemicist," *Jacobin*, September 30, 2013, https://jacobinmag.com/2013/09/alexander-cockburn-the-last -polemicist.

52. Frances Perkins, *The Roosevelt I Knew* (New York: Penguin Classics, 2011), 314.

53. Franklin D. Roosevelt, "Franklin Roosevelt's Address Announcing the Second New Deal," October 31, 1936, available at http://docs.fdrlibrary.marist.edu /od2ndst.html.

54. Thomas Jefferson to James Madison, October 28, 1785, in *The Papers of Thomas Jefferson*, ed. Julian P. Boyd (Princeton. NJ: Princeton University Press, 1950), papers 8:681–82, http://press-pubs.uchicago.edu/founders/documents /v1ch15s32.html.

55. Abraham Lincoln, "Speech in the Illinois Legislature Concerning the State Bank," January 11, 1837, *Collected Works of Abraham Lincoln*, vol. 1 (Ann Arbor, MI: University of Michigan Digital Library Production Services, 2001), available at https://quod.lib.umich.edu/l/lincoln/lincoln1/1:92?rgn=div1;view=fulltext.

56. See Adolph Reed Jr. "Race and the New Deal Coalition," *The Nation*, April 7, 2008, https://www.thenation.com/article/race-and-new-deal-coalition/.

57. Frank may overstate the degree to which the Democratic Party ever *was* a "party of the people," but his analysis of contemporary liberalism is correct nonetheless. Thomas Frank, *Listen, Liberal: Or, What Ever Happened to the Party of the People?* (New York: Picador, 2016). For a review emphasizing how bad the Democratic Party has always been, see John Halle, "Review: Listen, Liberal," *Current Affairs*, August 18, 2016, https://www.currentaffairs.org/2016/08 /review-listen-liberal.

58. Frank, *Listen, Liberal*.

CHAPTER 12: RESPONSE TO CRITICISMS

1. Rob Larson, *Capitalism vs. Freedom: The Toll Road To Serfdom* (Alresford, UK: Zero Books, 2018).

2. Edward Bernays, *Propaganda* (London: Routledge, 1928; reprint edition Brooklyn, NY: Ig, 2004), 37.

3. "'This Government Is Rightwing' Says Venezuelan Union Leader José Bodas," *Venezuelan Voices*, April 5, 2019, https://venezuelanvoices.home.blog/2019/04 /05/this-government-is-rightwing-says-venezuelan-union-leader-jose-bodas/.

4. Anatoly Kurmanaev, "The Tragedy of Venezuela," *Wall Street Journal*, May 24, 2018, https://www.wsj.com/articles/the-tragedy-of-venezuela-1527177202.

5. Francisco Toro, "As Socialist Venezuela Collapses, Socialist Bolivia Thrives. Here's Why," *Washington Post*, January 5, 2017, https://www.washingtonpost .com/news/global-opinions/wp/2017/01/05/as-socialist-venezuela-collapses -socialist-bolivia-thrives-heres-why/; Francisco Toro, "No, Venezuela Doesn't Prove Anything About Socialism," *Washington Post*, August 21, 2018, https://

www.washingtonpost.com/news/global-opinions/wp/2018/08/21/no-venezuela
-doesnt-prove-that-socialism-will-bring-about-a-zombie-apocalypse/.

6. The causes of the Venezuelan economic crisis are complicated, and hardly anyone who talks about the lessons of Venezuela for "socialism" has seriously studied the Venezuelan economy. For some beginning explanations of what's actually going on, see Francisco Rodríguez, "Crude Realities: Understanding Venezuela's Economic Collapse," Washington Office on Latin America, September 20, 2018, https://venezuelablog.org/crude-realities-understanding -venezuelas-economic-collapse/; Michael Roberts, "The Tragedy of Venezuela," Michael Roberts Blog, August 3, 2017, https://thenextrecession.wordpress.com /2017/08/03/the-tragedy-of-venezuela/.

7. For more on this argument, see Nathan J. Robinson, "What Venezuela Tells Us About Socialism," *Current Affairs*, May 29, 2018, https://www.currentaffairs .org/2018/05/what-venezuela-tells-us-about-socialism.

8. For discussions of various ways in which economies might be "socialized," and a dip into the "calculation debate" over how necessary markets and prices are, see Seth Ackerman, "The Red and the Black," *Jacobin*, December 20, 2012, https://jacobinmag.com/2012/12/the-red-and-the-black; Evgeny Morozov, "Digital Socialism? The Calculation Debate in the Age of Big Data," *New Left Review*, March-June 2019, https://newleftreview.org/issues/II116/articles /evgeny-morozov-digital-socialism.

9. Ludwig von Mises, *Socialism: An Economic and Sociological Analysis*, 1922.

10. Numa Mazat and Franklin Serrano, "An Analysis of the Soviet Economic Growth from the 1950's to the Collapse of USSR," second draft, unpublished, http://www .centrosraffa.org/public/bb6ba675-6bef-4182-bb89-339ae1f7e792.pdf.

11. Gur Ofer, "Soviet Economic Growth, 1928–1985," RAND/UCLA Center for the Study of Soviet International Behavior, 1988, https://apps.dtic.mil/dtic/tr /fulltext/u2/a220336.pdf.

12. "Revenue Statistics - OECD Countries: Comparative Tables," Organization for Economic Cooperation and Development, https://stats.oecd.org/Index.aspx ?DataSetCode=REV.

13. Leigh Phillips and Michal Rozworski, *The People's Republic of Walmart: How the World's Biggest Corporations are Laying the Foundation for Socialism* (Brooklyn, NY: Verso Books, 2018).

14. For more on the crazy Sears experiment, see Mina Kimes, "At Sears, Eddie Lampert's Warring Divisions Model Adds to the Troubles," *Bloomberg*, July 11, 2013, https://www.bloomberg.com/news/articles/2013-07-11/at-sears-eddie -lamperts-warring-divisions-model-adds-to-the-troubles.

15. Paul Krugman, "John Galt and the Theory of the Firm," *New York Times*, July 16, 2013, https://krugman.blogs.nytimes.com/2013/07/16/john-galt-and -the-theory-of-the-firm/.

16. Ben Shapiro, "What Is Intersectionality?," PragerU, June 17, 2018, https://www .prageru.com/video/what-is-intersectionality/.

17. Oscar Wilde, "The Soul of Man Under Socialism," 1891.

18. Ibid.

19. See Samuel Miller McDonald, "Capitalism Is Collectivist," *Current Affairs*, May 9, 2018, https://www.currentaffairs.org/2018/05/capitalism-is-collectivist.

20. James Otteson, *The End of Socialism* (Cambridge: Cambridge University Press, 2014).

21. Christoph Engel, "Dictator Games: A Meta Study," MPI Collective Goods Preprint, no. 2010/07 (March 1, 2010), http://dx.doi.org/10.2139/ssrn.1568732.

22. See Samuel Bowles and Herbert Gintis, *A Cooperative Species: Human Reciprocity and Its Evolution* (Princeton, NJ: Princeton University Press, 2013). For a clear refutation of the theory that human beings are innately selfish, see Herbert Gintis, "On the Evolution of Human Morality," *Edge*, June 18, 2012, https://www.edge.org/conversation/the-false-allure-of-group-selection#hg.

23. Garrett Hardin, "The Tragedy of the Commons," *Science* 162, no. 3859 (December 1968): 1243–1248.

24. Elinor Ostrom, *Governing the Commons: The Evolution of Institutions for Collective Action* (Cambridge: Cambridge University Press, 1990), 24.

25. Matt Bors, "Mister Gotcha," *The Nib*, September 13, 2016, https://thenib.com/mister-gotcha.

26. The Walmart cheer is a creepy corporate teambuilding chant that Walmart has made workers do at the beginning of shifts. It is proof that capitalism is collectivist. See Richard Metzger, "America Circa 2013: The Walmart Cheer Is the Most Depressing Thing You'll Ever See," *Dangerous Minds*, July 29, 2013, https://dangerousminds.net/comments/america_circa_2013_in_a_nutshell_the_wal_mart_cheer_is_the_most_depressing.

27. For more on poop emoji pool floats, see Rob Larson and Nathan J. Robinson, "Stubborn Detachment," *Current Affairs*, May 24, 2019, https://www.currentaffairs.org/2019/05/stubborn-detachment.

28. I do think there are serious questions about what obligations of interpersonal generosity the socialist ethic entails. See Nathan J. Robinson, "Why Bernie Sanders Should Give His Millions Away," *Current Affairs*, April 16, 2019, https://www.currentaffairs.org/2019/04/why-bernie-sanders-should-give-his-millions-away. For a more scholarly treatment see G. A. Cohen, *If You're an Egalitarian, How Come You're So Rich?* (Cambridge, MA: Harvard University Press, 2001).

29. Nathan J. Robinson, "Why Elon Musk's SpaceX Launch Is Utterly Depressing," *The Guardian*, February 7, 2018, https://www.theguardian.com/commentisfree/2018/feb/07/elon-musk-spacex-launch-utterly-depressing.

30. Louise Connelly, "The Most Expensive Doughnut in the World Is Covered in 24-Karat Gold," *CNBC*, October 11, 2017, https://www.cnbc.com/2017/10/11/worlds-most-expensive-doughnut-is-covered-in-gold.html.

31. My colleague Brianna Rennix and I have argued that contemporary architecture is distinctly capitalistic with its "efficient" abandonment of ornament and its aggressive minimalism. See Brianna Rennix and Nathan J. Robinson, "Why You Hate Contemporary Architecture," *Current Affairs*, October 31, 2017, https://www.currentaffairs.org/2017/10/why-you-hate-contemporary-architecture. Artist Molly Crabapple has argued sensibly that today's architecture is anti-life because its buildings do not have "places for the birds to live," which come with

intricate ornamentation. Birds have no value under capitalism, and their interests are thus disregarded entirely. See: "Molly Crabapple on the Power of Art," *The Current Affairs Podcast*, June 6, 2019, https://www.patreon.com/posts/27446318.

32. Justin Davidson, "I Have a Feeling We're Not in New York Anymore: Hudson Yards Is a Billionaire's Fantasy City and You Never Have to Leave— Provided You Can Pay for It," *New York*, February 18, 2019, http://nymag.com /intelligencer/2019/02/hudson-yard-billionaires-fantasy-city.html.

33. See Nathan J. Robinson, "Mardi Gras in Theory and Practice," *Current Affairs*, June 23, 2018, https://www.currentaffairs.org/2018/06/mardi-gras-in-theory -and-practice.

CONCLUSION

1. Chris Cillizza, "This May Be the Scariest Thing Donald Trump Has Said as President," CNN, March 5, 2018, https://www.cnn.com/2018/03/05/politics /donald-trump-xi-jinping-analysis/index.html.

2. Chaim Gartenberg, "Construction Begins on Jeff Bezos' $42 Million 10,000- Year Clock," *The Verge*, February 20, 2018, https://www.theverge.com/tldr/2018 /2/20/17031836/jeff-bezos-clock-10000-year-cost.

3. Quoted in Nicole Karlis, "Bernie Sanders Condemns Amazon's Worker Mistreatment Just in Time for Prime Day," *Salon*, July 17, 2018, https://www.salon .com/2018/07/17/bernie-sanders-condemns-amazons-worker-mistreatment -just-in-time-for-prime-day/.

4. Brianna Rennix and Nathan J. Robinson, "What's with Nationalism?," *Current Affairs*, December 30, 2018, https://www.currentaffairs.org/2018/12/whats-with -nationalism.

5. Danny Lewis, "Reagan and Gorbachev Agreed to Pause the Cold War in Case of an Alien Invasion," *Smithsonian*, November 25, 2015, https://www .smithsonianmag.com/smart-news/reagan-and-gorbachev-agreed-pause-cold -war-case-alien-invasion-180957402/.

6. Alan Boyle, "Jeff Bezos and His Blue Origin Space Venture Go All In on Moon Settlements," *GeekWire*, May 26, 2018, https://www.geekwire.com/2018/jeff -bezos-blue-origin-space-venture-go-moon-settlements/.

7. Douglas Rushkoff, "Survival of the Richest: The Wealthy Are Plotting to Leave Us Behind," *Medium*, July 5, 2018, https://medium.com/s/futurehuman /survival-of-the-richest-9ef6cddd0cc1.

8. For a good introduction to labor history see Erik Loomis, *A History of America in Ten Strikes* (New York: New Press, 2018).

9. Quoted in Ana Marie Cox, "Bree Newsome Thinks Allies Should Be Protesting," *New York Times*, October 18, 2017, https://www.nytimes.com/2017/10/18 /magazine/bree-newsome-thinks-allies-should-be-protesting.html.

10. Jocelyn Kiley, "Most Continue to Say Ensuring Health Care Coverage Is Government's Responsibility," Pew Research Center, October 3, 2018, https://www .pewresearch.org/fact-tank/2018/10/03/most-continue-to-say-ensuring-health -care-coverage-is-governments-responsibility/.

11. Andrew Buncome, "Bernie Sanders Is the Most Popular Politician in America, Poll Finds," *The Independent*, August 25, 2017, https://www.independent.co.uk/news/world/americas/us-politics/bernie-sanders-most-popular-politician-poll-trump-favorability-a7913306.html.

12. "We Rise Together, Homie: An Interview with Antoine Dangerfield," *Jacobin*, August 3, 2018, https://jacobinmag.com/2018/08/wildcat-strike-indianapolis-shut-down.

13. Ibid.

14. Ibid.

15. Ibid.

APPENDIX

1. Amber Frost makes a similar argument about the reason for reading the *Financial Times*. The *New York Times* thinks culture and politics make the world go round. The *Financial Times* and *Wall Street Journal*, like Marx, understand that it's capital that makes the world go round. See Amber Frost, "Why the Left Can't Stand the *New York Times*," *Columbia Journalism Review* (Winter 2019), https://www.cjr.org/special_report/why-the-left-cant-stand-the-new-york-times.php.

2. Dinesh D'Souza, for instance, is mocked by the left, but upon reading his book *The Big Lie*, I realized that he is an extremely compelling writer who is able to put dangerously stupid ideas into a highly persuasive format. Many on the left, because they would never pick up a book like this, do not appreciate how skilled D'Souza is and underestimate what a formidable enemy he is. See my review of his book, Nathan J. Robinson, "Who Are the Real Nazis?," *Current Affairs*, December 1, 2017, https://www.currentaffairs.org/2017/12/.

3. For a much more extensive list of lefty podcasts and YouTube channels, see this "Master List" on Reddit: https://www.reddit.com/r/BreadTube/comments/9kwkxa/master_list_of_leftwing_youtube_and_podcast/. I am grateful to those who compiled the list as well as to Peter Coffin for introducing me to these shows.

4. I wrote more about the books that inspired me here: Nathan J. Robinson, "Literature of the Left," *Current Affairs*, July 11, 2018, https://www.currentaffairs.org/2018/07/literature-of-the-left. The books I mention have been compiled into a Goodreads list here: https://www.goodreads.com/list/show/126110.Literature_of_the_Left.

5. For a discussion of how the reality show *Gordon Ramsay's Kitchen Nightmares* implicitly makes the case for worker-owned restaurants, see Oren Nimni and Nathan J. Robinson, "Bonus Episode: Kitchen Knightmares," *The Current Affairs Podcast*, July 23, 2018, https://www.patreon.com/posts/20274902.

6. For more on the way conservatives complain about being marginalized when it's leftists who are actually silenced, see my book *The Current Affairs Rules for Life: On Social Justice and Its Critics* (New Orleans: Current Affairs Press, 2018), particularly the chapters "Pretty Loud for Being So Silenced" and "The Real 'Dangerous' Ideas."

INDEX